LANDSLIDE

LANDSLIDE

THE FINAL DAYS OF THE TRUMP WHITE HOUSE

MICHAEL WOLFF

Henry Holt and Company New York

Henry Holt and Company
Publishers since 1866
120 Broadway
New York, New York 10271
www.henryholt.com

Library of Congress Cataloging-in-Publication Data is available.

ISBN: 9781250830012

Our books may be purchased in bulk for promotional, educational, or business use. Please contact your local bookseller or the Macmillan Corporate and Premium Sales Department at (800) 221-7945, extension 5442, or by e-mail at MacmillanSpecialMarkets@macmillan.com.

First Edition 2021

Designed by Meryl Sussman Levavi

Printed in the United States of America

1   3   5   7   9   10   8   6   4   2

For Paolo Lanapoppi

"We won. Won in a landslide. This was a landslide."
—President Donald J. Trump, January 6, 2021

CONTENTS

INTRODUCTION

From the *New York Times*:

... [an] examination of the 77 democracy-bending days between election and inauguration shows how, with conspiratorial belief rife in a country ravaged by pandemic, a lie that Mr. Trump had been grooming for years finally overwhelmed the Republican Party and, as brake after brake fell away, was propelled forward by new and more radical lawyers, political organizers, financiers and the surround-sound right-wing media.

In the aftermath of that broken afternoon at the Capitol, a picture has emerged of entropic forces coming together on Trump's behalf in an ad hoc, yet calamitous, crash of rage and denial.

But interviews with central players, and documents including previously unreported emails, videos and social media posts scattered across the web, tell a more encompassing story of a more coordinated campaign.

Across those 77 days, the forces of disorder were summoned and directed by the departing president, who wielded the power derived from his near-infallible status among the party faithful in one final norm-defying act of a reality-denying presidency.

January 31, 2021

Except . . .

In the days and weeks after Election Day on November 3, the president was deserted by his aides and staff. The legal establishment, at least anyone in it with a promising career, abandoned him. His hapless band of co-conspirators were too crazy or drunk or cynical to develop a credible strategy or execute one. It was all a shit show—ludicrous, inexplicable, cringeworthy, nutso, even for the people who felt most loyal to him. The election challenge never had a chance of success.

Trump's presidency was a mirror image of good government and the normal workings of the bureaucracy, but his final days were a further quantum-leap departure from any system capable of achieving support or successful results—or, for that matter, even an underhand and sham result.

The second impeachment trial of Donald Trump was to charge him with explicit plans and strategy and intent—his final days in office a calculated effort to do anything to remain in office. But for those who saw Trump up close, even for those who believed he was profoundly guilty of so many things, this was not getting it at all. Rather, the opposite: Trump's true assault on democratic norms was to have removed organization, strategy, method, rationale, and conscious decision making from the highest level of government.

From the beginning of Trump's intrusion into American political life, the striving, orderly, result-oriented, liberal world and its media were unable to fathom his carelessness and cluelessness or understand him or his supporters by any standard political measures. Hence, what might appear to be crazy and self-destructive must in fact have been a plan.

Politics could not be pure caprice or farce, could it?

This insistence on specific intent, on the calculated and "coordinated" misuse of power, keeps Donald Trump in the realm of knowable politics. But what if it was precisely the absence of intent and, instead, the swings of irrationality and mania that managed, even as his government collapsed, to hold so many people in thrall?

The fundamental modern assumption is that a crazy person cannot be elected president—a bad person, a corrupt person, an incompetent person, a mendacious person, a bigoted one, yes, but not someone who has completely departed reality. The age of modern bureaucracy demands, at the very least, being able to sit through a meeting without barking like a dog.

From the careening and calamitous last stage of his reelection campaign through the preposterous election challenge and the deadly mayhem of January 6 to the improbable buffoonery of his second impeachment trial, there emerges a much different picture from the one much of the media has painted of a corrupt, cynical, despotic effort to hold on to power and to subvert democracy. Here, instead, is a far more complicated human and political tale of desperation and delusion.

It is one that should by any logic have ended on January 6. But the most striking and determinative fact of the political age is that the Trump story continues, even in defeat, to be inspirational to so many—and why all Republican roads now lead to Mar-a-Lago. "Mr. President," said the pollster Tony Fabrizio, trying to explain to Trump what even he might have had trouble fully grasping, "your voters believe whatever you tell them to believe." Indeed, by mid-May 2021, new polling showed 67 percent of Republicans were of the view that Joe Biden was not the legitimate winner of the 2020 presidential election. Trump does nothing right. Cannot put one pants leg on at a time. His ham-handed, doomed, blundering, and embarrassing efforts to undo that election, together with his heedless call to arms on January 6, showed him once more to be the naked emperor, evident not only to his enemies but, with ever-deeper sighs of incredulity, also to his allies. And yet, here we are, him with his grip on the heart of only slightly less than half the nation, the once and future Donald Trump, licking his wounds and, eyeing his public, figuring what new, absurd, and rash exploit to embark on.

* * *

This is the third book I have written about Donald Trump in as many years. It's a chronicle that has put me in close touch with almost every phase of the Trump White House and with nearly every member of the revolving cast of characters around him. A great many of them, in the West Wing, the campaign, and in the greater Republican Party, have contributed to this account, including Donald Trump himself.

The former president's office has been supplied a detailed summary of much of the material set forth in this book. His staff has either confirmed events, conversations, and various details of Trumpworld life as I have portrayed them or offered corrections. In the event that factual matters have been disputed, they have been included only if confirmed by multiple sources.

Many who have discussed these events with me have asked to remain anonymous for reasons that will be evident from this tale.

LANDSLIDE

PROLOGUE

THE TRIAL

Typos drove him wild. He might lash out for days when he found one, or when someone else, more likely, pointed out a mess-up in a letter or document prepared under his name—the infuriated concern of someone thinking somebody else's laziness might reveal his own weaknesses.

He was spitting furious now because the legal brief was filled with botches, the second time in a week this had happened—the *Unites States*! In the first line! *A violent overthrown*! And plenty more. The press was already on him—complete ridicule, somehow a higher indignity and reason for fury than the second impeachment trial he was being subjected to.

He wanted someone fired—whoever had proofed it, fired. He wanted them gone immediately! He placed call after call to his remaining aides. "What is fucking wrong with these people? They can't hit spell-check?"—spell-check, in the mind of a man who did not use a computer, was the solution.

The miscreant here, however, could not, practically speaking, easily be fired because it was the president's lead impeachment lawyer, Bruce Castor. On the job for only days in the most important professional engagement of his life, Castor had rushed through reading the brief at 3:40 a.m. that morning, February 8, 2021, and had filed it straightaway. Nobody had proofed it.

Castor was trying to explain this to the former president, who kept interrupting, his voice sharp, curt, sneering, unabating, dismissing Castor's excuses. "Spell-check, Mr. President, doesn't pick up italicized words," said Castor, another man who did not perhaps use a computer much.

"*What?* That's the stupidest thing I've ever heard. Fix it! Get it back! Fix it! NOW!" the incredulous president yelled, not unusually losing his shit.

That's what the group huddled on the frozen sidewalk outside the Trump International Hotel in Washington, DC, later that Monday morning, headless chicken–like, was trying to do—while at the same time, without preparation or, really, forethought, trying to defend a president from gross ignominy. They were fixing the typos. NOW!

"Are these lawyers the stupidest?" Trump fumed on the phone to anyone who would listen. "Are they the stupidest?"

Quite the larger problem, now overshadowed by the typo drama, was that the fourth impeachment trial in U.S. history, scheduled to start the next day, was to be argued by lawyers who'd entered the case only a week ago. Of the three main lawyers, Castor, David Schoen, and Mike van der Veen, Trump hadn't personally met any of them and had not even spoken to van der Veen (who, indeed, would be the only lawyer to emerge with some lasting respect from Trump).

Castor sat in the Mercedes G Wagon waiting to go to the Capitol for a walk-through and to meet the Republican Senate staff. In addition, there were a Jeep Rubicon and a Range Rover waiting to take the new team to the Senate trial. Castor was still wounded because the Trump guys on the ground wouldn't let him drive his beloved Corvette to the Capitol door. That was how he had imagined it happening. That was one reason he'd taken the case: that image. "The Corvette is me. It's like my business card."

The Trump aides still hanging in—at this point, largely beyond surprise—could hardly believe it. Reading the room had often, to say the least, been a problem in Trump circles, but a Corvette at the U.S. Capitol still reeling from the violent attack being laid at the president's feet?

Trump's lawyers—not these lawyers, but the lawyers who had been Trump's lawyers, some on the first impeachment, but who were trying to be nowhere near out front on this impeachment mess—were, in turn, being reamed out by the former president over these new lawyers: "Who are they? Where did they come from? Who hired them? How come I always get the worst lawyers?"

Somehow, for no reason that seemed particularly clear to anybody, especially to Castor and Schoen and the rest of Trump's new lawyers, Trump's legal point person was Eric Herschmann. Herschmann had appeared in Trumpworld a year ago, during the last impeachment, and he'd continued to hang around, variously assigned to oversee the White House Counsel's Office and then as a campaign and West Wing political advisor—he was one more of the people the president's son-in-law and senior-most aide, Jared Kushner, had designated as a presidential babysitter.

Herschmann, too, was attached to his cars, parking his Lamborghini incongruously next to the government cars in the White House parking lot. But after the January 6 attack on the Capitol, and before the second impeachment, Herschmann had gotten himself out of Dodge. In fact, every single lawyer who had worked on Trump's first impeachment was conveniently unavailable. Still, like Trump's old lawyer Michael Cohen, who had remained with the president through all the offenses he, Cohen, had ever since been recanting, you did not relinquish Donald Trump so easily. Perhaps because he was always carping at you on the phone, or just because the drama, the runaway-train drama, called you back. How could you not stay to see the end: the most incredible train wreck ever?

And indeed, Schoen and Castor were now furious at Herschmann, who, even while taking cover, was still trying to hold on to his Trumpworld place and run everything. Or, really, more to the point, nobody was running anything; Herschmann was just running it more than they were because he was more often on the phone with the ex-president—who was furious, steaming, nonstop in his hectoring, ever certain in his certainties, as it was always thus.

Trump was ranting to his legal team that he didn't want this trial going down this way—technicalities, free speech, jurisdiction baloney. He wanted his defense to be that the election was stolen from him. It *was* stolen! Everybody knew it was stolen. Here was the chance to lay out the case! Indeed, the former president proposed he make the case himself on the Senate floor!

But here was the one argument Herschmann and virtually everybody else associated with the case had no doubt would get the former president convicted. Once more, everybody was trying to save Trump from himself, never a promising proposition.

There were more immediate problems. The unwieldy group, nobody necessarily speaking to anyone else, was stuck outside the hotel in the freezing weather. The Trump guys, the remaining retinue or remnants of Trumpworld, were trying to move everybody forward as a group—and get there ASAP to fix the typos. But after January 6, the Capitol had become a veritable DMZ. There were new roadblocks and checkpoints to navigate everywhere. It was thirty degrees Fahrenheit, bone-cold, and they'd been standing outside (except for Castor, in the G Wagon with the heat running) for twenty minutes. And nobody seemed to know why, except that somebody had said they needed to wait; Adam wasn't here.

Who, somebody finally asked, is Adam?

Adam was the legal intern who was going to drive the Jeep.

And why isn't Adam here?

"He's doing a law school quiz on Zoom."

A Trump wag noted: "We've gone through all the lawyers and are now down to law students."

The Trump guys finally piled everyone into two cars, leaving the Jeep and Adam behind.

At the Capitol, two dozen people crammed into Room S-211, the Lyndon Baines Johnson Room, across the hall from the floor of the Senate. Here was a scrum of Trump lawyers, support staff, comms team members, and people from the office of the Republican leader Mitch McConnell: David Popp, McConnell's comms director; Stefanie Muchow, his deputy chief of staff; and Andrew Ferguson, the minority counsel, all three sheepish in their sudden roles as Trump hand-holders, as unsure of their function here as everybody else.

This was the first in-person meeting of the Trump defense team and of the Republican leadership upon whom Trump's fate depended. To say that nobody on the defense side had the slightest idea what approach anyone else had in mind for the fourth impeachment trial in history and the second in thirteen months would be an understatement. Once again here was a familiar Trump nexus: everybody hoping that somebody else could make sense of the lack of plan and purpose that at all times attended Donald Trump, or at least step forward to try.

The McConnell people, who would somehow have to summon the pretense that there was a reasonable defense here and who, indeed, had four years of experience dealing with the radical peculiarities of the Trump White House, nevertheless seemed slack-jawed and stunned: the Democrats had a new majority, a righteous cause, and in addition, they had just done the impeachment-and-trial drill a year ago. The Trump team, for its part, rustled up from no one knew where, was certainly looking like a gang that couldn't shoot straight—indeed, they seemed likely to shoot one another.

Bruce Castor, who was still trying to fix the typos, was also micromanaging the seating of the defense in the Senate Chamber, where everyone would be positioned for the fixed television camera there. Television time was the payoff.

David Schoen, a solo practitioner from Montgomery, Alabama, had been designated by Trump as the lead lawyer. But then Bruce Castor announced to the team that *he* would in fact, damn it, be the lead lawyer. This was after the first set of lawyers, a group of local boys from South Carolina corralled by that state's senator Lindsey Graham after a golf date with Trump, had been dismissed within days of signing on.

Schoen now had gone into a sullen, alarming funk—a strike of sorts, it suddenly seemed, only a day before the trial was to begin. Here was the stop-the-trial crisis: Castor had not provided a place for Schoen's college-age son, Simon, to sit on the Senate Floor.

It was hard to know why someone would take on the defense of Donald J. Trump. Most lawyers—over and over again—had run from the opportunity. But now here might be an understandable reason: Schoen wanted to impress his offspring.

"Where is Simon going to sit? There's no place for Simon. I was told I could have Simon with me." Schoen seemed about to hyperventilate, as the McConnell aides stared in shock.

In the cold orbit of Donald Trump, where only one man's feelings usually prevailed, this was a weird human meltdown, and no one knew what to do.

"I was told I could have Simon," Schoen repeated, refusing to move on.

The room reflected a collective uh-oh, everybody trying not to look at anyone else, more confounded than ever about the basic mechanics of how Donald Trump was going to defend himself with one of his lead lawyers about to cry.

"You have assistants. I don't have anybody." Schoen folded his arms.

"But there are limited places, and your son doesn't have direct involvement with the case," Castor said, trying to mollify his new colleague.

"That's not the point. That's not the point!" Schoen said, his voice breaking. "I was told I could have him out there. I want him out there," said the indignant father—a greater role than defending the former president.

"Dad, Dad, it's okay," said the son, finally, moments before the second impeachment trial of Donald Trump looked about to collapse into absurdity, dysfunction, and tears, with each person in Room S-211—like all people who had found themselves in Trumpworld—wondering how they had arrived at this freaky place.

1

DEATH STAR

The president had heard something that filled him with fear and brought his campaign to a sudden standstill. The 2020 race was about to enter the key summer months. Joe Biden was sheltering in his basement while the president was taking all the grief for COVID-19, and without his fighting rallies. But attacking Joe Biden, really slaughtering him as only Trump believed he could, was just what the Dems wanted him to do—so he wouldn't do it. He wasn't that stupid.

Brad Parscale, the Trump family–appointed campaign manager, who had built one of the biggest political money machines in history, a true Cadillac campaign, was seeing poll numbers sink and everything going south because Donald Trump was afraid to go on the attack. *Because the Democrats were fucking with him.*

Jared Kushner, the president's son-in-law and the behind-the-scenes power in the campaign, told Parscale to make the call. They needed a new strategy. They needed the ultimate strategist. Call Karl Rove!

Parscale implored Rove to come to Washington ASAP. He had to sit down with the president. The Dems were screwing with his head. The Dem strategy was diabolical. Trump and the party needed him.

Rove was the political mastermind of the George W. Bush administration, and was on top of the Trump list of party doyens targeted for frequent slurs. ("He looks so fucking stupid up there with that white board," Trump would reliably mock Rove for his election night appearances doing hand tallies on Fox News.) But he was a professional, something in short supply in Trumpworld.

At the raging high point of the coronavirus pandemic, Rove, from his home in Texas, got himself to Washington, DC, for what was to be a secret meeting with the president. Except that, when he was shown into the Oval Office, a dumbfounded Rove found fifteen people there. Rove had spent eight years in an office near the Oval when it was a place of formal and select purpose. This was a bus station. Or, as Trump aides, as confounded as anyone by the Oval Office's crowds, ado, and unlikely characters, often put it, the *Star Wars* bar scene.

There was Parscale and Kushner; Ronna McDaniel, the Trump-picked head of the Republican National Committee; Mark Meadows, the newly appointed chief of staff; Dan Scavino, who managed the president's Twitter accounts; Hope Hicks, the president's personal advisor and hand-holder; and a slew of others Rove didn't know.

The president—to Rove's ear, sounding like Alec Baldwin's *Saturday Night Live* impersonation of him, an impersonation (of the impersonation) that Rove himself would often perform—outlined the dilemma: He had come to understand that the Democrats wanted him to attack Biden so as to weaken and destroy him. And then, when he had destroyed "Sleepy Joe" as only Trump could, the Democrats' plan, he had it on *super-secret* authority, was to replace Biden as the nominee with ... Andrew Cuomo. The governor of New York had been leading a popular daily television rebuttal to the White House's COVID response—a constant affront to the president.

"Even assuming they wanted to do this," said Rove, astonished by the ludicrousness of the assumption, "why would Bernie Sanders"— the clear Democratic runner-up—"allow it to happen?"

"Because," the agitated president said, lowering his voice, "this is all being coordinated by the Obamas. And," Trump added, more darkly "there is a very good chance that Michelle will go on the Cuomo ticket as VP."

As respectfully as he could, Rove offered that he found this to be, to say the least, a bizarre theory. Trump, with his signature shmear of flattery, acknowledged Rove's reservations, piling it on about his being the smartest, and yet the president was dead set on believing that here was an exceedingly clever conspiracy to bring him down— yet another one!

The conversation among the fifteen people in the room—some participating, some there for no reason that Rove could fathom— continued for an hour. Should they attack Biden and run the risk of Cuomo? Should they let Biden alone until it was too late for the Dems to replace him? But how strong might he become without being challenged in his basement? And wouldn't Michelle Obama certainly spell doom for them? What was to be done?

"My God, where did he get this from?" Rove asked Parscale as he was being shown out.

"Sean Hannity."

"Sean Hannity?" Rove repeated, incredulous that the Fox News anchorman, with his extravagant conspiracy theories, was dictating the course of a presidential campaign.

"POTUS believes it," said a helpless Parscale. "If you could call Hannity and tell him to let up, that might be good."

* * *

The campaign was a distilled reflection of the president's indecision, resentments, disorganization, constant sense of victimhood, plus the last thing that anyone had said to him—and, as well, his son-in-law's sagacious and self-protecting judgment not to challenge him on any of this. But right now the imploding campaign was all being blamed on Bradley Parscale, the website developer from San Antonio, Texas, who had risen from "digital guy" in 2016 to become Kushner's and the Trump children's handpicked campaign manager and who proudly called the billion-dollar Trump political enterprise the Death Star—an odd choice of metaphor because rebel forces in *Star Wars* were able to fly in and destroy the superstructure.

A crowd gathered in the Oval for a cover-your-ass meeting on July 13, with the on-the-verge-of-ripshit president behind the Resolute desk autographing pictures as he surveyed the room. The official purpose of the meeting was to assign blame for the fact that the Republican nominating convention was a month out and a looming catastrophe. Having been forced to move the convention from Charlotte, North Carolina—effectively run out of town by the city fathers because of COVID fears—the Trump campaign now had no plans for the new location, in Jacksonville, Florida. The program manager in Charlotte—already paid!—had simply walked away. There was no finalized venue in Jacksonville, no program, no program manager, no speeches written, no speakers locked in, and almost no money because the RNC had already committed to contracts in Charlotte.

The disarray was in fact largely a product of the president's own continuing reluctance to give up on the idea of a mass convention blowout, the ultimate Trump event. But now the blame fell on everyone else.

"I thought you were doing this?" a despairing Parscale had said days earlier to the RNC's McDaniel, who was here in the Oval to defend herself.

"Planning the convention? Excuse me. That's your job."

McDaniel, the niece of Mitt Romney, the 2012 Republican presidential nominee—she was previously, and proudly, "Ronna Romney McDaniel," but Trump had encouraged her to drop "Romney" from her name—was now Trump's adjutant as head of the RNC, a careerist good at holding her tongue. She was here with her chief of staff, Richard Walters, who was clutching renderings of possible convention venues in Jacksonville. Jason Miller, directly in front of the president's desk, was trying, maskless, to keep his social distance from the RNC pair. Kushner had recently brought Miller, a reassuring presence for the president from the 2016 campaign, back from disgrace: in 2016, Miller had had an affair with another staffer, who'd gotten pregnant and who had militantly and indefatigably taken to Twitter against him when he refused to leave his wife; she was still tweeting four years later. There was Lara Trump, who, in the competition among Trump brothers' wives and girlfriends, had become the most zealous in-law (although Don Jr.'s girlfriend Kimberly Guilfoyle was coming up strong). Beside her sat a stricken-looking Parscale. At six foot eight, Parscale seemed always to be slouching, not wanting to appear too much taller than the theoretically six-foot-three president, annoyed if he wasn't the tallest man in the room. Mike Pence, the ever-smiling vice president, sat to the president's left. Kushner; Bill Stepien, one of Parscale's deputies; and Marc Short, the vice president's chief of staff, faced one another on the couches, with a model of Air Force One between them.

But the president seemed unable to focus on the impending disaster of the convention. He reverted to another disaster from a few weeks before. He had wanted a blowout stadium rally—and not an outdoor stadium, an indoor one!—to show that the base was more committed to him than afraid of COVID, and for him to show the base that he was tougher than Sleepy Joe Biden hiding in the basement.

"I need my people. I need my people" was his refrain, translated down the chain by Parscale as "We have to get him his people."

The result had been the Tulsa rally. Parscale announced one of the biggest crowds of the president's career: there were a million requests for tickets, Parscale exuberantly and fatefully tweeted. Alas. According to the Trump campaign, the Secret Service put the final crowd size at twelve thousand, and the fire marshall at six thousand, for what was supposed to be among the largest (and most expensive) rallies in Trump history. A total screw-up and disaster! (What's more, it got out that quite a long list of Trump staff members at the rally had come down with COVID. A furious Trump ordered testing to stop so more cases could not be identified.)

"Has Brad actually ever done anything right?" The fuming president addressed the room as though Parscale weren't there. "He's fucked up everything." The president, looming over the now-photo-ready clean surface of his desk, only the red button for summoning his Diet Cokes visible, exploded: "How can you be so stupid? Answer me!" he demanded of Parscale in front of the group.

Parscale tried to stutter out a defense but then just shut up and took it.

"I'm asking you how you can be so stupid? I can't believe I have such a stupid campaign manager," Trump stormed on at Parscale. "You've fucked up everything!"

Everybody in the room had seen this story before. In a way, it was a Trump set piece, a venting that seemed not to exhaust him but to create more fuel as it went on. Everybody endured their own mortification, appreciating the lesson—for most everyone, not their first lesson—that the president always needed someone else to blame; that nothing bad happened to him that was not directly caused by the failure or active malice of someone else.

"Stupid, stupid, stupid . . . just tell me how stupid you can possibly be? I want to know. Really. Tell me." He continued whipping his campaign manager.

The next day, Trump and Kushner demoted Parscale, and turned the operation over to Parscale's deputy, Bill Stepien. They would have to restart the campaign.

* * *

George Floyd was killing him. A week after Floyd's murder caused by a Minneapolis policeman kneeling on his neck, setting off mass protests across the country, the president, in order to show his strength, had walked across Lafayette Park to St. John's Church with his generals—the park cleared of protestors by tear-gas and other riot-control measures—and he'd been killed for that. He looked weak. And it wasn't just the lamestream media on him—Tucker Carlson on Fox was calling him weak and ineffective. What's more, he was being screwed by his own Justice Department and attorney general, paralyzed, afraid to move, Bill Barr, such a suck-up, but as worthless, it turned out, as Jeff Sessions, the man he'd replaced for being worthless.

Now Trump had had enough. He needed legal action and media pushback.

"I'm getting killed on Tucker and we're not doing a damn thing," he sat in the Oval Office and screamed at Mark Meadows, the former North Carolina congressman, only a few months into his job as Trump's fourth chief of staff, and White House counsel Pat Cipollone, one of Trump's favorite White House targets for mockery and abuse.

Protestors in Portland and Seattle were taking over everything. They were toppling statues and nobody was doing anything—making him look . . . weak! Looking weak was as bad as you could look.

Cipollone said they had things in motion.

"I don't give a shit what you have in motion, I want them in jail. They should get ten years in prison for toppling a statue. And that Mayor Wheeler . . ."—the mayor of Portland—"what a loser. Can't we just send in the Guard?"

Cipollone, stammering, tried to explain the procedures for employing National Guard forces.

"You've been telling me that shit for weeks. I'm getting killed.

Tucker is talking to millions of people. But you and Barr and all of my 'great lawyers' aren't doing a damn thing. Shut it down! Arrest them! Do what you have to do! I have the worst lawyers. Get the radicals locked up! You guys can't even do that! What is wrong with you? I have to do everything myself."

* * *

It was, so often, a White House of one.

It was him on the phone.

Much of the business of the Trump White House was conducted or influenced through Trump's lone dialing. He reached out at will and on a whim, often to people he had just seen on television or to random people who inexplicably were able to get through to him.

Now he had Dick Morris on the phone.

Morris was a political operative who was expert at showing up at propitious moments of American negativity, a divisive genius behind the American political curtain.

In 1994, after the disastrous midterm election following Hillary Clinton's health care overhaul, Morris was called in to help bring the Clinton administration back to its tougher, dunk-on-the-liberals roots. Morris was liked by almost nobody and forever trapped in the amber of a too-good-to-be-untrue sex scandal—nailed sucking on a prostitute's toes—his very distastefulness somehow allowing him to be the agent of everybody's harshest political go-to moves.

In some ways, this was quite an unexpectedly conventional move for Trump, to need such a Dr. Darkness.

Morris—"weaseling his way in," in the frustrated view of the White House staff—had a hook. His father, Eugene Morris, had been, several generations before, a real estate lawyer who represented Trump interests; Trump remembered him fondly: "A real tough son-of-a-bitch."

Morris now offered Trump an attractive proposition:

COVID and its mounting deaths were being put on the president. And they were trying to lay the death of George Floyd on him, too—just as they'd tried to *wrongly* pin Charlottesville, the 2017 white supremacist rally that ended in mayhem and violence, on him. But, obviously, said Morris on the phone, it was the protestors who were America's problem—not COVID!

If someone was trying to blame you, you needed to defiantly blame somebody else, a reliable practice in politics, but one embraced by Trump to a new self-defining extreme. The buck, every Trump aide understood, always stopped somewhere else.

Morris had endless suggestions for the president and articles to print out and read—not that he would read them, but Morris would call and offer a recap of them (not that Trump would necessarily listen to the details of the recap). While never showing up at the White House or visiting the West Wing or campaign headquarters in Rosslyn, Virginia—or getting paid, a willingness to work for free being a high recommendation for anybody employed by this president—the seventy-three-year-old Morris suddenly became the president's whisperer, with even baser political instincts than Trump's own.

At Kushner's instruction John McLaughlin, the president's favorite pollster, was supplying Morris with his data. Kushner was trying to triangulate: keep the president happy with this new voice in his ear, but keep Morris at arm's length from the campaign and, hopefully, minimize his influence on it.

Morris's presence was mostly kept secret. The only indication was that a series of discordant questions with a racial tilt started showing up in the weekly tracking polls. "Where are these fucking questions coming from?" wondered the Trump pollster Tony Fabrizio. Then Morris sent an email mistakenly copied to the top campaign team. The secret was out of the bag: the campaign's message was now, officially, despite Kushner's triangulation, chaos in America—the social order in turmoil, criminals on the loose.

While the nation in a sea change of attitude seemed in sympathy with the Black Lives Matter movement, the new Trump message, in an abrupt turn, one following an old script, was all in on law and order and bad things about to be done to white ladies in the suburbs.

And, hey, chaos *was* engulfing the streets. At least, if you watched Fox News, it was. While virtually the entire media was otherwise focused on COVID, BLM, and economic meltdown, Fox News was nearly 100 percent focused on the burning of America.

Morris's law-and-order campaign, his backlash against the protests, his darkness at noon in America, would certainly, Morris convinced the president, fire up the base. "Firing up the base" was a Trump White House term of art meaning a set of Trump tweets that would get Fox to double-down on an issue, thus amping up the passion at rallies, getting poll spikes, and, as well, in a perfect circle, reassuring the president that he was doing the right thing.

That was always the goal: assuring the president that he was right.

In this, foreshadowing much that was to come, little intruded on the president's chosen version of reality.

Morris sketched a series of ads, malevolent and dark, that he sent to the president—in fact, written by his wife, Eileen McGann:

Phone rings:

Thank you for calling 911, the police emergency line. Due to defunding and increased call volume, we cannot take your call right now. Either leave your name and number and we'll call you back. Or wait your turn on line while we help your fellow citizens. Estimated wait time is one hour thirty minutes.

In the weeks before his demotion, Parscale started to test the new messaging. Ever sensitive to what the president wanted reported, Parscale duly reported that Morris's scare ads, as tonally far from the greater media's sympathetic picture of the Black Lives Matter movement as could be, were scoring off the charts in pre-air testing.

And there followed two more ads in the Morris "insurrection" series. This was saturation placement: some $40 million would be sunk into the summer law-and-order campaign.

But nothing moved. Not an uptick in the polls anywhere. Forty million spent for nothing—quite the first time in modern American politics that law and order failed as a hot-button issue.

* * *

To say that midsummer was the absolute nadir of the campaign—a failing message, an effective logistical collapse, and an overhaul of the leadership—would not be true, because there were greater nadirs to follow. Immediately.

Bill Stepien, the new campaign manager, shortly discovered a $200 million gap between what the campaign intended to spend and what it would likely take in.

Stepien, also a Kushner choice, was a Brooks Brothers young Republican campaign op type, forty-two but, with a thick hat of boyish hair, looking ten years younger. In Trump's preferred circle of tall men (though not, preferably, as tall as him), Stepien was short. A New Jersey boy, he had been a key aide to the state's governor Chris Christie. But in 2014, Christie threw Stepien under the bus when his administration was accused of punishing an unfriendly mayor with massive traffic jams in his town—"Bridgegate." Stepien was cleared of all responsibility but reduced to menial political jobs until Kushner—always looking to slap down Christie, who, as a federal prosecutor, had put Kushner's father, a New Jersey real estate developer, in prison—hired him during the 2016 campaign. Quite the opposite of Parscale, Stepien, a veteran of many races, understood that presidential campaigns were as much a function of budgets as they were of rallies and even of a candidate's magnetism and celebrity appeal.

The Trump campaign had raised more money than any campaign in history, but Parscale had spent more to get it than any campaign prudently would. The campaign would be bone-dry by the first week of October. There would be no money for media, salaries, or even campaign swings on Air Force One.

"Was he stealing from me?" the president now demanded about Parscale in meeting after meeting, confounded by this predicament and adding Parscale's alleged perfidy to his continual monologue. "Where did all that money go? Was he ripping me off? I knew he was ripping me off even in 2016!"

Part of the answer was that the money had gone to raise even more money in order to inflate the numbers that kept the president happy. Trump held in his head a running tally supplied to him on a constant basis by Parscale, and lifted by flights of exaggeration of his own, of every cent the campaign had raised. Yes, the Trump campaign could brag about more online donors than any campaign in history, by a factor of ten to one, but the costs of online fundraising, while it might seem inexpensive with free email, was in fact 35 to 40 percent more than traditional in-person events. Customer acquisition costs—list acquisition, social media ad buys, the buildout of a digital marketing arm—bedeviled every online direct-to-consumer business, which is what the Trump campaign had turned itself into. Whereas, with the old ways, the only costs for in-person events at which you might raise $10 million or $20 million were an hors d'oeuvre platter and some cheap white wine and the use of a rich supporter's house.

And in a Trump world of constant freelancing, and in an atmosphere of surprise revenue streams and general cheerfulness and congratulations about personal gain, it was even harder to know where the money was going, whether it should or shouldn't be going there and even if you should be asking that question.

Katie Walsh—a longtime RNC advisor and consultant, a Parscale ally, and briefly the deputy chief of staff in the Trump White House before she fell out with Kushner—had been installed as the interface between the campaign and the RNC. After Parscale's departure, she was confronted by campaign aides who demanded to know why she was drawing fifteen thousand dollars a month from Parscale-controlled companies that were billing the fees back to the campaign. "Am I?" she responded, a disingenuousness that was also a reflection of the labyrinthine difficulties of knowing who in Trumpworld was paying whom and for what.

Months after the campaign, there would be continuing questions about how much money had flowed from the campaign through out-side companies controlled by Parscale, with estimates going as high as $30 or $40 million. Gary Coby, who ran online fundraising, was sending close to five million text messages a day to potential donors. The cost of a text message at this volume should have been one or two cents apiece, but the Trump campaign was spending more than seven cents a message, much of that going through Coby's outside company.

"Whatever Gary is making is worth it," said Kushner, cutting off any questions. "He's the one bringing in all the money." In Kushner's platitude-friendly management style, if you had the big stuff—that is the money (and in the Trump political world, like the Trump business world, you focused on the bragging rights of gross rather than the harsher reality of net)—the little stuff would follow.

As for Trump, the consternation, rumors, and blame over mis-spent and misdirected (if not misappropriated) funds within the White House and the campaign organization all had one thing in common: agreement that the president had no idea where the money was going. He was "blissfully unaware," in one campaign official's description.

* * *

On July 20, the pollsters came into the Oval Office—John McLaugh-lin and Tony Fabrizio.

McLaughlin reliably tried to make his poll numbers say what Trump wanted them to say. Fabrizio didn't give a shit and, indeed, made little effort to hide his disgust for the president. Fabrizio was sixty years old, overweight, and—quite an anomaly in the Republican circles in which he made his living—had been out of the closet for several years. He was snarly and gruff and more and more seemed to enjoy being a Debbie Downer, just telling you what the data showed.

Trump, for his part, thought Fabrizio charged too much and leaked to the *New York Times*. The president seemed personally repelled by him, settling on him the obvious sobriquet "Fat Tony."

Fabrizio was leading the presentation. It was Stepien, Fabrizio, Miller, McLaughlin, and White House political director, Brian Jack, lined up in front of the president's desk, with Scavino, Kushner, Meadows, Hicks, and policy advisor Stephen Miller, and random others wandering in and out of the Oval. There was a PowerPoint deck, but it was handed out in hard copy. Trump held up a page at a time with distaste: "What am I looking at here?"

He pressed the red button on his desk for another Diet Coke.

An impatient Fabrizio was trying to talk him through it. But Trump was resisting, a combination of his not wanting to hear what he was being told, not being able to understand what he was being told, and not being interested enough to want to understand it.

It was hard to hold Trump's attention when he wasn't the one talking.

But Fabrizio's message was clear: the president was on the wrong side of COVID. No longer did the "China virus" rhetoric work; it had run out its shelf life.

It was plain, and Fabrizio spelled out the numbers almost with delight: a large majority of voters saw masks and testing as the way to open the economy, with nearly 70 percent of voters in agreement on this. When the president was perceived as taking COVID seriously, his approval ratings spiked. Most people blamed the spread of the virus on the lack of social distancing and failure to wear masks; most voters and a majority of Trump voters favored requiring masks to keep the country open; most favored an executive order requiring masks for indoor public places; two-thirds of Trump voters thought the president's wearing a mask would set a good example and be an act of patriotism; and eight of ten of Trump voters supported wearing masks as a preventative measure.

There really wasn't any room for debate.

"This is a no-brainer," said Kushner, seemingly awestruck by the numbers, wandering in and suddenly paying attention to the meeting.

Even McLaughlin came down clearly in favor, at the very least, of less hostility toward masks, suggesting an indoor mask mandate in federal buildings.

The scowling president dug in harder. "I know my people. They won't have it. They don't believe it. No mask mandates!" He clenched his shoulders and lifted his hands to ward off the mask mandate, his whole body seeming to revolt at the very notion.

Meadows, four months into his new chief of staff role, understood the president's COVID phobia and now willingly yessed him: "A mask mandate? People would go crazy."

"Mr. President," said an equally immovable Fabrizio, "I'm going to tell you what your voters truly believe about masks. They believe whatever you tell them to believe."

Trying to move Trump one way often resulted in moving him the other. Telling him what he should do made him not do it.

But the president suddenly went from sourness to delight. And inspiration! He had another way of dealing with COVID. If the Democrats were using COVID against him, he would use it against them: they could just use COVID as a reason to delay the election. "People can't get to the polls. It's a national emergency. Right?" He looked around to everybody for their assent—and for congratulations on his great idea.

There was often a small moment of silence and a collective intake of breath whenever Trump, with alarming frequency, went where no one wanted to go or would have dreamed of going. The reaction now was somewhere between gauging Trump's being Trump, with everybody understanding that nine-tenths of what came out of his mouth was blah-blah and recognizing that here might be a hinge moment in history and that he really might be thinking he could delay the election. If the latter, then there was the urgent question of who needed now, *right now*, to go into the breach?

A reluctant Meadows did: "Mr. President, there isn't any procedure for that. There would be no constitutional precedent or mechanism. The date is fixed. The first Tuesday . . ." Meadows's sugary North Carolinian voice was tinged with panic.

"Uh-uh. But what about—?"

"I'm afraid—no, you can't. We can't."

"I'm sure there might be a way, but . . . well . . ."

* * *

The next week, the president brought up delaying or avoiding or somehow bypassing the election again. This time at a debate prep session at his golf club in Bedminster, New Jersey.

These were more golf sessions than debate prep, and the president was in a relaxed mood. Indeed, aides had often thought he was at his most inane or dangerous at Bedminster, freely musing about the extent of his powers (it was in Bedminster that he made his "fire and fury" threat against North Korea).

Chris Christie, the former New Jersey governor and on-again, off-again Trump ally, was participating in the mock debate session, which was quickly digressing into the usual Trump rambles and monologues.

"I'm thinking about calling it off," said Trump, as though without much thought.

"The prep?" said Christie.

"No, the election—too much virus."

"Well, you can't do that, man," said Christie, a former U.S. attorney, half chuckling. "You do know, you can't declare martial law." Christie followed up: "You do know that, right?"

It was both alarming and awkward that he might not.

Trump's preposterousness often combined with the possibility of his dead seriousness to create a moment in which embarrassment and crisis seemed indistinguishable.

* * *

He juggled the election in his mind not necessarily as a win or lose proposition. Rather, it was a roadblock or technicality to get around, like taxes or zoning regulations or refinancings, or some advantage the competition might employ unless he came up with a sharper countermove.

Back in March, in the first days of the lockdown, nearly thirty people had gathered, maskless, in the Oval Office, the president behind the desk, a lineup of chairs in front of him, the couches filled, people behind the couches in the back, more at the sides— people from the White House, from the campaign, from the RNC, and from the Trump family. The subject was the Democrats' efforts to steal the election.

Steal was rather a term of art, meaning not really *stealing* the election, but lobbying state and local authorities to liberalize election rules to make it easier for people to vote who were less inclined to vote—that is, getting more Democrats to vote.

"Steal" in the president's mind extended beyond voting. The "Russia hoax" and the two years of the Mueller investigation were attempts to steal his presidency. He repeatedly returned to his claim that he deserved two extra years, bonus years, because of "the steal."

The Democrats, under the guise of COVID, were out to "rig" the election, albeit (it was sometimes added) "legally."

In this, they had a "genius," or a "Dr. Evil": Marc Elias. An election lawyer, Elias had served as the top lawyer for both the Bill Clinton and John Kerry campaigns and—to Republicans, even worse—was a partner at the Democratic law firm Perkins Coie, which had played a key role in funding the "dossier" that purported to place Trump in a Moscow hotel room with hookers urinating on a bed where the Obamas had once slept.

Elias was, most Republicans seemed to agree, the best election lawyer in the country. He could really *steal* an election. He was the center of a "system" and a "machine" that would bend election laws in the Democrats' favor. That's what they were up against.

One of the people in the meeting was a young lawyer named Jenna Ellis, whom Trump had personally recruited after seeing her on television and who had recently joined the campaign. She was now a favorite for, in addition to her pleasing television performances, telling the president that Democrats were challenging "election security standards" (i.e., rigging the election). Another person in the meeting was Justin Clark, a longtime election lawyer and Trump White House staffer and now campaign aide. Ellis and Clark had clashed the week before, on a panel at CPAC, the yearly gathering of professional conservatives. Ellis, with no discernible expertise on election issues, other than that the president had posted her to his campaign, argued that the Democrats were trying to undermine the system and, in fact, the Constitution itself. Clark, the professional election lawyer, said mostly that, actually, both Democrats and Republicans traditionally fought to maximize their procedural advantages at the polls and that, in the end, mostly fighting to a draw, elections were won by the better candidate with the better campaign and with the better message—and not because of election rules.

Clark felt personally sure that the Trump campaign, in these still-early COVID days, was well-positioned for a convincing win and that they had election process issues under control. Ellis, as the meeting ended without clear resolution or plan, huddled with the president with the urgent message that the Democrats could win only by letting every Tom, Dick, and Harry vote. That's how they would steal it, in some unacknowledged irony, by making it easier for people to vote.

* * *

He also often seemed to see the election as something personally directed against him, inherently somehow unfair, putting it remarkably bluntly: "They are using the election against me."

On August 7, Trump aides and pollsters reconvened at Bedminster—McLaughlin in person, Fabrizio on the phone. Bedminster had hopeful airs of a British gentlemen's club, but looked more like a steak restaurant. Everybody was gathered around a conference table, each with Trump-branded water bottles—and with intense air-conditioning.

The message was clear: mail-in voting, which the president was so bitterly trying to oppose, would be the sea-change factor in this election. Almost 70 percent of the electorate would vote early.

The advice was unambiguous: while mail-in ballots would help the Democrats, militant opposition to mail-in ballots would dramatically compound the Republicans' disadvantage.

Trump's resistance to the logic here was painful.

In the age of COVID, in-person voting would surely be depressed and, already clear, mail-in ballots would be the attractive default option—hence, the Trump pollsters argued, you obviously wanted to encourage your supporters to vote however they might want to do it. But, in the president's mind, this now had become part of the COVID forces and strategy aligned against him. COVID was the way for the Democrats not only to ruin his beautiful economy but also to steal his election—by getting people who would otherwise not vote, the "low-propensity" voters, Democratic voters, to cast ballots.

Stepien, the new campaign manager, only a few weeks into the

job, tried to argue that they had a better ground game than the Democrats and could get mail-in voting to work in their favor.

In an effort to lessen his own exposure to the president's wrath
and resistance, Stepien brought in the Republican House leader,
Kevin McCarthy, for a follow-up meeting in the Oval Office to help
argue the case—"My Kevin," in Trump's term of endearment and
ownership. The Republican Party was sending out voter request
forms and getting a 2 or 3 percent response, McCarthy explained,
where they should have been getting closer to 15 percent.

The president seemed not to understand.

He, argued McCarthy, with surprising pointedness, was depress-
ing the response rate.

Of the various kinds of mail-in voting (Trump himself was a
mail-in voter in Florida)—absentee, request, universal mail—Trump
generally confused them all, casting aspersions on people who voted
in any way but at a polling station on Election Day, and making it
somehow a Trump virtue to show up in person. Couldn't he just
shut up a bit on the subject?

No, it had to be fought. He made the obvious point: most of the
people who voted by mail wouldn't be voting for Trump.

Somehow, to accept mail-in voting or even not to oppose it was,
for Trump, to capitulate to a greater effort to attack and undermine
him—mail-in voting was a symbol of the forces against him. Already
he was far down the rabbit hole of predicting a stolen election on
the basis of mail-in voting. He could not now encourage people to
vote by mail, even if by doing so he might increase his share of the
mail-in vote by enough to win the election.

Stepien and McCarthy tried painstakingly to explain the different kinds of mail-in voting, some of it not at all part of what the
president was against, and to point out how he was discouraging all
Republican mail-in voters.

"What if the weather is bad in Pennsylvania on Election Day?"
a frustrated Stepien asked.

"Unsolicited," Stepien and McCarthy suggested as the word he should use, unsolicited ballots, that's what he was against, right? "Can you just say you're against unsolicited ballots?" They hoped that message adjustment might help at least a little bit.

He didn't like it—it all still seemed suspicious to him and wrong not to show up on Election Day. It was how they would steal it.

But as with many meandering Trump meetings—well, they were all meandering—if you stayed long enough he might get bored and agree. So, yes, he would say "unsolicited"—at least until he stopped saying it.

* * *

By the time of the Democratic National Convention, on August 17, Trumpworld had reached another new polling low.

Jason Miller had suggested in a convention planning meeting, only half humorously, that they send the president to Taiwan on the day of Biden's acceptance speech, which, while it might start World War III, would at least get them the news cycle.

At this point, among Trump enemies and allies, earnest conjecture began about how a man with a long history of refusing to acknowledge defeat would handle a precise numerical reckoning against him. Trump enemies, those associated with the Biden campaign and other outside liberal groups, began strategic discussions and planning for far-flung Trump scenarios (i.e., how he might try to hold on to office), reports of which fueled Trump's conviction of an organized effort to deny him reelection and force him from power—"the steal" was fast becoming anything that might keep him from winning the election.

* * *

And yet the president also had a preternatural confidence. How could he possibly lose to Joe Biden?

He had really never wavered in his belief that he was a natural winner and Biden an obvious loser. Such was Trump's own salesman-like certainty that Andy Stein, a New York City political figure and a Democrat who had known Trump for many years, was absolutely convinced by his frequent and sometimes daily calls with the president that, despite almost all polls saying otherwise and despite his Democratic friends telling him he was smoking something, there was no way Trump could lose.

Trump's entire world was construed from what he saw on television. Accordingly, most of his perceptions about Joe Biden were based on Biden's inability to dominate the screen, with Trump cackling at Biden's lapses and mimicking his verbal hesitations and stutter. He was certain that Biden could not survive a debate with a full-on Trump. The sleepster would wilt and sink into inarticulateness against his more voluble and charismatic (or at least hyperaggressive) opponent. Whatever had been wrong in the campaign, whatever challenging circumstances COVID had created, nonetheless, debating Biden was the simple solution.

Trump had nothing but contempt for Joe Biden. He found Hillary Clinton—"Crooked Hillary" now known simply as "Crooked"—almost endearing compared with Biden. This was perplexing to many because Trump's great level of animosity seemed to have no personal basis. It was hatred without history. Trump and Biden hardly knew each other and had seldom, if ever, interacted. And yet Biden had become his bitter nemesis, a symbol of failure, whereas Trump was the symbol of success—and that was, for Trump, a mortal divide.

Biden was not only a perennial also-ran and second-rater and hapless swamp creature, but he was now old and fragile in a way that Trump seemed to need to exaggerate to compensate for his own age. Biden with his hair plugs. Biden with his face lifts. Biden with his shades. It was disgusting (pay no attention to Trump's own myriad comical vanities). Nobody was passionately going to follow Joe Biden. Likewise, against the background of his own dubious aca-

demic history and defensiveness over his own intelligence, Trump
had come to see Biden as not just stupid, but the stupid*est*; not just
lackluster in school, but the *last* in his class; not just prone to verbal
errors, but *senile*.

If he lost to Biden, what would that say about him?

Here was another piece of the constant running monologue: "How
could I lose to this dummy, last in his class, busted for plagiarism,
dumbest guy in the Senate—even Obama thinks he's a joke—total
has-been, never was . . . *He's* going to be president? Yeah, right."

It was therefore more than just frustrating that Biden was holed
up in his basement, sheltering from the pandemic, his vulnerabili-
ties and weaknesses kept hidden from the public. Weeks and weeks,
months and months virtually, without appearing in public. This was
frustrating! But to Trump, it was also a clear sign of an opportunity.
The very fact that Biden's people wouldn't let him out in public
demonstrated that all you had to do was get him out. All you had
to do was get Joe to stick his head out of the basement—and then
kick it.

This was reinforced by Trump's campaign staff. The analysis was
that Trump had gone way too easy on Hillary in their first 2016
debate. Now they were defining a new strategy. Journalists write
about debates based on the first half hour, and audiences drift away
after that, too. Trump therefore was set to bring Biden down in the
first thirty minutes—one typical Biden mess-up, in the face of a
towering and mocking Trump, was all it would take.

There were a half dozen practice sessions over the summer, in
the White House or Bedminster. Trump was more focused than he
usually cared or was able to be. He seemed to be enjoying the easy
layup here. Shooting fish in a barrel. The prep team ran old video
clips of Biden. Since 1988, Biden had been saying the same old
things. Economy, military, race—same canned answers every time.
Anytime he went off script, he crashed and burned. "Everybody has

a plan," said an even-more-confident-than-usual Trump, quoting Mike Tyson, "until they get punched in the face."

If Biden's insubstantiality got under Trump's skin—quite the personal insult that they would be considered equals on a stage!—the president was also in an ever-building fulmination against the moderator, precise and unshakeable Fox anchor Chris Wallace. Wallace had become, for Trump, a fly in the Fox ointment. The president regarded Fox's devotion to him as his due and took its slights more personally and more bitterly than all others. Doubts on Fox struck Trump as the deepest disloyalty. A fifth column. If he couldn't count on Fox, what could he count on? Also, in his mind, these feelings had gotten mixed up with memories of Wallace's father, Mike Wallace, a grand figure of a former media age—*60 Minutes* correspondent, talk show host, New York City social figure, confidant of the rich and famous—with whom Trump seemed to identify. Chris Wallace was a shadow of his father, and why did Trump have to deal with him? (Trump made this comparison explicit in various tweets and constant mutterings. It seemed to amuse him to compare the seventy-three-year-old Chris Wallace with his dead dad.)

There were scores to be settled in this debate, and Trump was always at his most satisfied—most expansive, even—when he was set to settle a score.

Hope Hicks, whose presence reliably calmed the president, was in the prep sessions. There was also Dan Scavino, who'd worked at Trump's golf course in Westchester County, New York, and then become his social media guy (his Twitter guy), and who, after most everyone else in the administration had fallen aside, had become the person who probably spent the most time with the president.

Bill Stepien was there with Jason Miller and Stephen Miller, the president's speechwriter and primary holder of the right-wing policy portfolio. Meadows and Kushner drifted in and out of the room. Kellyanne Conway, who had recently left the White House—largely because of the obstreporous public campaign against the president by her husband, George Conway—was back playing Chris Wallace. Chris Christie was playing Biden.

Debate prep was a sought-after ticket, partly because Trump was in a reliably good mood. Reince Priebus, the president's first chief of staff, managed to grab an invite for a session. Sean Hannity and Laura Ingraham tried but failed. Rudy Giuliani came once, but no one wanted him back. His phone rang constantly, and he couldn't shut it off. He shuffled endless pieces of paper without being able to find what he was looking for. He couldn't work his iPad to bring up what he wanted to show, reliably stalling meetings. And he went down rabbit holes—they could get Hunter Biden, if they could just find the guy who signed the forms to get Hunter the waiver to get into the military. And he passed gas, constantly.

On September 27, two days before the first debate, ABC News called the campaign for comment because the ABC affiliate in Florida was reporting that Brad Parscale was holed up in his house—shots may have been fired; it was possibly a hostage situation. Shortly, a video would surface of Parscale, bare-chested in cargo pants and holding a beer, being tackled by a police officer.

"Man, that guy has some fucking problems," acknowledged an astonished Trump. The psychotic break of the architect of the Trump political operation seemed to many in the Trump orbit consistent with the campaign's troubles.

On debate day, the key group gathered in the Map Room at the White House for a final prep session to pump up the inner (and outer) Trump. Chris Christie—maliciously or tactically or both—suddenly turned the practice session, by now a rote affair, into something much different: "You have blood on your hands," said Christie, sitting directly across from the president and, theoretically, channeling Biden. "You're a complete failure. All these people have died from the virus. And it's your fault." Worst of all, said Christie playing Biden, Trump had attacked Biden through his son, when Trump's own family was full of problems! Christie appeared to be trying to reinforce the plan to attack Biden aggressively, at the same time profoundly misreading how his old friend would respond to this approach—even as the president glared at Christie, arms tightly crossed and becoming clearly agitated.

"Mr. President, you have only ever shown callous indifference at every point when you should have shown concern and compassion. It was your coddling of the racists in Charlottesville . . ."

Looking back, people in the room judged Christie's attack on the president to have worked, to have turned up Trump's fury—but to have turned it up way too much. All challenges to Trump meant, invariably, a response at an always greater level of ferocity, and Christie had vastly raised the bar. This not only set Trump toward an attack on Biden, but also, as observers would judge in hindsight, broke his relationship with his old crony.

In the history of televised U.S. presidential debates, this one was the most disastrous. In the Trump camp postmortem, it was Biden's fault. (It could not, certainly, be Trump's fault.) They were foiled by, and had no reasonable way to anticipate, the extent of Biden's weakness. Biden was not strong enough to counter or object to Trump's interruptions. Hence, there was no drag on Trump's unrelieved attack—which, unbound, became more determined and furious, if not incomprehensible and, at moments, seemingly deranged.

And compounding everything, there was Chris Christie afterward, being interviewed on television saying what a rotten job the president had done.

* * *

And then, at the point where little could have gotten worse, in the succession of falling West Wing dominoes, the president got COVID.

Trump's rush to the hospital on Friday, October 2, was a black ops affair. The immediate staff knew no more than the outside world. Stepien assumed Meadows knew, but he could not get Meadows on the phone. The others closest to the president, Hicks and Scavino, didn't know—or, if they did know, they weren't letting anyone else know. (In fact, it was Meadows on the helicopter with the president to Walter Reed hospital—with Scavino following.) The family didn't know. The vice president didn't know. Never a model of effective communication, the Trump White House now with the king's life in the balance, closed down authoritarian-style. Was he dying?

More than a few staffers went so far as to mordantly suggest that this was his way out of a hopeless campaign.

And then he rose like a phoenix. Again.

As surprising as the rush to the hospital was his apparent recovery a day later. Although they tried not to admit it, there was a not-infrequent sense among the president's aides that he had magical properties. To the extent that people stayed with him, this was one of the reasons. Not just that he survived, and not just that he survived what nobody thought he could survive, but that he did it so often. Why bet against him?

Trump blamed getting COVID on Chris Christie, who would himself come down with the virus a few days later (and spend a week in the ICU). Christie had sat across from him at the debate prep table, and Trump had seen the spittle come out of his mouth and tried to duck from the droplets.

Blaming Christie probably had less to do with the reasonable likelihood that the former governor had in fact given COVID to Trump—or, for that matter, Trump might as easily have given it to him—than with how incensed he was at Christie for viciously attacking him "like he meant it" during the debate prep, and for the part this had played in getting the president so wound up that he overplayed his hand with Biden.

In fact, among those in the debate sessions, it was Hope Hicks who got COVID first, and the president would accuse her as well of giving it to him, but affectionately, teasingly, because, in fact, it was Christie who had really given it to him, he was convinced—and who would be, from thereon out, exiled from the Trump circle.

Kushner, Scavino, and Meadows, all in elaborate PPE gear, took up their posts in the president's hospital room. Stepien and Jason Miller were on the phone. The president's nearly overnight COVID resurrection was, to Trump if to no one else, a sign that the campaign—dragged down by COVID, the economy, and the Black Lives Matter protests and whacked, in the eleventh hour, by the debate and now, unimaginably, *insurmountably*, by the weird poetic justice of his being struck down by the virus he had worked so hard to deny—was itself going to rise again.

Thinking this might be a humbling moment, Stepien pitched Trump on the idea of coming out of the hospital and taking a new, softer tone: You're a grandfather . . . and we need to be safe . . . and all do the right thing . . . and look after one another. Here was an opportunity, Stepien saw, to show a completely different side of this guy. And Trump got it, Stepien thought. He bought it. He understood.

Except, then the president broke out of the hospital and did his indomitable, nothing-touches-me, boss-man ride around the hospital grounds, exposing aides and his Secret Service detail to the virus, and on his return to the White House, proclaimed how "powerful" he felt—taking, Stepien noted to others dryly, "a different approach."

* * *

Crises in Trumpworld almost always became an opportunity for sycophants and promoters promising to save Trump from whatever trouble he was in.

Fox's Sean Hannity, whose own career and identity were now intricately tied to Trump and who was despairing about the state of the campaign, was calling the president in a daily panic about the campaign's advertising—it sucked. "You're not speaking to people the right way," he told the president.

In turn the president, complained to his campaign aides: "We're not speaking to people the right way."

But Hannity had a solution. He'd personally written just the ad Trump should be running. ("Joe Biden: Radical, Corrupt, Extreme, and Dangerous." And then a further enumeration, with pictures: Socialist; Green New Deal; Amnesty and Sanctuary Cities; Law Enforcement.)

"I'm just trying to be helpful," Hannity said, now constantly hectoring the campaign team. "I don't want anything."

To keep Hannity from complaining more to the president, who would then complain more to the campaign, the campaign produced Hannity's sixty-second ad—and, at the cost of nearly $2 million, ran it only on Hannity's show.

Rudy Giuliani, the ultimate Trump freelancer, repeatedly sidelined, now stepped forward again with a deus ex machina that resembled nothing so much as Nixon's discovery of Alger Hiss's Pumpkin Papers (notes and microfilm said to prove that Hiss was a spy stashed in a literal hollowed-out pumpkin in his backyard). In the final days of the election, Giuliani had located, in a computer fix-it shop in Delaware, a hard drive purported to belong to Hunter Biden which Giuliani claimed contained emails linking Joe Biden to the same alleged foreign corruption to which Giuliani and Trump had previously tried to link Hunter and, hence, his father, resulting in Trump's 2019 impeachment.

If the Democrats seemed briefly stricken by what might be revealed by Hunter's alleged hard drive, the confusion, oddness, and general harebrained quality of all Giuliani's efforts and gambits reliably overshadowed any point he was trying to make.

Here, too, was another Trumpworld theme: the president's need to be proven right. Hence his refusal to give up on bad hands that had been played before. Trump, temperamentally unable to let almost anything go—mental loops hardened in place, obsessional and fixated—was yet convinced that Hunter Biden was Joe Biden's mortal weakness; Trump could hardly believe this prospective Hunter Biden scandal hadn't played. Hunter Biden was Trump's answer to the great Russia hoax. It was really the Clintons, Obamas, and Bidens tied up in foreign corruption—not him! And he could prove it. Hunter Biden was the smoking gun.

But here was, he hotly felt, the media establishment circling the wagons, unwilling to see Democratic scandal where Democratic scandal so obviously was, with even social media blacking out Hunter Biden news. Come on! There on video was Hunter Biden blowing crack and getting a foot job! Giuliani had given the hard-drive scoop to the *New York Post*, which headlined it for days—but it was an October dud. Hardly any other pickup. If anything, it was seen as yet another sign of Trump desperation.

Eric Herschmann, another insider-outsider, now popped up to save the day. A former partner of one of Trump's former lawyers, Marc Kasowitz—who himself had briefly been a White House presence before being routed by other White House factions—Herschmann had joined an energy company in Texas and cashed out with, depending on who was telling the tale, tens of millions, hundreds of millions, or hundreds and hundreds of millions and a collection of high-end autos that often made much-commented-upon appearances in the West Wing parking lot. He was one of the billionaire types (or almost-billionaire types, or would-be-billionaire types) whom Kushner courted and trusted. Plus, he was willing to work for free. He had become an official come-as-he-wanted Trump whisperer.

Now he came with Tony Bobulinski.

Bobulinski was a former Hunter Biden business associate of unclear status—at best, a business partner scorned. Bobulinski, where all other efforts had failed, had a tale that—really, truly, this time—would link the Bidens to international corruption, various Trumpers now believed.

Herschmann and Stefan Passantino, a lawyer who used to be with the White House Counsel's Office, trying to promote Bobu-linski into the campaign's October surprise, were sure they had the

Wall Street Journal taking this story. Trump even let it slip that there was a big story coming in the *Journal*. But the story they got was a story in the *New York Times* about how the *Journal* wasn't going to run the story. The best they could do was Breitbart, the online right-wing outlet once run by Steve Bannon. (Curiously, Bannon, now a Trumpist podcaster, had joined with Giuliani to promote the Hunter Biden hard-drive story.)

Passantino phoned Jason Miller the morning of the second debate, with the Trump team on its way to Nashville. An off-the-books plot to get Bobulinski to Nashville, to make him an official guest at the debate, was instantly hatched. It recalled Steve Bannon's recruitment of a lineup of Bill Clinton accusers—Juanita Broaddrick, Paula Jones, and Kathleen Willey—to attend the last Trump-Clinton debate after the "grab-'em-by-the-pussy" *Access Hollywood* tape came out.

The plan: they'd confront Biden with his son's accuser and make the accuser available to the press.

Except that it was 8:30 a.m. in Nashville, and Bobulinski was in Los Angeles, and COVID flight restrictions meant he'd never get there in time. So, he'd need to fly private.

Who was going to pay for that?

Well, they'd worry about that later. So, yes, do it.

Except that Bobulinski, now in the air an hour before debate time, couldn't land because when the president is on the ground, air traffic control shuts down all private flights in the vicinity.

"Oh—wow," said the president, when told about the plan (and the plane). "Just like when Bannon brought in Juanita Broaddrick."

They got clearance to land Bobulinski at an airfield a half hour out and sent a fleet of Suburbans to fetch him. He arrived without a dress shirt, requiring an emergency trip to Nordstrom.

The campaign team decided not to risk setting up an official campaign press conference, just in case Bobulinski was nuts; instead they just walked him into the press pool. There Bobulinski displayed the three phones on which he claimed he had texts from Hunter Biden discussing the foreign payoffs with his father.

Still, they were faced with establishment skepticism—October surprise PTSD, aides were calling it—and what, in the president's mind, would be another aspect of the plot to steal the election from him: the media continuing its blackout on the Biden "scandals." Fox News covered the press conference live, but everybody else ignored it.

Mostly the press wanted to know who had paid for Bobulinski's private plane.

Oh, and then Bobulinski lost the phones with the Biden messages, the only "proof" for any of his claims ("proof" now conveniently beyond scrutiny). They were in a toiletry bag and . . . somebody put it down. (Ten Trump aides searched the debate auditorium and surrounding areas, finally finding the phones in the parking garage.)

Months later, Trump would still be citing postelection polls that found that 1 out of 6 Biden voters would have had serious doubts about their vote if they had only known about Tony Bobulinski—if only the media hadn't protected the Bidens.

And yet who is to say that the president's determination to sully Hunter Biden—indeed, his absolute belief that the Bidens were among the most corrupt political families of all time—even in the face of a dubious media, didn't have some effect.

Something did. The polls were rising.

* * *

The calamitous nature of the Trump campaign, handicapped by both candidate and organization—here was an incumbent president who, inconceivably, was being outspent down the home stretch by nearly three to one—helped convince liberals that a landslide was coming for the Democrats. They would take the White House and the Senate and would vastly expand their House majority.

But, equally, with sudden movement in the numbers, the Trump team—given that you just never knew what was going to happen when Donald Trump was involved, and with calamity always the background to their victories—was far from giving up on its own hope for a landslide.

Suddenly, even in the face of COVID, you had Trump rallies in the final days of the campaign showing new, unmistakable enthusiasm—crazy stuff! Four, five, six rallies a day—all giving Trump a druglike high and, more than any polls or data analysis, a deep sense of the political landscape and a conviction, not something he had ever really wavered from, that he was absolutely going to win.

His last rally was in Grand Rapids, the same place it was before Election Day 2016.

"Who has voted so far? Has anyone voted?"

Tepid response.

"Okay, good. Because you're saving it, right? You're saving it for Tuesday? Right? No, we're cool. We're going to have a red wave—they call it the great red wave—like nobody's ever seen before. Like nobody's ever seen."

His closest campaign staffers were still hesitant—few had illusions that this was anything but the most cursed and hapless campaign in history. And yet, seeing the numbers move and the crowds build gave them a new sense that they might in fact make it, that, if only they had a few more days or a week more, they could surely get there.

From an internal campaign memo days out from the end:

> The Biden campaign has begun to see their polling numbers take a turn—and they're now talking openly about it as a warning to their allies.
>
> They fear what we know to be the most important factor in the race: momentum at the end. The momentum has clearly shifted in our direction over the last week.

On a state by state basis, the trendlines from mid-October 2016 are starting to reappear—and that's why the Biden campaign is sweating. . . . History is beginning to repeat itself.

Trump's timing might be off, but his instincts were so often right: Joe Biden, even given all the breaks, was sinking, and Trump was rising.

2

ELECTION NIGHT

Miami-Dade came in first, and it blew out all Trump team expectations.

"This is good, tell me this is good!" shouted Jason Miller across the Map Room to Matt Oczkowski, who ran the data operation.

"This is *very, very* good," muttered Oczkowski, hardly looking up from his screen.

Florida had become a key bellwether. It counted its early voting tallies ahead of Election Day. Returns here would be some of the first in the nation for a battleground state. If Trump lost Florida, he faced a virtually insurmountable map.

The more realistic of the Trumpers understood that there was a good chance that older people, a dominant Florida bloc, usually Republican swinging, would this year, fearful of COVID, come back to the Democrats. What's more, Michael Bloomberg had committed to pouring $100 million into the state for Biden—although many in the White House, most of all Trump, believed he wouldn't make good on that promise.

It was clear by 8:10 p.m., Donna Shalala, a Democratic personality with strong Clinton cred—she served as his secretary for health and human services—who had come to Congress in the 2018 anti-Trump backlash, was out. She was followed by Debbie Jessika Mucarsel-Powell, another liberal Democratic pickup in 2018. By 8:30, a CBS News exit poll had Florida seniors breaking heavily for Trump.

The Republicans had doubled down on their Florida spend (digital, radio, and television), with a singular message: The Democrats were socialists. *¡Socialistas!*

To Democrats, a ridiculous message. To Hispanic voters, apparently a resonant one.

After Miami-Dade, the I-4 corridor came in, "the road where presidents are picked," the 130-mile stretch of Florida between St. Petersburg and Daytona Beach, passing through Orlando. The Trump campaign had beaten Matt Oczkowski's numbers in Miami-Dade with Cubans; now they were beating them in Orlando with Puerto Ricans.

Florida represented a set of key communities. If the campaign performed at the levels Oczkowski predicted, not only would Trump win the state, but his win would be a strong indication of what might be expected across the country. Now, down the line, the campaign was holding or beating Oczkowski's model for seniors, Hispanics, women, Blacks, and even the most difficult group in Oczkowski's model, eighteen-to-forty-four-year-old independents.

The doubts about the campaign and, among some, the realistic notions about the difficulties they were going to have that evening, potentially insurmountable difficulties, began to evaporate for many in the innermost circle.

Several campaign aides registered Kushner's uncharacteristic hand pump.

Before 9 p.m., Kushner called upstairs to the Executive Residence and told his father-in-law that the Florida numbers meant fantastic news across the country.

"Holy shit," said Miller, standing up from the horseshoe set of tables in the White House Map Room.

* * *

There were four giant screens in the Map Room, side by side against one wall, like a polyptych on a Renaissance church altar.

With its nineteenth-century still lifes and portraits, the formal and ceremonial nature of the Map Room was a slightly discordant setting for the boiler room nature of the final hours of a political campaign, with everybody intensely bent over laptops, fortified by Diet Cokes and gummy bears.

The White House Election Day operation had begun in the Eisenhower Executive Office Building (EEOB) in the predawn—the first hours of voting across the country were key moments for spotting any suspicious business (people not showing up to open the polls, polling stations without ballots, poll watcher issues). There was a station for each of the seventeen battleground states, staffed with a lawyer and a political pro who knew the state. The rapid-response media operation was based out at campaign HQ in Rosslyn, just across the Roosevelt Bridge. There banks of computers were staffed with people fresh out of college, who sat staring at two massive walls of TV screens following social media, scouring platforms for any mention of voting problems or irregularities or funky stuff. But the true brains of the operation were here in the Map Room.

Oczkowski, up late the night before, was in his seat by late afternoon. He had come into the 2016 campaign through the back door of Cambridge Analytica, the behavioral target–marketing company that was owned by far-right billionaire Robert Mercer, which had, controversially, scraped Facebook profiles for its own data banks and for its own use—an effort, with at best mixed results, to use social media data mining for right-wing causes.

After 2016, Oczkowski left Trumpworld to run his own company, HUMN Behavior. He billed himself as an expert on "Middle America"—that is, the people who might otherwise not be captured in the typical marketing grid, the more-than-not unhappy and dis-satisfied American. "Using tactics from the worlds of behavioral science, data science, growth marketing, sentiment graphing, and geographic analysis," HUMN, per its official description of its methods, could reach the hidden Trump voter. Oczkowski's models had proven uniquely and, in many ways, eerily correct in 2016. In 2020, Parscale, trying to buttress his own claims of vast data omni-science, had pulled "Oz" back into the reelection effort (Parscale always introduced him as an MIT graduate, when in fact he was a graduate of James Madison University in Harrisburg, Virginia).

Still, there were reservations that Oz's head was perhaps too far in the clouds, or up his ass. Of the three possible Great Lakes states—Wisconsin, Michigan, and Pennsylvania—with one abso-lutely required for a Trump Electoral College win, Oz analyzed that Michigan was the likeliest. Why?

"Candor," Oz said. "Trump's candor."

"Candor?" said one incredulous campaign staffer. "Not immigra-tion, or taxes, or jobs? Candor? What the fuck does that even mean?"

In strong measure, the optimism that had grown inside the Trump campaign over the last two weeks and that was filling the war room at the EEOB on November 3, and the rapid-response room at HQ in Rosslyn, and the more elite war room in the White House Map Room, was Oczkowski's. His models were clear—as had been the case in 2016, the Democrats had stalled, and Trump was fast com-ing up from behind. They were going to win.

Nearby was Gary Coby, the online fundraising point person—portly and bespectacled, missing his usual camouflage MAGA hat (Coby was being hailed by Kushner as being the true MVP of both campaigns for his ability to raise obscene amounts of money and perhaps also for making obscene amounts for himself). Mike Hahn, who ran the campaign's social media—the hyperaggressive finger behind the ubiquitous Team Trump Twitter account—was at the horseshoe desk next to Justin Clark, the deputy campaign manager and lawyer, buttoned up and by the numbers, who oversaw Election Day ops. Then there was Matt Morgan, the campaign's general counsel, who had come over from the Pence team, and Meadows, Stepien, and Miller.

A more typical Election Night war room would have had, by early evening, the beginnings of a great litter of pizza boxes and beer bottles, but there was tonight a self-conscious effort to observe White House decorum, with everybody anxiously policing their own trash.

As the first polls closed—parts of Indiana and Kentucky in the Eastern Time zone closed at 6 p.m.; Florida, Georgia, South Carolina, Virginia, Vermont, and the other parts of Indiana and Kentucky in Central Time closed at seven o'clock—the Map Room got more crowded. There were no masks and no social distancing. The president's sons Don Jr. and Eric, and Eric's wife, Lara, pushed into the tight crowd. Tony Ornato, who had been uniquely promoted from the Secret Service into a Trump White House political job, was in the room, too. Now there was Jared Kushner and Ivanka Trump, in a double-breasted blazer; Stephen Miller, in a double-breasted suit; Kayleigh McEnany, the White House press secretary; Ronna McDaniel; Laura Ingraham, the Fox News anchor; and Jeanine Pirro, the Fox News personality—"the Judge," as Trump invariably greeted her, because she was once a New York State judge and now played one on television—who, by early evening, was already on unstable feet. Rudy Giuliani wandered in and out.

On most Election Nights after hard-fought and expensive races, and especially Election Nights in a presidential race, there is among senior-most professionals and those closest to the candidate a heightened sense of probable outcome—uncertainty existed only within a narrow margin. But in the Trump war room that evening, there were any number of people who believed it might be a landslide *either way*.

One floor up, in the East Room, four hundred guests (cabinet people, congressional allies, contributors, friends of contributors, and friends of White House friends) were gathered. The mood, a true believer's mood, was full of excitement, a palpable thrill that it was going to happen again, all the more thrilling for the coming smackdown of liberal certainty.

"They're dead, they're dead, they're dead; we won, we won, we won," repeated the weaving Pirro in the Map Room—or similar words that were growing harder to decipher.

Upstairs, in the Residence, the president was watching election coverage with Melania, his tie off, shirt loosened. The phone wasn't leaving his hand, one call to the next. He kept checking in with various people in the Map Room, often having each confirm what the person sitting next to them had just told him. He was looking not so much for information, here in a holding pattern before first results, as for confirmation that all was as he had convinced himself it would be: it wasn't going to be just a win but, kicking it up several levels, a really, really big win. A landslide.

Now . . . Trump ought reasonably to have had enough information to have maintained a nuanced sense of a complex and teetering map—indeed, he ought to have had as much information on the vagaries and micro-indices of the night as anyone anywhere. But, in fact, he was still getting most of his information either from television, with the networks now confused, if not panicked, by the early Trump numbers; or from the highly edited picture supplied to him by aides who, if bad news was not absolutely necessary to deliver, would surely deliver only good news.

The president was data averse. He was a seventy-four-year-old businessman who did not use a computer and could not work a spreadsheet. He could receive neither email nor texts. He was, in some sense, among the more information-limited people in the nation. In addition, he was averse to his own data expert.

Among the Trump team, where most everyone had an *Apprentice*-like geniality and firm handshake, Matt Oczkowski was grossly introverted, deeply inarticulate, and often entirely unresponsive. At best, you'd finally get his views at the end of a long series of strangled ahems and stammers. Oz was almost everyone's point of constant reference and authority on the campaign, but the president was kept carefully away from him; he was too nerdy for the president. Occasionally, Trump would inquire further—"Oz? Like the Wizard of Oz?"—only to be told, as part of the pay-no-attention-to-the-man-behind-the-curtain theme, that it was short for an unpronounceable Polish name and that he was just the numbers guy.

The president's best data set was crowd size, and he was still reliving the overflowing and tumultuous rallies of the past week. By this measure, he and his data wizard were on the same page: once again, polls had been unable to accurately measure the true passion and fealty of the Trump nation.

* * *

The president, calling down, went over the Florida numbers again and again, taking an extra amount of pleasure in another defeat for Michael Bloomberg (doubly sure now that the former New York City mayor hadn't put up the money he'd said he'd spend to support Biden—although in his telling this would shortly become, even with Bloomberg spending all that money, Trump had won anyway!).

In the space of a few minutes, the anxieties of COVID, the economy, and an underdog and nearly flat-broke campaign were replaced by the sense, inexplicable to even the most dedicated Trumpers no matter how many times they had experienced it, that the president possessed some otherworldly power. And suddenly, many Democrats, in a new nightmare scenario, were equally having to consider the sorcery by which Trump held and might expand his base.

The overwhelming number of political analysts and media commentators believed that the polls, chastened by 2016, had been corrected for those anomalies. The experts had convinced themselves and, by this time, most Democrats and likely a considerable proportion of Republicans, that a decisive victory was about to unfold for

Joe Biden and many of the Democrats running with him. The insider's joke going into the evening was that anything less than a definitive rout would, finally and deservedly, kill the polling business forever. Even pollsters were making the joke—the point being that there was simply *no* chance at all that the pollsters, and the meta pollsters analyzing the pollsters and creating the complex models on which liberal certainty was built, could be wrong again. Liberals had convinced themselves—on the basis of COVID, Trump's debate catastrophe, Biden's stealth campaign, and of course on the strength of the seemingly incontrovertible numbers themselves—that the vaunted base would crack. The base's allegiance to Trump, the sort of devotion and awe seldom seen in modern political life, one that appeared to hold a reliable 40 percent or more of the electorate, locking down the leadership of the Republican Party in fear and cultish adherence, would turn from solid bloc to broken pieces.

And then the results started coming in from Ohio.

At their most confident, Democrats had been seeing Ohio as competitive. Even if they could just hold Trump's margin below the level of 2016 it would be a good night. Such hope, and such an optimistic barometer, collapsed in just about twenty minutes. Oczkowski had Ohio as a safe win, but Trump was beating the model among African Americans, seniors, and women. Even Cincinnati, which had been lagging behind 2016 Trump numbers in polling in the final weeks, was coming in strong in virtually all categories.

Meadows was in the Map Room, concentrating on his home state of North Carolina, a must-win state where they had been behind. He was now putting them ahead.

Iowa then followed, stronger than predicted. That was the theme: they were not only strong where they had to be, but much stronger than anyone had expected.

Early leads in the Great Lakes states, Oz reported, were holding.

Kushner called his father-in-law to say they were going to win: "It's happening."

Jason Miller tweeted: "It's happening."

Trump kept calling down to the Map Room to hear this same report from anyone who would give it; repetition was not a problem for him.

Family members kept going upstairs with positive reports, a small competition to be the bearer of good news, every one of them raising expectations.

* * *

Having spent a career of Election Nights, Bill Stepien tried to get into a dispassionate numbers place: it was all math. But the opposite was happening now. The professional was being overwhelmed by the emotional. Passion was getting in the way of the rational. Donald Trump had made magic happen in 2016, and he was making it happen again, it seemed. All magic.

Stepien had tried to explain to the president that the early evening would be unstable and the tallies unreliable. "The initial figures will be good for us, but they will tighten." He had hoped he had made this point clear to the president, but had no illusions that he actually had.

Somewhere before 10 p.m., the president formed the absolute conviction—that is, confirmed the conviction he had already formed—that he had again, overcoming all odds, won the presidency. He was in a relaxed, easy, I-told-you-so mood and, with his outside callers, basking in his victory.

Karl Rove called the president at about 10:30 to congratulate him on his win—which became another pillar of Trump's conviction that he had won. Why would Rove—a man as in with the Beltway Republican establishment as anybody, who didn't like Trump much and whom, to be honest, Trump didn't like—call to say he'd won if he hadn't?

The only information flowing to the president was positive information. And as he reported it to others, it became only more positive.

At just this point in the evening, Tim Murtaugh, the campaign's communication director, overseeing the campaign headquarters operation in Rosslyn, with access to the same information arriving at the Map Room, was glumly concluding that the odds were against their making it. At that same time, all his colleagues, ten minutes away in the White House, were into early celebration. The closer you were to Trump the more *you* believed what he wanted to believe.

* * *

Fox News's coverage was itself celebratory, if not ecstatic.

Trump's reelection would be a big payoff for Fox. The fortunes and future careers of so many Fox personalities had become tied to Trump, from Laura Ingraham and Jeanine Pirro celebrating at the White House that night; to former Fox anchor Kimberly Guilfoyle, the president's son's girlfriend; to Tucker Carlson and Sean Hannity, who doubled as Trump advisors and, to the extent Trump had any, personal friends.

At the same time, behind the network's overwhelming success pandering to the president and supporting the Trump narrative, there was another, more crucial story. Rupert Murdoch, the man who controlled the network, detested the president. He had always detested him. The fact that Fox News had come to so depend on Trump had helped divide the Murdoch family. The fact that the network was making so much money because of Donald Trump meant it could not truly be managed, other than to acquiesce to Trump. Two of Murdoch's children, his daughter Elisabeth and his son James, had all but turned on the family company because of Fox, sundering the patriarch's succession plans. In 2018, Murdoch sold the bulk of his empire to Disney, in no small part blaming Trump for his family's enmity and for ruining his dreams of an ongoing Murdoch dynasty.

But the Murdochs had been left with Fox News because it was too toxic for Disney.

Fox News had been the first network in 2018 to call the House of Representatives election for the Democrats—when polls still were open in the West, a Murdoch family guerrilla action against Trump. Ever since, Trump, as much as he needed the network, had heaped on it his frequent invective. Indeed, the marriage between Trump and the Murdochs, in some ways the foundation of the Trump movement, was quite a sadomasochistic one.

Shortly after 11 p.m., Murdoch's son Lachlan, in direct charge of the network, got a call relayed from the Fox News election data operation: the desk was ready to call Arizona—still, by most measures, hotly contested and still a definite Trump win in the Oczkowski model—for Biden.

The Fox News election desk was a data operation run by Arnon Mishkin—"a Democrat," Trump would always add—on the premise that it was independent of Fox News's otherwise partisan views. But this was merely cover for the election desk to bypass the news desk and to be directly answerable to the Murdochs.

Certainly, there was every reason, if you wanted a reason, to delay the Arizona call, to yet forestall it and still have no fear of being preempted by anyone else. Lachlan got his father on the phone to ask if he wanted to make the early call.

His father, with signature grunt, assented, adding, "Fuck him."

* * *

Bret Baier and Martha MacCallum were the Election Night anchors at Fox, with Bill Hemmer at the vote board.

At 11:15, with nearly everyone in the Map Room assuring the president about how good everything looked (the celebration in progress), Jason Miller heard from Bill Hemmer that they were going to call Arizona for Biden.

Miller involuntarily rose from his seat. "What the fuck?" he said out loud, looking around and seeing the still-merry and untroubled faces in the Map Room; optimism had become exhilaration. Here, in the Map Room, on the verge of Trump's reelection, was the inner circle of Trumpworld at its happiest. Jeanine Pirro was not the only wobbly one.

"That's what they're doing. That's what they're going with," said Hemmer, helpless.

"Who?"

"The election desk."

"When?"

"It's going up now."

Fifteen minutes before, just as the president was retaking the lead in North Carolina, Justin Clark, the election lawyer and deputy campaign manager, in a buoyant mood, had headed over to check in on the roomful of lawyers at the EEOB. Clark and Matt Morgan, also shuttling between the Map Room and the lawyers in the EEOB, both noted that it was quite a calm Election Night—no reports of widespread irregularities. It was a good night. Everything smooth. Clark got back to the Map Room at almost exactly 11:20, when Fox's Arizona call was made—flabbergasted.

All certainty and belief seemed to crumble in a second.

It was a campaign more of signs and superstitions than numbers.

* * *

Donald Trump saw an election emotionally rather than quantitatively.

For him, the blow from Fox News was the ultimate treachery. What's more, it was a direct challenge to Oczkowski's numbers. Oz had Arizona for Trump by a narrow but certain margin—between 10,000 and 20,000. The map now was full of narrow-margin states, and if Oczkowski hadn't gotten it right in Arizona, then other narrow margins might need to be questioned, too, necessarily plunging the celebratory mood into one of uncertainty and doubt.

Uncertainty and doubt were not places Trump could easily occupy.

And the stakes here weren't psychological only for the president or for the celebration already in progress or for the supporters on hand, but for the broader map. If this was a squeaker, if this was going down to the wire, then perception easily became the margin of victory. If Fox, the president's certain ally, was calling an extremely close state for Biden, then that might empower other close calls by other networks. It was a hell of a lot harder to claw back from a called race than it was from an undecided one.

What had just happened was also a tell. The astonishment at the Fox call in the Map Room—that it seemed like such a senseless slap across the face—meant that the Trump team had truly thought Arizona was safe and not in any way equivocal. This was not disappointment that Fox had made the call against them; it was incredulity. Meaning: all their expectations could be off, way off. The Trump premium on good news was pushing all the narrow margins solidly their way. This was the illusion that Fox was now challenging.

But, more to the point, the immediate downer here was going to be the president. So far, up in the White House Residence, he had been happy and optimistic; that was easy to deal with. Now the entire enterprise would have to shift to Trump maintenance.

* * *

Meadows, Kushner, Miller, Stepien, and Clark, with Oczkowski in tow—Hicks, still recovering from COVID, was a noted absence—assembled and went upstairs. The president, Ivanka and her brothers Don Jr. and Eric, and the First Lady's chief of staff and press secretary, Stephanie Grisham, were waiting. You exited the elevator into a big hallway on the main Residence floor—the hallway ran the entire length of the White House. Everyone stood in a distended circle outside the Trump bedroom area, in some halfhearted or half-embarrassed effort at social distancing.

Trump was back in his suit and tie, dark, grim, ripshit, muttering, repeating to himself, "What the fuck? How can they call this? We're winning. And everybody can see we are going to win. Everybody's calling to say that we're winning. And then they pull this." Again and again, the same refrain.

Oczkowski, stammering—this among the few times he had ever come face-to-face with Trump—tried to argue that his model was correct, that they would win. Arizona's governor, Doug Ducey, had his own model, which also had them winning, said Oczkowski. They *would* win.

Eric Trump kept grilling members of the campaign staff: "Where are these votes in Arizona coming from? How is this happening? You said we were good."

The Fox call was just wrong, insisted a flustered Oz. It was inexplicable.

It was, interjected Trump, the fucking Murdochs.

Here was a delicate and worried circle, with everyone trying to avoid eye contact. Making matters even more excruciating, Stephanie Grisham was utterly wasted, keening as though there had been a death.

Desperately, Oczkowski kept repeating, "When the votes come in, we'll win," and then doubling down on his certainty: "Absolutely, we're going to win." He had the numbers for anybody to see.

The president's rage was entirely on Fox—it wasn't Arizona; it wasn't Oczkowski's model. He knew they had won. It was Fox. It was about the Murdochs, who were always trying to fuck him. He was the golden goose at Fox, and what did that get him? They owed him, but they had screwed him. In his Hobbesian worldview, people were always trying to take things from him. Indeed, it seemed clear—clear as day to him. He had won Arizona, everybody said. But Fox and the Murdochs, for perfidious, disloyal, and very mean reasons, were trying to steal it from him. This was for him, in a psychological realm beyond an election tally, a vastly more personal place. It was not about the numbers; it was about the motives. The motive was to fuck him.

Trump, fulminating, crossing over into fury, directed everybody to call somebody: Jared to call Rupert; Jared to call Hope and to have her call Lachlan; Miller to call Bill Sammon, the Fox News Washington Bureau chief and part of the election decision desk. *Call. Do something. Call everybody. Fight this. They have to undo this. They have to!*

Undoing became the president's focus. *This has to be undone!*

The Murdochs, in repeated calls, washed their hands of the matter. It wasn't their decision . . . no. Nothing, you understand, they could reasonably do. Even if they wanted to.

* * *

There was a *Rashomon* version of the president's call with Karl Rove that evening. In this, it didn't take place at 10:30 p.m., but long after Fox's Arizona call at 11:20. Kushner reached out to Rove and said the president was coming apart about Fox, and could Rove call him and say there was still a long way to go. Rove made the call and told the president to hang in there. This wasn't congratulations. It was solace.

* * *

The president was still hearing a tempered yet optimistic—though significantly less so as the night went on—report on election data: Oczkowski's numbers were slipping but showing that they would make it.

Still, Stepien was hearing that Rudy Giuliani, who had begun the night at a table amid the four hundred guests in the East Room (one of Giuliani's guests, Healy Baumgardner, would come down with COVID the next day) but then roamed through the White House, was getting through to the president with a message that had a much different emphasis, initiating what aides knew to be a dangerous game: *You've won the election, and they are going to try to steal it from you.*

"He's just telling him things that are not true," an unnerved Stepien relayed to the inner circle of Trump advisors, Meadows, Miller, and Clark.

The four men got Rudy aside—in the China Room, with its display of pieces from every president's table settings. Rudy had had too much to drink, which seemed perilous among all the porcelain and fine dishes lining the walls, and was fumbling through his devices, looking for numbers. He was full of intensity and weird math.

Clark noted that he had not seen Rudy for the entire campaign.

"We've won! We need to declare victory!" Rudy kept saying.

"What do you know that we don't know?" said Stepien, trying to delicately humor him.

"Because if we don't say we won, they will steal it from us," declared Giuliani in a new twist, again rifling through his devices for random numbers. "Look, we've won Michigan!"

"We haven't won Michigan," said Stepien.

"We have to say we won it! Otherwise they will steal it!"

Giuliani was instructing Clark, the election lawyer on election issues, and separately, on the phone to the president, outlining how they had to start to position for a fight. If it was close—and it would be close, because they were trying to steal it!—they had to get to higher ground.

Meadows, the Southern Baptist, with small tolerance for drunks, turned to the obviously hammered former New York City mayor: "No, we are not going to do that because we will look foolish. Things are moving too fast. We can't put the president in the position of looking like he doesn't know what he's doing."

Rudy had been trying to make this argument for weeks now—that they had to prepare for the worst—but everybody (Meadows,

Kushner, Hicks, and the campaign team, really, everybody) had tried to shut him out. To the degree that the Trump White House was united about anything, it was united in keeping Giuliani out.

But now Rudy had the president's ear:

The Democrats would do what they had to do to undermine a close call for Trump. Trump had to do what he needed to do to protect himself and to undermine a close call for the Democrats. He was winning, he would win—the accruing down-ballot victories for Republicans in Senate and House races made that clear: the GOP had lost in 2018 because Trump was not on the ballot; they were winning now because he was. But, if this was to be a fight—and of course it would be a fight, because the other side was surely going to do anything it had to do to win—this was, obviously, a death match. Trump had to put his stake in the ground.

There was another march up to the Residence. The original group was now joined by Giuliani; Vince Haley and Ross Worthington, the speechwriters; Derek Lyons, the staff secretary (the chief of staff's chief of staff); Pat Cipollone, the White House counsel; and Eric Herschmann. Everybody milled around; the not-too-ambulatory Rudy sat in a chair. The president wanted numbers, but no one was giving him numbers, so he got them himself, from the television. Why had the counting stopped in Pennsylvania, he demanded to know? And Wisconsin? What was happening in Wisconsin? But no one knew. No one actually knew if the counting actually had stopped. Well, it *had* stopped, the president insisted, because they were going to steal it. There was no other reason.

If the counting was going to stop, his logic now went, it had to stop for good—with him still ahead. The counting couldn't continue later or tomorrow; that was how they would steal it. They would know how many Biden ballots were needed and would come up with them. It was crystal clear to him. It had to be clear to everybody. They had stopped the counting so they could stuff the ballot box!

Obviously.

He had to say something. They had to go public.

Everybody left the Residence and headed with the president to the Green Room, one of the formal parlors on the first floor, to get ready for a speech—some sort of speech. Trump started rambling, with aides trying to get his words down. It wasn't so much a victory speech, which Giuliani was urging him to give, as an ongoing list of Trump grievances. Indeed, the script would stay remarkably consistent in the coming weeks, filled with random numbers that he had been informed of at some point in the evening and an impressionistic math that proved what he wanted it to prove. There was an effort to talk him down from his dark mood. If he was going to go out there, he should rally the troops, shouldn't he? Let's project optimism! But he had gone into a bad place.

At 2:30 a.m., Trump, with his wife, and followed by the vice president and his wife, came out and delivered a petulant, rambling, defensive, wounded cap to the evening—demanding, sore-loser style, that vote counting be stopped, with the final tally being an Election Day tally, while he was still ahead.

We won the great state of Ohio. We won Texas, we won Texas. We won Texas by seven hundred thousand votes, and they don't even include it in the tabulations. It's also clear that we have won Georgia. We're up by two-point-five percent, or a hundred seventeen thousand votes, with only seven percent left. They're never gonna catch us. They can't catch us. Likewise, we've clearly won North Carolina. Where we're up one-point-four percent. We're seventy-seven thousand votes with only approximately five percent left. They can't catch us. We also—if you look and you see Arizona—we have a lot of life in that ... But most importantly, we're winning Pennsylvania by a tremendous amount of votes.

We're up six hundred ... Think of this. Think of this. Think of this. We're up six hundred and ninety thousand votes in Pennsylvania, six hundred and ninety thousand. These aren't even close. This is not like, "Oh, it's close . . ." With sixty-four percent of the vote in, it's going to be almost impossible to catch. And we're coming into good Pennsylvania areas, where they happen to like your president. I mean, it's very good. So, we'll probably expand that. We're winning Michigan, but I'll tell you, I looked at the numbers. I said, "Wow." I looked. I said, "Woah, that's a lot." By almost three hundred thousand votes, and sixty-five percent of the vote is in, and we're winning Wisconsin. And I said, "Well, we don't need all of them. We need . . ." Because when you add Texas in, which wasn't added—I spoke with the really wonderful governor of Texas just a little while ago, uh, Greg Abbott. He said, "Congratulations." He called me to congratulate me on winning Texas.

I mean, we won Texas. I don't think they finished quite the tabulation, but there's no way. And it was almost complete, but he congratulated me. Then he said, "By the way, what's going on? I've never seen anything like this." Can I tell you what? Nobody has. So, we won by a hundred and seven thousand votes with eighty-one percent of the vote. That's Michigan. So, when you take those three states in particular and you take all of the others, I mean, we have so many . . . We had such a big night. You just take a look at all of these states that we've won tonight, and then you take a look at the kind of margins that we've won it by, and all of a sudden, it's not like we're up twelve votes and we have sixty percent left. We won states. And all of a sudden, I said, "What happened to the election? It's off." And we have all these announcers saying, "What happened?" And then they said, "Oh."

So, Florida was a tremendous victory: three hundred and seventy-seven thousand votes. Texas, as we said. Ohio, think of this. Ohio, a tremendous state, a big state. I love Ohio. We won by eight-point-one percent, four hundred and sixty thousand . . . think of this. Almost five hundred thousand votes. North Carolina, a big victory with North Carolina. So, we won there. We led by seventy-six thousand votes with almost nothing left. And all of a sudden everything just stopped. This is a fraud on the American public. This is an embarrassment to our country. We were getting ready to win this election. Frankly, we did win this election. We did win this election. So, our goal now is to ensure the integrity for the good of this nation. This is a very big moment. This is a major fraud in our nation. We want the law to be used in a proper manner. So, we'll be going to the U.S. Supreme Court. We want all voting to stop. We don't want them to find any ballots at four o'clock in the morning and add them to the list. Okay? It's a very sad moment. To me, this is a very sad moment, and we will win this. And as far as I'm concerned, we already have won it.

Afterward, the president moved with some seeming uncertainty, even aimlessness, into the Map Room, followed by his family and stay-close retinue. Suddenly, the Map Room was overcrowded and, most everyone noted to themselves, a super-spreader setting.

Oz was still focused on Arizona, with confidence that it would come back to them, but this did not yet seem reassuring to the president. Then the focus moved to Wisconsin. A big data release was due at 3:30 a.m. The expectation was that this might nail it for them. They could leave Election Night in a strong position, the momentum with them. Except, 3:30 passed without new numbers from Wisconsin. Everybody waited, without much to say, anxiety ramping up, the president muttering: Why the delay? What was happening? Had they stopped counting? What was going on?

Giuliani was hotly remonstrating—exactly what he said would happen was happening, he insisted. They now knew how many Biden votes they needed to offset Trump votes, and they were producing them! That's what the delay was about.

The president stayed for twenty minutes longer, becoming more and more agitated and angry before leaving for the Residence.

Matt Morgan, the election lawyer, who had been in the Map

Room for much of the evening, left shortly after 4 a.m., driving home for a few hours of sleep before getting back in first thing. On the drive home, it struck him that Wisconsin was on Central Time. The new data would hit when it was supposed to hit. They had just gotten the time zones wrong.

3

NEW VOTES

If Arizona was the gut punch, the 4:30 a.m. Eastern Time drop from Wisconsin was, at least for the realists when they woke up on Wednesday morning, the seeming knockout blow.

Nick Trainer, the campaign's political director (at home with COVID, the second time he'd contracted it during the campaign) with the closest contacts in the state, gave an early morning assessment that their four-figure lead in Wisconsin was soon likely to slip away.

Without Wisconsin, they had minimal chances of holding the map.

And yet . . .

"I spoke to state party guys up there, and they think there are some scraps that might allow us to claw back. Going to be a fight into tomorrow to see what is really left out," Oz reported after the Wisconsin data drop.

The innermost team (Kushner, Hicks, Scavino, Stepien, Miller, Clark, and Herschmann) convened on a call on Wednesday morning. Each was perfectly aware of the equivocal nature of where they stood. But the emphasis in the discussion that morning was still on the potential for a positive outcome in Pennsylvania, Georgia, and Arizona (despite Fox). They were under pressure but still up in Pennsylvania and Georgia, and trailing but seeing the potential for recovery in Arizona. The discussion, however, was not about the difficulties of holding on, difficulties apparent to all, but that the current numbers would be an encouraging balm for the president.

In fact, Oz had found his way to a positive place: "We're going to win this thing—assuming they don't find new votes."

Kushner called his father-in-law and outlined their strength in each state. Maintaining the current map, they would win, the president was told.

* * *

Another view began to develop as well: that they had to prepare for war. By 9:30 on Wednesday morning, the pollster John McLaughlin wrote the top White House and election team:

> The media is setting us up to allow the Democrats to steal the election.
>
> We need to prove fraud. Are there any precincts in Milwaukee or Detroit or Phila[delphia] where the vote count exceeds the number of registered voters?
>
> Monroe county in Michigan where the President won 43k–26k in 2016 hasn't reported?
>
> We should treat the leads as victory in AK, ME2 [Maine's 2nd Congressional District sends an elector separate from the rest of the state], NC and GA so our electoral count is 248 and is higher than Biden's to counter the media refusing to call those states for the President.
>
> We need to counter their public opinion push.

Dick Morris, copied on McLaughlin's email, responded to the others on the list with his projections of a win in Pennsylvania by 117,000 votes and a win in Michigan by 147,000.

James O'Keefe, the conservative activist specializing in sting videos, started to circulate a video of a U.S. Postal Service "insider" outlining a litany of abuses in Pennsylvania (all of which would be debunked by federal investigators).

Matt Schlapp, the CPAC moderator and Trump operative, started to tweet about a rumor in Arizona that a large number of Trump-area ballots were being invalidated because of the use of Sharpie markers. (This, also, was untrue).

Boris Epshteyn, who had worked in the White House in the administration's early months and who was now trying to reinsert himself, announced that, without any clear authorization, he was proactively heading to Arizona for the fight that was sure to happen there.

In some sense, the truest point was that the Trump campaign had no idea what was going on. The campaign's grip on the numbers, its structure for reporting and disseminating numbers, and its overall information management systems were as chaotic as any in recent presidential campaign history. What's more, this allowed a large range of outside and unvetted views into the mix and, among the many that found a direct route to Trump, often gave primacy to them.

Not knowing what they should do, they had to do something.

By Wednesday afternoon, fifteen campaign operatives and party heavyweights were dispatched to contested locations to appear on local media. But this, too, was a chaotic process, with the campaign protesting in a panicked email that it hadn't enough manpower even to handle hotel accommodations. A press conference was scheduled on a street corner in Philadelphia with Eric and Lara Trump, but protestors chased them away.

* * *

It was not only the campaign's chaos and competing power centers that gave it a problem with numbers and a confused sense of the playing field. The basic premise of election modeling and Election Day gaming and projecting is knowing where the votes are. The location of votes judged against turnout, past history, comparable demographics, and knowing when they have appeared in the ongoing count is part of a reasonable and generally reliable data analysis. But this goes amiss, radically amiss, if you don't know where the votes are, how many there are, who is casting them, and when they will be counted and reported.

COVID-prompted mail-in voting had seriously upset the models. Mailing in your ballot was a significantly different action from showing up at a polling station, and because it hadn't been done on such a massive scale before, it was difficult to anticipate or model that behavior—who would vote, how many would vote, and from where. Indeed, in the constant seesaw of trying to maximize your voters and minimize your opponent's, here, finally, was a curious work-around for the Democrats' longtime problem of getting "low-propensity" voters to the polls—and a way to counter the Republicans' longtime successful efforts to discourage those same voters from turning out. Now the low-propensities didn't have to go to the polls. It was this loss of an advantage that Trump found personally galling and somehow, by turning COVID into an opportunity, downright unjust. COVID was being used to the Dems' advantage—hence, *rigging* the election. That is, in Trump's mind, it was rigged, because, by putting this advantage to work, the Dems had taken the advantage back from the Republicans (even if, in the past, the GOP had used low-propensity behavior to *their* advantage). In a zero-sum world—worse, a world in which the Republican Party was getting ever smaller—you couldn't let any advantage go. If somebody stole your *advantage*, they were stealing your *vote*.

Democrats, by gaming the potential advantages of this mail-in behavior, had a lot better sense of the nature of this new voting paradigm. Whereas the Republicans—having, by the Trump diktat, written off mail-in balloting as somehow fanciful or illegitimate or ephemeral, or even by denying its existence (another general aspect of the party's COVID head in the sand) and believing it could somehow be rolled back or undone even as millions of ballots went out—were left substantially more in the dark.

COVID-inspired mail-in voting had created a blind pool of votes—at least to the Republicans. The mail-in ballots were a sword of Damocles over their heads

Oczkowski's level of confidence was exceedingly high with regard to the votes they knew about, but he was shaking off responsibility for what they didn't know about. And indeed, he had no real idea about the extent of what they didn't know. "We don't know what we don't know" became the curious cover for what was supposed to be the all-knowing data operation. And now Oczkowski was subtly shifting from "We are going to win" to "We should win."

"*Should* win? What is that?" many on the campaign team found themselves asking one another.

* * *

And there was another counting issue, arguably the most serious one.

Trump had a problem with numbers, or perhaps an alternative view of them. Where numbers were, for most people, the thing most fixed, for him they were surprisingly, even magically elastic. This was a particular real estate view. A buyer's $1 million property was a seller's $5 million property. There wasn't a number he couldn't naturally inflate. Of the many legal cases slowly proceeding against Trump, several involved the real value of his assets against the fabulously greater value he had vouched to his lenders. A few years before his run for president, various of his children had gotten into trouble for making assurances about the lineup of deals and buyers they had for apartments in a Trump building that, in fact, they could hardly give away.

Numbers were what you needed them to add up to.

What's more, it took a particular stomach, which almost nobody had, to bring Trump bad numbers. Even numbers of an equivocal nature somehow reflected on the weakness of the person bringing them. Hence, all numbers, in the telling, became Trump numbers— that is, good numbers for Trump.

Oz numbers were progressively more negative and pessimistic numbers, but they were much less negative and pessimistic than they should have been and yet still far more equivocal than anything Trump was hearing—by the time they got to Trump, they were positively rosy.

"We will win, if no new votes are found"—but this would have been better phrased as: realistically, with the votes still coming in, we will lose.

Still, as long as the reports were positive (that is, not negative), Trump, on the phone, was retailing this out to his long call list, who in turn, because that was what was required, assured him of what he was assuring them. Again, here was the information loop—if its intention was not to mislead, it was certainly determined to put off bad news as long as possible and, indeed, to find every possible avenue to good news. And it was a closed loop. Trump, incapable of, or uninterested in, looking at the data himself, relied on what people told him; and to the extent possible, they told him what he wanted to hear. And often, the people he was speaking to, which was why he spoke to them, strayed beyond even the good news he wanted in the assurances they offered him. They gave him ecstatic news.

Trump, having discouraged Republican mail-in votes, insisted he would prevail in a "red wave," a vast, unprecedented turnout of Republicans at the polls on Election Day. And, indeed, at this point, twenty-four hours after the polls had first started to close, the red wave seemed a certainty: the Republicans had seen a massive, record-breaking Election Day turnout. Fearing this, and fearing that Republicans would claim a win, the Democrats in the week before the election had promoted a counter view: the "red mirage." Don't be distracted, they said. The Republicans might pile up big early tallies on Election Day at the polls, where votes would usually be counted first, but the Democrats would pile up even bigger tallies in the mail-in votes, which register later. This, too, was now clearly happening.

Trump, however, was personally satisfied that the red wave had won.

He clung to a specific set of numbers given to him by the pollster John McLaughlin: if Trump could raise the 63 million votes he received in 2016 to 66 million votes—and he was on track to do this and, even, substantially exceed it—he would absolutely win. This was, Trump kept repeating (and would do so for months to come), "absolute."

By Wednesday evening, Oz was reporting that they were down by 93,000 votes in Arizona, but he believed that the outstanding votes would put them up 100,000, so they would win by 7,000. In Georgia, they were up by 46,000 and would lose the outstanding votes by 41,000, but still win by a slim margin. In Pennsylvania, they were ahead by 207,000 votes, and while they would lose the remaining outstanding ballots by 157,000, this still meant they'd win by 50,000. So, all good. These were the numbers being relayed to the president.

"We should still be okay . . . We should be able to pull this off . . . assuming no new votes," Oz assured the campaign team throughout day two.

Only a few caught the nagging afterthought that Oz now persisted in adding to every assessment: . . . *assuming they don't find new votes.* It certainly had an inexact, if not downright existential, ring, suggesting shadowy forces . . . or awfully poor analytics.

At 9:30 p.m. on Wednesday, MSNBC's Steve Kornacki said he believed Arizona was still in play, and Rachel Maddow could be heard saying, "Oh God," in the background, which was interpreted as a strong tell in the Trump camp: the libs were scared.

Wednesday closed as if still not a done deal, then at least a net-positive day: they *should* win. For many, this continued to translate into: they *would* win. Tuesday's despair had been replaced by Wednesday's optimism.

They had done it again.

"It's a landslide, they're telling me," Trump assured friends.

* * *

"How do you feel about Arizona and Pennsylvania?" Oz was asked on Thursday morning, before the roundup meeting.

"We're getting some info ready now for when we meet. We're still in the ball game in both places. Arizona didn't count as many as we thought last night, but it broke to us by 59 percent. Penn[sylvania], we still have room—assuming they don't find new votes." The margin of victory in Pennsylvania, the night before, at a firm 50,000, was now holding at 35,000. But Oz had also included a question, in all caps, in his report: "IS PHILLY TOTALLY REPORTING?"

Still, the numbers were holding up:

At 10 a.m. on Thursday, Eastern Time, in the next report, the numbers team was projecting a win by 7,000 in Arizona, by 5,000 in Georgia, and now down but holding by 25,000 in Pennsylvania.

* * *

The innermost team (Kushner, Hicks, Scavino, Stepien, Miller, Clark, and Herschmann) convened late Thursday morning. Kushner was advocating a largely positive spin, taking his cue from Oz. Nobody was seriously pushing back.

But every number that came in seemed to be an erosion of the last report. The Georgia margin was disappearing.

Oz reported near noon: "Every key takeaway is no one has a good read on GA—every outlet is all over the place. At this point people are putting out numbers based completely on conjecture and gut feelings."

It was hardly encouraging that the data guy didn't know what the real numbers were.

At 12:50, another 36,000 votes were added to the Pennsylvania tally, 35,000 of them mail-in. Biden won 25,000. There were rumors, but no confirmation, of 735,000 uncounted mail-in votes in Pennsylvania.

At 1:12 p.m., all of Oz's numbers and margins were down farther.

Fifteen minutes later, their lead in Pennsylvania was slashed by two-thirds. Within the hour, they were wiped out.

In less than two hours, they had gone from buoyant to fucked—and with an increasing sense that all their numbers had largely been a crapshoot.

Stepien, Clark, and Miller sat down together on the L-shaped couch in Stepien's office. Just sitting there, not saying anything.

* * *

Trump existed in a peculiar vacuum of information throughout Thursday.

It was clear what was happening, but no one wanted to tell him—or, at least, everyone wanted to wait as long as possible to tell him.

Good news still flowed, at least tidbits of good news, some of which, months later, he would still be repeating: He was likely to get more votes than any sitting president had ever gotten. In many Democratic states, Biden was underperforming Obama. Trump might beat his own 2016 count by as much as 10 million votes (it would be 12 million). He was certainly going to beat his own 63 million votes in 2016 by well more than the 3-million-vote threshold he had been told he'd need for victory.

Kushner, who had so eagerly brought his father-in-law the good news on Election Day and on Wednesday morning, now delegated others to convey and couch the less-promising reports.

Here was the fact—one set of facts: They were going to do vastly better than most anyone thought they would do at most points in the campaign. If they lost, it would be by the thinnest of margins in the key states. It was clear that the down-ballot success might nearly reverse Republican losses from 2018. And they would likely hold the Senate. Trumpism—here was a headline for the 2020 election—was winning. As a minority political movement, Trumpism was remarkably strong—strong not in spite of Donald Trump, but, inexplicable to many (including many in the White House), *because* of him.

But this good news made it more difficult to give the president the bad news. If all the former was true, then the corollary, that he might lose, must be wrong. If you told him the former and then presented him with the latter—that he had, in fact, lost—*you* were wrong. The very fact that there was so much down-ballot success when, two years before, without him on the ballot, it had been a disaster everywhere was stark evidence that something was wrong on top. The Dems' meager margins meant not that Trump was losing, but that there *had* to have been some funny stuff.

On Thursday, Mark Meadows, the next in the ever-increasing line of dominoes, and the West Wing linchpin, came down with COVID. He was out for almost two weeks.

* * *

Meanwhile, a gung-ho group, recasting 2020 as 2000, when Republican operatives and lawyers amassed for the Florida recount, was out putting boots on the ground in tight-race states in Pennsylvania, Arizona, Georgia, Nevada, and Wisconsin.

Dave Bossie went out to Arizona, where he found Boris Epshteyn (with an annoyed Bossie asking, "Who invited Boris?"). Matt Schlapp, the emcee and organizer of CPAC, the annual conservative conference, whose wife, Mercedes, had been in the White House comms office before going over to join the campaign, was off to Nevada with Ric Grenell, the acting director of national intelligence. Pam Bondi, the former Florida attorney general and frequent Trump TV surrogate, and Corey Lewandowski, the Trump operative, went to Pennsylvania.

In Phoenix, twenty lawyers hastily gathered at the old Ritz-Carlton (recently converted into a cool, new boutique hotel less hospitable to an old-fashioned backroom election operation) to begin the process of reviewing discarded Republican ballots. Under Arizona rules, if a ballot signature seemed not to match the signature on file, it was thrown out. But if you contacted the voter and he or she affirmed their vote, it would be added back, all quite an exhausting and time-consuming effort.

In some sense, it was reasonable to see this as just what political operatives in tight races did. This was not yet out of the norm. Partly, the president was being appeased. But at the same time, elections were often contested. A process was put in place. This was recognizable behavior. Recounts were frustrating but were standard operating procedure.

The process was still being run by Matt Morgan and Justin Clark, the campaign's two main lawyers and its elections specialists.

A midthirties, always-wear-a-tie sort, Morgan had worked for Pence before coming over to the campaign, a sign to some that he was a hopeless establishment type. He had coordinated most of the preelection lawsuits over changes to voting rules. All this, though, was less to-the-barricades than it was procedural, by-the-book stuff. If there was a rap on Morgan, it was that he was too much of a paint-by-numbers lawyer, too straight.

Clark, forty-five, was a Wesleyan graduate (possibly the only graduate from the famously liberal school to work for Trump or even vote for him) and a close associate of Bill Stepien's. He had become a kind of self-appointed sheriff, trying to keep the grifters, kooks, and obvious self-dealers out of Trumptown—and away from the campaign's money.

In the days after the election, Morgan and Clark came to represent both the procedural election efforts and, even more clearly, the limits on them. They would direct the standard efforts and, it was a given, give up when these were exhausted

Rudy Giuliani, in his growing drumbeat, would put it to the president that his biggest issue could be, as much as voter fraud, Morgan and Clark, who, if there was a problem—and of course there were going to be problems—were not out there, were not getting ready for a fight, would fold like a cheap suit. Who knows where this is going? Rudy argued. But it could go way beyond nobody-type lawyers arguing about a few thousand votes to become quite a different matter, a going-to-the-mattresses matter, of needing to disqualify hundreds of thousands, maybe millions, of illegal votes.

Morgan and Clark (not unlike most of the rest of official Trumpworld) saw Giuliani as willing and eager to move beyond standard procedure and into an unknown and unimaginable world.

* * *

Here was the Trump White House pattern that in any even momentary relaxation of the palace guard—and now Meadows, the chief doorkeeper, was out with COVID—the waiting peanut gallery slipped in.

The president had spoken to Giuliani throughout Tuesday night and become grimmer because of it, and then, on Wednesday, largely rushed him off the phone as he got fairly good news from others. But on Thursday, Giuliani, full of warnings and news of dark stuff, got a longer hearing.

Trump was canvassing for what he wanted to hear, and it was the outsiders who clearly understood the advantages of telling him precisely that: there was no way of explaining it if he hadn't won, other than that it had been stolen from him—that was the logic proceeding from the "fact" that he couldn't lose.

Likewise, there was a struggle to be the *one* who told him what he most wanted to hear. At the same time, while it was important to be extreme, it was equally important to be less extreme than the other extreme voices in a world quickly filling with people competing to be even more extreme. A new insider hierarchy was forming among the outsiders.

Jenna Ellis, Trump's handpicked television lawyer, was getting a serious hearing. Ellis, an ambitious young woman with scant legal background, had positioned herself on television as a "constitutional lawyer," according to her frequent chyron. "I love the Constitution," she would state as her particular and overriding credential. She had gone from a small-town DA's office in Colorado, to radio and television appearances with a self-published book comparing the Constitution to the Bible, to becoming an official Trump campaign surrogate, to then, with the president catching her frequent appearances, getting an invitation to the Oval Office. Whereupon, after taking admiring notice of both her television performance and her chyron, he hired her in early 2020 as another of his "personal lawyers."

"You work for me . . . ," said Trump . . . and did not have to add . . . *and you report to me . . . got it?*

Ellis had gone with record speed from a person who would say what was necessary to get time on television to a person who would say what was necessary to be Donald Trump's lawyer. It was confusing to almost everyone else in the White House and the campaign that, at the same time that Ellis was formally attached to the campaign, she seemed able to operate outside it, reporting directly to the president and, through most of the 2020 campaign, whispering election warnings in his ear. Here was a person with no discernible relevant experience and, in a universal opinion, not exactly a legal scholar, helping to provide the basis for a broad constitutional challenge to an American presidential election.

Now, in the days after the election, and going over the heads of the White House and campaign leadership and its ranking lawyers— White House counsel Pat Cipollone and presidential advisor Eric Herschmann in the West Wing and Morgan and Clark on the campaign—Ellis told the president that great constitutional offenses had been committed against him.

Still, to the degree that she was trying to position herself as the outsider saying what the president wanted to hear to the insiders, who weren't saying what he wanted to hear, she was nevertheless trying to keep within basic, if outer, bounds. In a midweek discussion, the president asked her about the "mayor"—that is, Giuliani. Ellis heaped fulsome flattery on the mayor—a passionate advocate, she said. But she suggested, too, that, given the complicated dimensions of the legal struggle ahead, perhaps, she now recommended, it ought to be led by a litigator (that is, a real lawyer, rather than merely a television one)—someone, she suggested, like Jay Sekulow, who had been the president's lawyer (his actual rather than television lawyer) during the Mueller investigation and his impeachment.

But Sekulow was among the insiders not rising enough to the pitch of certainty, outrage, and war that Trump was looking to hear. In fact, he was telling almost everybody else on the campaign and White House legal teams that he wanted nothing to do with this mess.

Even the gung-ho and opportunistic Ellis understood with some trepidation that to be part of this new team she was going to have to accept quite an open-ended sense of mission.

* * *

To the campaign and West Wing staff, there was now little doubt about the trends that would lose them their must-keep electoral votes. It was a clear and, for many, an I-told-you-so outcome: the

Democrats, seizing on the COVID excuse, had pushed for mail-in voting and had encouraged their people to use this new privilege, while the Republicans had discouraged it, and therein lay the Democrats' thin margin—and it would be thin. Indeed, the Democrats, clearly without the landslide they had predicted, were saved by this lucky emphasis; that was all they were saved by.

But it was enough.

And so little that you could believe that mail-in voting was the margin of fraud—that is, if that's what you wanted to believe. After all, they would not have won without their mail-in votes, which, even with no one identifying precise issues, were technically more susceptible to funny business than votes cast at the ballot box. Hence, well, fraud . . . maybe, which became obviously.

If there was widespread fraud, nobody in the Election Day operation had picked up on any of it, certainly not on the mass of irregularities that would surely have surfaced if fraud existed at a game-changing scale in multiple states. At best, some in the campaign and White House were willing to entertain the constitutional argument that election procedures in some states had been, due to COVID, altered to accommodate mail-in voting, in steps that had bypassed the formal approval of state legislatures, as stipulated in the Constitution. Far from a fraud or a steal, but rather, a theoretical argument—one that, even if you could get some judicial buy-in, would yet be unlikely to result in many millions of votes being thrown out. The President's election lawyers, Morgan and Clark, could not have been more explicit on this point: judges were always reluctant to interfere in elections and *no* judge was going to cancel thousands, let alone millions, of votes.

At the end of the day on Thursday, Trump was announcing to the Oval Office entourage that he'd had enough of Morgan and Clark and he was going to put somebody else in charge.

In fact, by Friday morning, three days after the election, there was not a single insider voice who believed there was anything greater than the remotest, pie-in-the-sky fantasy that the vote count could be challenged in the (at least) three states they would need to overcome the Biden electoral count, one of them likely needing to be Pennsylvania, with its big electoral vote haul and with its now-substantial Biden lead.

The insiders were planning for at least a somewhat normal future, and indeed, unaware of the other conversations the president was having, or at least the extent of them, they had already begun to leak their version of normalcy. "Hi guys," wrote the *Washington Post*'s Ashley Parker on Friday the sixth to the campaign's comm director, Tim Murtaugh, and the comms staffers, Ali Pardo and Erin Perrine, seeking official comment or confirmation about what her campaign sources were saying: "We plan to report that advisors have broached the idea of an electoral defeat w[ith] Trump on Thursday and Friday, and how he should handle it. We also plan to report that some advisors/allies are coming [*sic*] that Trump will offer a concession speech where he doesn't necessarily admit defeat, but says he commits to a peaceful transfer of power to Biden."

Yes, the insiders, leaking like the Trump White House always leaked, were preparing for the end, letting the media know that, at least for some people, reality and sanity still existed (always one self-protecting thread of Trump leaks).

It was Hicks, on the Friday morning call, who firmly shifted the conversation to the preservation of legacy, that the election issues should not become a distraction to the work they now had to do to complete the story of their four years in office—this was now history making. They needed to pick the issues they would want to define them. Unspoken was the understanding that if they did not pivot to a formal ending of the Trump presidency, a futile attempt to hold on to it would be their legacy.

But Trump was locking in on a different view.

In effect, the function of the outsiders was to jazz him up about what he wanted to believe was right and to further assure him that everybody else was wrong.

The West Wing and campaign insiders, no matter that they were members of the often-outré Trump White House, had become part of a standardized political process. They had played the game. They had been focused on winning, and that hadn't happened. They certainly did not now want to dwell on loss. What's more, having played, they all pretty much knew why they had lost.

And therefore, the old campaign organization became the enemy, and a new campaign organization, the post-campaign organization, rose in its place. And they were leaking, too. "Advisors have expressed a lot of frustration over the campaign's legal strategy, saying there was no comprehensive planning ahead of Election Day," wrote the *Wall Street Journal* on Friday, November 6, "and little follow through on decisions made this week. Some aides have criticized Kushner, saying he claimed control of the legal strategy ahead of the election but was distracted by other issues such as Middle East peace efforts." (To which a resentful Bill Stepien replied, in an email chain circulating the *Journal* article, "This is BS.")

The outsiders were speaking not to standardized political process, but to the Trump MO: always seize the opportunity for public drama. This gave you control of the narrative and, of course, gained the attention of the public. Conflict, the essence of a reality show, offered a more promising result than doing nothing.

It's important to note: the only game any of the outsiders had was, regardless of sense and reason, to tell Donald Trump what he wanted to hear and to tell it more forcefully than the other people who were telling him what he wanted to hear.

As always, Trump had two conversations going: what people were saying to him, which he may or may not have been listening to, and what he wanted to hear, which he sought out if it was not forthcoming on its own.

In a discussion among his close aides always trying to under-stand what they were dealing with, all of them ever struggling to rationalize or explain the Trump phenomenon, one participant offered the view that Trump was like flowing water: he would go where he wanted to go, around whatever obstacle was in his way.

* * *

Finally, on Friday afternoon, the insiders went in to see him in the Oval Office, the chairs lined up in front of his desk, the president tight in behind it, his fist in his palm—Kushner, Stepien, Miller, Clark, and, at the president's invitation, Dave Bossie joining them. Meadows phoned in from his sickbed. Here was the first real conversation, the formal one, almost three days out, about things not looking real good.

"There is," Kushner told his father-in-law, "still a statistical chance, but, in general, it's an uphill fight." That was the team's characteriza-tion of what might more reasonably be no chance at all.

"What do you mean? We're winning." Trump had been, as always, watching television nonstop and would have known that even though a definitive call had not yet been made, any sign of optimism was gone from the air. For some in the room, there was the uncomfort-able, if not worrisome, sense that the president had frozen himself in the most optimistic moment on Election Night.

"Our margins," said Kushner "are not large enough."

"What do you mean 'not large enough'? How did it go from Elec-tion Night, where I'm up by a million votes? Right? A million votes in Pennsylvania? Tell me how that goes? Because they're stealing it. They're still counting votes. Where did these votes come from? They've got to stop counting right now! Why are we letting that hap-pen?" His anger washed over the room. "Where's Oz—get him on the phone!" Indeed, the others felt that Oczkowski was already gin-gerly trying to fade out of the war room and the campaign, having been in scant evidence since election night. "Molly," Trump called to his assistant. "Get Matt Oz."

"He's on," said Molly Michael, a no-small-talk, late-twenties, strawberry blonde who had replaced his last assistant, Madeleine Westerhout, after she drunkenly told Trump family stories one night in a Washington bar.

"Matt . . . Matt . . ."

A stammering Oczkowski now seemed at his most strangled, nearly unable to talk.

"Matt . . . Matt . . . you said we'd be fine. We were up by a million votes in Pennsylvania. They're stealing this. We've got to do something."

"Ummm . . . yeahhhh . . . I . . . well . . . it's that . . . we just don't know how many ballots are out there," said Oczkowski. "We just don't know. But there's more than we know."

"They have to stop counting them! They are still coming in after the election. That's illegal!"

"Hmmmm . . . yeah, well . . ." Oczkowski was mumbling.

"What? They have to stop counting!"

"Yeah, but . . . we're just not likely at this point to pick up any of these contested states. I don't see that we can. I'm sorry, Mr. President."

With disgust, Trump got off the phone with Oczkowski and then angrily threw it back to the people in the room. "Get them to stop counting. That's what you have to do. Get them to stop counting these illegal votes."

This immediately devolved into an attack on his own lawyers, with an evocation of Roy Cohn, the long-dead fixer who had become in his mind the ultimate protector, and bitter comments about the lack of fight among the lawyers who now worked for him.

Kushner and Meadows, treading water, outlined some possible further legal steps and offered an initial report from the campaign lawyers.

In Trump fashion, this meeting, in some ways quite a categorical reckoning, rolled into and overlapped with the next meeting—"like an Allman Brothers concert," in one aide's description, "people just show up and start playing"—in which the world of possibility and fight and the promise of reversal yet existed.

Matt Morgan and Rudy Giuliani were now sniping at each other in front of the president. This was ostensibly over hiring local lawyers for the Pennsylvania lawsuit the campaign had filed—Porter Wright, a national firm with a large Pittsburgh office, had agreed to handle it.

With considerable frustration, Morgan was trying to weigh resources against possible rewards. They could not, after all, fight every battle. Even if Rudy had reports of fraud, if that wasn't, in any event, going to be enough to win them a disputed state, then why bother? They needed to focus on where they had a chance to win and where a win in court would give them electoral votes—a very small target.

A heated Rudy rejected this as defeatist. "If–you–just–put–me–in–charge," said Rudy, slashing his hand through the air on each word, he would go to battle. They would go to the mattresses.

Giuliani told the president that they already had eighty sworn affidavits attesting to specific incidents of voter fraud that they were immediately in a position to act on, which both surprised and impressed Morgan.

Giuliani kept repeating, "Eighty! Eighty!"

Morgan began almost to doubt himself. Maybe Giuliani's team had found evidence of a great, unseen, election fraud.

When Morgan got back to the campaign office, he called the lawyers at Porter Wright to tell them to make sure they had reviewed the Giuliani affidavits. Those lawyers then called the Giuliani team, which shortly sent someone over to collect the affidavits from Morgan. In other words, a furious Morgan now understood, most of the affidavits Giuliani was referencing were not his at all, but just the collection of unverified reports and allegations piling up in the campaign's office. It was just more Rudy bullshit.

The president, with his fine radar for who was all in and who was holding back, had already made the decision to cut out his weary, and skeptical, campaign leadership and legal team—too stiff, too slow, too by-the-book—but he was not yet desperate enough or crazy enough to put Rudy in charge.

He was choosing Dave Bossie.

Bossie was a right-wing gadfly, organizer, and attack man, a Yosemite Sam figure ever blasting at liberal rabbits, but at least a pro. In 2016, on the plane during a campaign swing, he had famously confronted Trump (the only one willing to), telling him he had to stop tweeting, insisting on this heatedly enough that many suspected this was the singular reason Bossie had been deprived of a spot in the White House, which he'd desperately wanted.

Bossie ran assorted conservative efforts and not-for-profits out of a small town house on Capitol Hill, producing films and books and other materials. One of his key accomplishments was the *Citizens United* lawsuit that ultimately removed all political spending restrictions on for-profit and not-for-profit companies. His other, arguably major accomplishment was Donald Trump. As far back as 2012, Bossie had been recommended to the developer and reality television star as a political advisor. Bossie had first introduced Steve Bannon to Trump. In 2015, he had recommended Corey Lewandowski, whom Trump hired as his campaign manager. More recently, Bossie and Lewandowski had been among Parscale's main antagonists, trying to force him out. Returning at the end of the week from Arizona, where he was trying to coordinate the recount efforts, Bossie was told by Trump that he wanted him to run the overall election legal challenge.

This was another reality-inversion moment—Bossie was not even a lawyer. A willing Trump soldier and always ready to please the boss, even Bossie was confused, or appalled, by his sudden elevation.

"I don't know if congratulations or condolences are in order," wrote one campaign aide to him.

"I want to fucking kill myself," Bossie replied.

* * *

The country had lived in weird and anxious limbo for something near seventy-two hours. Tuesday evening to Saturday morning may have been the greatest period of collective uncertainty (and dread, for many) since the Cuban Missile Crisis, almost sixty years before. And if, by Saturday morning, it seemed quite surely clear that Biden would win and Trump would lose, it seemed equally clear that if this were not shortly made definitive, the nation would enter an existential moment the likes of which it had never known.

But then, suddenly, during the anxious morning, it *was* definitive, as clearly definitive as an election can be, all traditionally reliable sources and all underlying analytics in agreement.

CNN called the election for Joe Biden at 11:24 a.m. Eastern Time on Saturday, November 7.

The Trump campaign staff had been anticipating a call, hoping it might not yet come, but also understanding that, its having come, the election and reasonable efforts to challenge it or even forestall it were over.

It was done.

NBC, CBS, ABC, and the Associated Press—everybody who had been holding back until the others moved shortly followed. Fox came in at 11:40 a.m.

Almost immediately, people everywhere poured into the street, the week's tension broken in an instant. Within moments of the call's being made, the area around the White House (now called Black Lives Matter Plaza) was filled with spontaneous revelers. In surrounding blocks, people banged pots and pans and maniacally tooted car horns, the evening COVID lockdown ritual now redeployed against the Trump election virus. The greater White House area from Fifteenth Street to Seventeenth Street and from K Street to Constitutional Avenue was enveloped in sudden and joyful gridlock.

In every Democratic city across the nation—that is, basically, every city—and liberal burg, from cappuccinos in the streets of Santa Monica to cocktails on the lawns of the Hamptons, it was a vast national (or, at least, anti-Trumpers) celebration.

It was an unseasonably warm day, and Trump, as it happened, was at his golf club in Virginia, where both Trumpers and anti-Trumpers shortly gathered at the door to heckle one another.

* * *

A group had slowly been assembling in the Rosslyn HQ all morning. Everybody was there largely to wait for the network call, although with no one quite acknowledging that that's what they were doing there; that this was a deathwatch. It was nearly the full brain trust: Kushner, Hicks, Stepien, Clark, Morgan, Miller, Herschmann, and Bossie.

Everybody, as though more out of inertia than plan, found themselves together in the conference room. Kushner and Hicks began trying to force an answer to the question they all already knew, but that nobody seemed yet willing to say.

"Is there any way you guys see us getting over the top?" asked Kushner, knowing of course that there wasn't, but officially still hanging on to the Trumpworld sense of elasticity, or fight, or magical thinking.

But even with the results as certain as they could be, the campaign found itself not wanting to say no, even though it could surely not say yes.

There were outstanding legal challenges. There were instances of fraud. There were questions.

But . . . could those issues, even assuming they were decided in the Trump campaign's favor, push them over the top?

Not really. No.

It was Hicks who again tried, with some determination, to move things forward. They had two and half months left to accomplish things and to remind people of what they had already accomplished.

Kushner, keeping himself out of the line of fire, then sent Stepien, Clark, Miller, and Herschmann, along with Bossie, to deliver the status report to the president—in effect, although it was not exactly framed this way, the final report.

* * *

Meanwhile, Rudy Giuliani was holding a press conference in Philadelphia. If the inner circled struggled to keep Giuliani away from the president, they worked just as hard to keep him away from the cameras.

Trump seemed to have understood what Rudy was up to, tweeting it out that morning. But few others in the immediate Trump orbit seemed to grasp much about what Rudy was doing. They were just grateful he wasn't in Washington.

What Rudy was apparently doing, without any clear structure in the election-challenge operation, was staking his claim to it: doing this as he had done during the "grab-'em-by-the-pussy" scandal in 2016 and during the Mueller investigation in 2018. If you defended the president hotly enough, especially if you were the only person defending him, then you were in with him. It was another critical theme of Trumpworld: The people who were in charge were the people who took charge. It was an anarchic, even *Lord of the Flies* org chart. (And, as Meadows would note to people, just because the president might say you are in charge doesn't mean he's really put you in charge.)

The press conference in Philadelphia was organized mostly by Giuliani's team—or lack of a team. And, indeed, because they did not have a team, they blamed the organization, or lack of organization, on the campaign team's refusing to assist them and its undermining them in malicious ways. Hence, in comic or absurd

confusion, the occasion morphed from, theoretically, the Four Seasons Hotel in downtown Philly to a strip mall business called Four
Seasons Total Landscaping, a ... well, landscaping business, soon to
enter history, on the edge of an interstate and across from an adult
bookstore, in its parking lot.

This was in every sense a Rudy affair: chaotic, disorganized, scattered in result and purpose, and not unlikely conceived and executed
with its key actor a few sheets to the wind. But Rudy, despite his own
befuddlement and every attempt by others to sidetrack him, pushed
through, however ludicrously, to the end. With his retinue behind
him (including Bernie Kerik, the disgraced former New York City
police commissioner whose presidential pardon Giuliani had previously arranged), Rudy set out to take over the Trump election fight:

"So, I'm here on behalf of the Trump campaign. I am an attorney
for the president," he said, introducing himself to this sudden and
unlikely gathering of the international press and, at the same time,
trying to bring the microphone down to his ever-shrinking stature.

I am here to describe to you the first part of a situation that is
extremely ... extremely ... troubling. First of all, for the state of the
Commonwealth of Pennsylvania and for a number of other states.
These lawsuits will be brought starting on Monday. But the first time
it was discovered was here in Pennsylvania just a few days ago. The
people you see behind me are just a few of about, I'd say, fifty to sixty
poll watchers, who will all testify that they were uniformly deprived
of their right to inspect any single part of the mail-in ballots. As you
know from the very beginning, the mail-in ballots were a source of
some degree of skepticism, if not a lot of skepticism, as being innately
prone to fraud.

With quite a poker face, he outlined the case for uninspected ballots, replacement ballots, and a sweeping Democratic effort to add
millions of illegal and illegitimate votes in Pennsylvania, a case he

had frantically and almost single-handedly assembled over the past forty-eight hours.

The case, in Pennsylvania and in several other swing states—which would not change very much over the coming weeks and which would be rejected by every court it went before—was different from most election challenges that centered on the counting and qualification of a limited number of ballots in races with razor-thin margins. Instead, the Trump case, propounded by Giuliani with confounding brazenness or shamelessness—quite to the astonishment of everyone in Trumpworld, who was suddenly paying attention to Giuliani's eccentric effort—was to challenge millions of votes and to demand their disqualification mostly because a Republican had not been there to observe their being counted.

* * *

That afternoon, Kushner's appointed delegation (Stepien, Clark, Miller, and Herschmann, joined by Dave Bossie) assembled in the White House. This was to be the ultimate mission. They were now, finally, to tell the president that there was no possibility of winning this, that all scenarios had been played out, and that the overwhelming likelihood was that legal challenges would prove futile. The group was agreed that when the president asked for their recommendation, it would be that the time had come to concede.

The five men got on the elevator together, nobody in a mask except for the elevator man.

They went up to the Residence.

The president was in golf attire—red hat, white polo shirt, golf slacks.

White House waiters brought in platters of meatballs and pigs in a blanket. As a way, it seemed, for everyone to avoid talking, they stuffed food into their mouths.

Clark gave the initial recap and up-to-the-minute appraisal—except that, instead of the no-chance conclusion, he punted and said there was little more than a 5 percent chance that the election could be successfully challenged.

At this, the president scowled and seemed to decide that Clark was a less-than-able messenger: "You're wrong. I think you're wrong. It's much higher." He said that there was at the very least a 25 to 30 percent chance, throwing out his view (details of which had largely been supplied by Giuliani) of a systemic fraud with massive discrepancies around the country. Indeed, how could they not prevail?

As they ate the meatballs (per Trump: "the greatest recipe ever") and pigs-in-a-blanket, with vats of mustard for dipping, and wave after wave of Diet Cokes appearing, the plan for real talk floated away, and instead, the group found itself repeating what they had heard about numbers of dead people and malfunctioning voting machines, each desperately offering the random reports that had come in since Election Night.

Yes, yes, they should play this out, of course. That was the right thing. Obviously, the evidence should be looked at. Of course, of course, that's your right, Mr. President.

What was supposed to have been the off-ramp from the 2020 campaign had now, suddenly, for everybody rushing to the exits, turned into a weird new on-ramp.

"You've got to fight harder. You're not fighting hard enough. They stole it. We've got to fight. We have to keep fighting," said the president, angry and certain, furiously trying to direct his weary generals.

So . . . not an end and acceptance and an honorable and realistic way forward at all, but somehow, a whole new agreement to pursue election challenges across the country.

Each of the men was silent as the group rode down in the elevator, uncomfortable in their incomprehension and bewilderment as they left, walking through the portico and then down the stairs near the Oval to "West Exec," the street that divides the West Wing from the EEOB, with its VIP parking spaces (Hicks, Herschmann, Stephen Miller), looking at one another abashed and disbelieving.

* * *

To the best recollection of some of the campaign and White House staffers most closely involved in the reelection effort, Matt Oczkowski was never seen or heard from ever again after the race was called on Saturday. This had a symbolic and functional significance: the Trump campaign, such as it was, had left behind the world of actual vote counting and empirical data.

4

RUDY

Almost everybody from the West Wing and the campaign stayed home on Sunday, November 8, five days after the election. This was, even in the face of the president's refusal to concede, a determined act of normalcy. A hard, emotionally fraught campaign was done—and lost. The readjustment needed to begin. Everyone's life would be going in another direction.

In many ways, the Trump White House was reacting normally to defeat. People were packing up. Even senior figures in the West Wing, such as Hope Hicks, were slipping out the back.

While it might be required for many to still show up for work—and COVID made it all the easier not to show up—it would not be the same, not with the same hopes, not for the same purpose. Everybody understood the nature of political defeat. That was the other reason to take a day, to recompose, to come up with a new bearing and attitude with which to face what had to be done, to be a team player and all, but to understand that the game was over.

That Sunday, Dave Bossie, newly in charge of the election challenge, came down with COVID.

"Really?" some of the team needled him. Given that the Saturday call by the networks and the Associated Press had made a Biden victory a certainty, and any challenge to it largely chimerical, there was no small amount of speculation on the part of remaining campaign staffers that Bossie's diagnosis was a convenient one. "How did you get so lucky?" noted one.

"Fuck you," replied Bossie.

With Bossie down and Meadows having fallen a few days before, COVID as pressing a threat to the Trump White House as defeat, this meant nobody was leading one of the most ambitious challenges to a presidential election in American history except the president himself.

While the White House was filled with Trumpers who were more Trump-like as the years went on and as the less-Trump-like washed out, no one, with the possible exception of Rudy Giuliani, was as Trump-like as Trump. That, in itself, was a unique characteristic of this White House: that the president himself represented the most extreme and purest impulses of his administration, unmindful of political consequences.

Even Bossie and Meadows, politically intemperate in their own ways, were yet careerists cognizant of the longer game; if they could help it, they were not going to self-immolate. Both men, along with everybody else in Trump's inner circle, understood what was going to happen: Trump would depart the presidency on January 20. They were counting on the dudgeon and posturing to wind down as the president found his own path to rationalizing and accepting his defeat.

Kushner, contained to the point of inscrutability—never breaking character—was absent more than he was present. The election had established his deadline for completing the set of Middle East peace deals that he had begun and that he saw as the administration's, or his own, lasting monument. But in a world where the obvious could not necessarily be spoken, the meaning of his absence from the West Wing was clear. In some sense, it was even an optimistic sign: while the president might not grasp reality, the people closest to him did.

On Monday morning, Bill Stepien, who himself had been scarce since Election Day and who would shortly be almost entirely absent from the scene, called a staff-wide meeting at the campaign offices in Rosslyn. The staff was to be paid until the fifteenth of the month. Ordinarily, this would have been a time either of celebration and jockeying for new positions if it was a winning campaign, or for good-byes and getting out your résumé if it was a losing one. But now the president wanted the campaign, in its remaining days, to continue with full intensity. Stepien had to send a tricky message, mediating the demands of both the President and reality. He said to the gathering, with some awkward hesitation, well, yes, it was a hard road, but there was still a pathway to victory, however limited, and what's more, important principles were at stake, and that he knew everyone would be professional and continue to give it their all. He hoped he was getting through but couldn't quite be sure. It was an especially young and green staff. Here was another Trumpworld theme: a lack of political sense and sensitivity. Not long after he took over the campaign, Stepien, in a staffwide meeting, had asked for a show of hands of those who had worked on a presidential campaign before; fewer than a quarter had. So, like the president himself, the young staff might not truly appreciate the very arbitrary nature of campaigns, that they ended, and that what Stepien was actually saying was: it's over.

For the other senior advisors, still healthy and still determined not to abandon the president in these final weeks (some combination of professionalism, loyalty, and concern holding them in place), this sense of finality—they all did know that they would be moving on—came with a further sense beyond dutifully working to the last day: they were witnesses. Sometimes guiltily and sometimes helplessly, they were seeing things never before seen in politics, even if they saw themselves as also trying to help restrain those things. They could not look away.

* * *

The persistent effort of Trump's closest aides, lawyers, and high appointees to keep Rudy Giuliani out of the White House and far from the president had once again failed.

Trump wanted to be right about everything and to be advised that he could do anything he wanted to do, and everyone, to a man and woman, knew that their first priority as a Trump staffer was to impede or distract him from this tendency. But Giuliani, willing to tell Trump not only that he could do whatever he wanted to do, but that he could go beyond this, offered Trump vastly more power, right, and discretion than even Trump himself thought possible.

"Rudy is Rudy, and Donald is Donald, and together that's an equation which adds up to a loss of contact with most other rational people, if not reality itself," said a laughing Fox News founder Roger Ailes, a close friend of both men, returning one day from a debate practice session with Rudy and Trump at the Bedminster golf club in the summer of 2016—well before their worst excesses together in the White House.

There was not just concern over Rudy in the West Wing, but deep resentment and even hatred of him.

"Everything Rudy has touched in the four years of this presidency," said Matt Morgan in disgust one afternoon as the election challenge began to unfold, "has gone bad." You would have been hard pressed to find anyone in Trumpworld who had not thought or said as much.

The former New York City mayor was a figure who seemed to have come loose in history—irrepressible, uncontrollable, reckless, runaway, daft. It defied credulity on the part of virtually everyone in the White House that, for the third time, after Mueller and

Ukraine, Giuliani, with all the havoc he brought with him, was back in the White House with unchecked influence, reporting to no one but the president himself. And his return had happened virtually overnight.

It was a measure of Giuliani's need, character, and stamina in the face of mockery, rejection, and a wide range of bureaucratic remedies to block his access to the avenues of power—these measures in place from the very beginning of the administration—that he nevertheless became such a central figure in Trump's presidency. It was a measure, too, of Trump's own constant search for alternatives to standard advice and counsel. As much as even he mocked Giuliani—and Trump was often withering in his contempt—he invariably turned to Rudy when he was the only man saying what the president wanted to hear.

In the days after Giuliani's return, Trump, in a nearly reflective or perhaps slightly shamed moment, explained to a caller that he knew Rudy took a drink too many, and that he was a loose cannon, and that he said a lot of shit that was not true. But Rudy would fight. He could be counted on to fight even when others wouldn't. And, too, he would work for free.

Giuliani was, many around Trump believed, always buzzed if not, in the phrase Steve Bannon made famous in the Trump White House, hopelessly "in the mumble tank." Many believed he had the beginnings of senility: focus issues, memory problems, simple logic failures. A vast disorganization of papers and files and tech malfunctions followed in his wake. His weight had ballooned to almost three hundred pounds. His popping eyes and poorly dyed hair made him seem like a pre–television age character, a past-his-time and gone-to-seed former official hanging around the courthouse steps regaling anyone who will listen with tall tales and wild theories of the shameful secrets and gothic underbelly of politics. Except, in fact, this not-ready-for-prime-time gargoyle was on television all the time. His life seemed to be singularly sustained by his being on television.

It was an implausible tale.

One of the few willing to defend Trump publicly after the "grab-'em-by-the-pussy" tape that seemed surely to doom the 2016 campaign, Giuliani had pushed to turn such kamikaze loyalty, one of the few debts Trump owned up to, into a high position in the new White House—ideally, secretary of state. The objections were obvious. Giuliani's clients around the world, dubious individuals and questionable regimes, raised a host of conflicts. Plus, he frequently drank himself insensate. His current marriage, like his others before it, would shortly pass into public shambles. His mental capacity was an open discussion among Trump staff and family. Trump couldn't get past Rudy falling asleep as soon as he got on board the plane on campaign trips, and he worried he'd nod off with foreign leaders. Giuliani was offered the Department of Homeland Security but thought that was beneath him—he did not want to forever be "9/11 Rudy." He was offered attorney general, but he said he was too old to go back to practicing law. Trump briefly suggested a Supreme Court position for him—risible for, among other reasons, Giuliani's long pro-choice history and the impossibility of his confirmation by a pro-life Republican Senate.

Out in the cold, Rudy bid—in Trump's telling, begged—to be brought in after the appointment of Robert Mueller as special counsel to investigate the president, but he was rebuffed by the White House Counsel's Office and by virtually every West Wing advisor. Still, he back-channeled Trump "intelligence" from the Justice Department, where he had worked more than thirty years before, and after the first set of lawyers washed out and a lineup of prestige firms declined the assignment, the president turned to Rudy, who was offering to work for free and was fully committed to the deep-state conspiracy version of the Russia investigation, appointing him in the spring of

2018, in a designation Rudy embraced both for reasons of ego and personal profit, his personal lawyer.

The actual lawyering, in fact, occurred quite removed from Giuliani (who had not practiced in decades), leaving Rudy to be the public media face: a performance at times so outlandish and, many assumed, drunken that it actually might have helped distract from and confuse the investigation.

At the same time, Rudy, ever money hungry, continued his other occupation: representing dubious international figures, many with issues before the U.S. government. Rudy went from defending the president against charges that he had conspired with Russian state interests to helping (likely, encouraging) him to conspire with or strong-arm Ukraine government interests to aid him in the upcoming 2020 campaign, resulting in Trump's Christmas impeachment in 2019. "What happened to Rudy?" became a significant American political question. The need to be at the center of attention, regardless of what he had to do to get there, had smashed his reputation as New York City's crime-fighting mayor and 9/11 hero. Asked at one point during the Ukraine impeachment trial if he had concerns about his legacy, Giuliani said: What did it matter? He'd be dead.

Much of the State Department, the intelligence community, the White House Counsel's Office, the president's family, and Trump's allies in Congress placed blame for the Ukraine fiasco on Rudy—so overt and heedless was Rudy in his actions that it might even seem to excuse Trump's responsibility. Rudy, after the impeachment, was cast out into the cold again.

But a Trump given is that he is always looking for affirmation, dialing for affirmation.

So, with Bossie and Meadows out of the picture, and with his son-in-law and just about everybody else hardly to be found from November 8 to 11, that crucial dead zone after the networks called the election, Trump was talking almost exclusively to Rudy. Rudy had found his way back in again, and Trump—while hard to believe he needed one—had found his inner demon.

* * *

Still, there was resistance, a resistance that Giuliani would use to help argue that only *he* was prepared to fight for the president to the death.

Kushner directed the campaign lawyers to meet with Giuliani, but with the clear caveat not to hand over the keys.

Bernie Kerik, Giuliani's longtime wingman, who signed on to the election challenge as its chief investigator, showed up to meet the mayor at campaign HQ in Rosslyn, expecting to find a war room preparing for battle—this was, after all, an effort bigger than the Florida recount of 2000. They would need hundreds of lawyers, a crisis operation, comms professionals, and volunteers ready (to use one of the mayor's favorite expressions) to go to the mattresses. The Giuliani team, without resources or, hardly, contacts of its own, needed the campaign to produce a legal infrastructure to support its as-yet-unclear strategy.

But Kerik found only Rudy at one socially distanced end of a conference table talking to the campaign's general counsel, Matt Morgan, at the other end. To Kerik, Morgan was taking notes with quite some evident lack of interest as the mayor spoke.

"Are there other lawyers coming?" Giuliani pushed.

"Well, yeah. I'm going to try to get some others to help," said an unmoved Morgan. "I hope."

For Kerik and Giuliani, the conspiracy to steal the election was not just a Democratic effort, but one aided by the Trump inner circle.

* * *

Morgan shortly received an email from Giuliani's girlfriend, Maria Ryan, now acting as his aide-de-camp. Ryan said Giuliani's fee for the election challenge would be twenty thousand dollars a day.

Morgan, unclear about what his authority was here, and believing he would be on the hook for either authorizing or not authorizing the payment, copied the email to many in the campaign and West Wing hierarchy, guaranteeing, he knew, that it would immediately leak—which it promptly did, to Giuliani's fury and flat denial. Anyone who had said he wanted that kind of money was a "liar," Giuliani declared, causing Morgan to ask Ryan how it felt to be called a liar in the *New York Times* by her boyfriend.

The president harshly clarified the situation: Rudy would get paid only for a win. He was a contingency lawyer.

* * *

Early on the afternoon of November 11, Stepien, Miller, Clark, and Herschmann joined Pence and Short, the VP's chief of staff, in the Oval Office for what was supposed to be a briefing for the vice president about the outreach to state legislatures, because Pence had a relationship with so many of them.

With the aggrieved president behind the desk, the meeting turned into both a recapitulation of Giuliani's growing case for nationwide election fraud and an excited discussion of his plan to import delegations from the legislatures in contested states to Washington, where the evidence could be presented to them (and where they could all get a visit with the president). They would not be able to ignore the evidence, all of it now overflowing from Giuliani's briefcase.

One of Giuliani's titles since leaving City Hall was "security consultant," implying a set of police and military and technology skills he did not have. Now he had enlisted Kerik, the former police commissioner, in this effort. They had set up a national election fraud hotline. The reports of what someone had seen, or might have seen, or knew that someone else had seen, came tumbling in: dead voters, double names, machine malfunctions, and far deeper conspiracies.

(Lots more came tumbling in: thousands of dick pics, animal porn, and virulent screeds, with nearly everybody who was manning the phones begging for other duties.)

In part, here were the usual anomalies of any election involving more than 155 million voters. And in part, this was another bounty of the Trump movement: Trumpers everywhere intent on producing what the president wanted. Trump had asked the Trump movement to confirm what he believed, and, with supporters rushing to offer him a stew of allegations and anecdotal reports, Trump now doubly believed it. Incident upon incident, egregious report, rumored or otherwise, on top of egregious report—all this, pouring into Trump's ear, was fast becoming the closed echo chamber confirming vast, nationwide election fraud.

Giuliani was proposing both a systematic legal challenge to millions of ballots—well beyond the quixotic, it was inconceivable that millions of votes would be tossed out—and a pitch directly to the bodies that, in his view, had the power to vacate the election: the individual state legislatures.

What was most stunning to the others in the room was that Rudy and the president clearly believed it would work: an American presidential election, otherwise orderly and without serious complaint from any overseeing authority or governing body, one where the margins between winner and loser appeared substantial and where few (if any) experts were disputing the underlying analytics, could be vacated and the purported winner replaced by the purported loser.

To mount such a fight would require an organization that would need to come together into a nationwide campaign in a window of weeks, one pulled together by a detail-resistant president, his almost empty White House, and a television talking head former lawyer without a law firm or meaningful staff or apparent resources.

Even if there was an organization of more than two old codgers spurned by everybody else, the plan here depended on something close to revolutionary zeal in state and federal courts to overturn election results that few established authorities were doubting—arguably, that none was doubting.

But, Giuliani insisted, if that didn't work—he seemed to acknowledge that, yes, courts were usually leery of inserting themselves into elections and especially of throwing out votes—they would mount a campaign to convince state legislatures to refuse to certify the election results. Instead of sending Biden's electoral votes to the Electoral College, Trump-supporting legislatures would decertify Biden electors and send Trump electors.

With the exception of Trump and Giuliani, this was a room of workaday political professionals, all with both local and national experience. What Giuliani was proposing and what Trump was embracing was a political world that was not remotely recognizable to anyone else in the room. State reps are a practical group—unexceptional, to say the least—content with modest political careers, paid nominal amounts by the state, with most dependent on law firms and other businesses in their communities for their livelihoods. A statehouse was not a place where you might count on finding people full of fire, with a yen for headlines and drama. Local (not to mention national) headlines sent your average state rep running for deep cover.

And yet the president believed that there was a movement out there. It was, in some sense, the main issue he was testing: the true nature and ultimate use of the Trump passion he had seen so many times in so many places.

More mundanely, the follow-up steps from this Oval Office meeting involved planning the logistics of bringing delegations from the contested states to Washington, DC, and making up a display of poster boards on easels—Trump disliked PowerPoint—documenting election fraud, all of which now had to be prepared.

* * *

Miller, Morgan, and Zach Parkinson, the campaign research director, met in the Rosslyn office the following morning—Thursday, the twelfth. Their purpose was to prepare for the gatherings of these state reps, who Rudy and the president imagined would be streaming to the capital on a daily basis. In short order, they'd have to harness Rudy's network of fraud allegations—Giuliani was passing around hard copy with hundreds of links that now had to be retyped—double-check the mountain of scattered and incomplete reports, and get everything onto the poster boards the president liked.

"Ain't gonna happen," said Morgan, as the meeting broke. "Nobody's going to come." (In fact, a handful of legislators from Michigan showed up ten days later for a meeting at which the state reps reaffirmed that they could do nothing, and a rump group from the Pennsylvania legislature, without anyone from the leadership, showed up for pictures with the president. But that was it.)

* * *

At 11:30 that morning, the president, picking this up from a broadcast on the right-wing news channel OAN, tweeted for the first time about Dominion, a manufacturer of voting machines:

REPORT; DOMINION DELETED 2.7 MILLION TRUMP VOTES NATIONWIDE. DATA ANALYSIS FINDS 221,000 PENNSYLVANIA VOTES SWITCHED FROM PRESIDENT TRUMP TO BIDEN, 941,000 TRUMP VOTES DELETED. STATES USING DOMINION VOTING SYSTEMS SWITCHED 435,000 VOTES FROM TRUMP TO BIDEN.

That evening, Sean Hannity, channeling the president—or the president having previously channeled Hannity—went hardcore on

Dominion, using his show to put Dominion at the nexus of the election fraud.

* * *

The next day, the president wanted to go over "messaging" strategy for the upcoming barrage of lawsuits Giuliani was planning to launch. This mostly meant organizing surrogates for national and local media, a job that fell in part to campaign aide Erin Perrine, herself a frequent TV spokeswoman for the president.

Trump had once walked into the television greenroom at the Rosslyn headquarters and found Perrine (pronounced Peh-REE-nee) in the makeup chair. "My favorite person, my favorite person"— indeed, he had been particularly enthusiastic about her television performances—"Erin *Pe-ree-nee!* You know what, great idea, you should change your name to just 'Pe-reen.' A classic name. Perfect TV name."

Perrine now waited with Miller, Stepien, and Clark in the Cabinet Room, across from the Oval Office. Trump was in with some of his usual assortment of attendants: Herschmann, Scavino, Pence, and Short, with Kushner and Stephen Miller and aide Johnny McEntee milling in and out and Meadows, recovering from COVID, there by phone.

Giuliani was also on speakerphone. In his intense, barely-take-a-breath, mouthful-of-spit, speeding-motor voice, such that it was particularly hard to make out what he was saying on the poor speakerphone audio, Giuliani pressed the case that the president's lawyers had fucked up the recount process in Georgia and that they weren't paying attention to the even greater issue of the wholesale corruption of the voting machines.

Giuliani had a point about the campaign lawyers: what the president was being offered by his lawyers was a long and winding road of complicated process. Election lawyers—and that's what Morgan and Clark precisely were—are playbook and procedure guys.

In Wisconsin alone, before they could get into court, they had to go through the recount process—and pay for it! As much as $8 million! Days would turn into weeks, weeks would turn into a month or more, boring everyone, including the media. And by then, Joe Biden would be president.

They needed, Giuliani was now nearly shouting, to break through. They needed confrontation, disruption. To go to the mattresses.

Trump often seemed amused to let others, in cockfight fashion, do battle, and now he sent Scavino to bring in Justin Clark from across the hall, telling Clark that Rudy was saying the campaign's lawyers were asleep at the switch.

"You have to file a suit in Georgia," insisted the disembodied Giuliani.

"We are going to get dismissed," said an impatient Clark, open in his contempt for the former mayor, trying to spell out the specific procedures for challenging an election in Georgia. "Georgia election law requires you to do this post-certification. They've just started the hand recount." That is, you could sue only after the recount was completed.

"We should never have requested the recount," declared Giuliani.

"Regardless, we have to wait."

"They are lying to you, Mr. President. Your people are lying to you," Giuliani pressed.

"Jesus, Rudy, you are such a fucking asshole," said Clark, hardly able to take Giuliani seriously and walking out of the meeting and back to the Cabinet Room.

In the ebb and flow and restless style of the Trump Oval Office, the group from the Cabinet Room now shortly joined the Oval Office group—with the president, as though it were a new idea, repeating his brilliant notion about Erin Perrine changing her name.

The president, at a pitch somewhere between deep offense and theatrical hyperbole, moved briefly off the election fraud to recap another point he would often make—that he deserved another term because of the "Russia hoax." "Can we demand that?" he asked Giuliani.

Rudy, on his part, seemed to have forgotten Clark and the Georgia issue, and was now banging hard on the subject of the Dominion voting machines, where Trump (and Hannity) had left off the day before.

The Dominion machines had moved from a story of what local officials characterized as "human error" involving a few thousand votes in a small county in Michigan—acknowledged and corrected almost immediately on Election Night—to the center of a great conspiracy. Not only was the company owned by the same people funding the Clinton Global Initiative, Rudy heatedly explained, but George Soros, that liberal billionaire and bête noire of the conspiracy imagination, had a role in its financing. What's more, their machines were made with Chinese parts. Here was a theory apparently associated with QAnon and other internet conspiracy channels—i.e., the machines were programmed to switch millions of Trump votes to Biden votes and were part of a campaign of foreign interference—that had then surfaced in the credulous report on OAN that Trump had retweeted the previous morning.

The meeting drew the current sides in the White House: there were people yet hoping to maintain their reputations and professional standing, and then there was Giuliani, who was willing to surrender or burn his. Indeed, he had long since done that.

The former quickly assembled a report assessing Giuliani's claims about Dominion, disputing virtually all of them. This was circulated in the West Wing and pointedly shared with Giuliani. He ignored it.

* * *

Reading the room became a process that required reading who was not in the room. Where, in fact, were Jared and Ivanka?

The four-year history of the Trump White House was, in one sense, the unlikely story of the rise and strange effectiveness of Jared Kushner. Much of the West Wing and campaign staffs were made up of people whom Jared had picked. Their common characteristic was that, while they were tolerant of Trump, they could be counted on to slow-walk his worst excesses; some, like Herschmann, acting for Kushner, even often sought to put a brake on them. Kushner, both for temperamental and strategic reasons, would not, in almost any circumstance, directly confront his father-in-law. Instead, his management approach was to layer in a kind of soft accommodation—a time lag that allowed the president's short attention span to pass. There was a Trump White House on steroids, and then there was Jared's Trump White House on a more limited dose. Put another way, everything that happened in the Trump White House was a product of the president's fevered impulses: a combination of resentments, dramatic flair, score settling, lack of knowledge or understanding, and a sense of what moved his audience. But this was filtered through a management system Jared had created to lower the immediate temperature precisely to the point where the president would not notice and Jared would not be blamed. One of Kushner's own consistent justifications for his role, and one of his stated reasons for being in his father-in-law's White House, was that he made things less bad than they would otherwise have been.

Meanwhile, against what Jared regarded as the "managed" Sturm und Drang of the Trump White House, he and Ivanka pursued their own separate efforts for good press and notable accomplishments, sometimes as though they were running their own separate administrations. Ivanka was particularly regarded as seeing herself as the center of Trumpworld and her father as in a different orbit. Jared, for his part, had put down clear markers for himself: among them what he would argue was the most successful Middle East diplomacy in generations, the Abraham Accords, a series of agreements between Israel and the Arab states. He regarded this effort as his own, quite independent of the president.

Kushner now, in the final weeks, seemed to make a sort of triage decision to focus his remaining time and energies on wrapping up more deals in his peace efforts and securing his legacy at the expense of trying to mitigate or manage the election meltdown—that is, he was willing to sacrifice his father-in-law's legacy, or was cutting his losses trying to save it. Ivanka, ever noted for a high level of self-centered efficiency, was already setting up their new life in Florida and arranging midyear admittance of her children to private schools.

Their absence was a sign to everyone else in the West Wing and the campaign that they had better be making immediate plans, too—indeed, that "management," however weak it had been in the Trump White House, however much Jared's "less bad" had seldom produced something actually "good," had entirely departed.

As notable as Jared and Ivanka's disappearance: Hope was gone.

And it was doubly telling and unsettling that Trump did not seem to take much notice of this—or perhaps couldn't bring himself to admit it. Hicks was as much a part of the Trump White House glue and character, even moral center (to the extent it had one), as anyone. Hicks had worked for Ivanka's fashion company as a PR person, then had been one of the first in the Trump orbit to be seconded to the Trump campaign. Of all the exceptions you had to make for most of the people around Trump, Hicks seemed personable, professional, hardworking, normal. (Indeed, this had spurred a kind of parallel view of someone who must simply be *hiding* deep peculiarities.) She liked Donald Trump, and Donald Trump liked her. She tried to protect him, and he looked after her. It was nearly . . . sweet. For many in Trump's circle, Hicks represented what might actually be an indication of Trump's humanity. When she left in 2018, Trump got her a job working for the Murdochs in Los Angeles, where she was regularly mocked and threatened in restaurants and Pilates classes. Trump spent the ensuing months trying to get her back. She returned in 2019.

"What do you think?" he pressed her about the election challenge as he allowed Giuliani to step in. She had been openly warning everyone that this was the only thing people would remember of the Trump administration, his refusal to accept the election.

"You know what I think," she said. "I don't think this is going to work."

"You're wrong. It's going to work." He suggested to her that there was a world of intrigue she was not privy to—evidence, experts, powerful individuals all coming together to make his case.

Beyond the election mess itself, Hicks had been hit hard by COVID, and was angry that the White House had been so cavalier about protecting the people in it from the virus. What's more, she had been hurt by the president's accusations (even if he was teasing) that she had given the virus to him. By the middle of November, she was effectively gone from the White House.

And if anyone still needed a reality check, there was Don Jr., who, in a heroic grab for his father's long-withheld approval, had become the president's designated second to the base, often even more rampant in his rhetoric than the president himself. Trump's eldest son was now excusing himself from meetings with the Giuliani clique and telling people he was a "realist."

Indeed, the room—as in "being in the room," the most vaunted place in politics—had become a perilous place: anyone who started to talk with any reservations about fighting on, or even about the difficult hurdles an election challenge faced, drew the ire of the president, whose defiance seemed to grow in inverse proportion to the ever-clearer certainty that there was little hope that a challenge could succeed.

* * *

Among the campaign's existing legal staff, Jenna Ellis was the only member to embrace the challenge effort. A week after the election, she had become Giuliani's effective number two, not just as a

legal strategist—strategist was not an important function—but as
a TV defender. On one day alone, she did more than ten television
appearances, followed by a lineup on talk radio.

A clear Trump administration theme was that a position in the
Trump White House was an enhanced route to a television career.
Also, your career within the administration advanced much more
quickly if your television career was advancing. In some sense, television was the singular point of the Trump administration. There was
a fine line (or no line at all) between working for Trump and being
on television for him. Television, in many ways, was the job.

"Bill," said Trump, shortly after Bill Stepien took over the campaign, "do you do TV?"

"I'll do anything that you want, although I actually prefer to stay
out of the spotlight, sir. That would be my choice."

"Well, you need to," said an uncomprehending president. "I
don't know how you do this job if you're not on TV. That's what a
campaign manager is supposed to do. What else is there?" (After
Stepien appeared on *Fox & Friends*, in obvious hostage video–style,
the president never brought up television with him again.)

Trump's view of the world (and how he understood the world's
view of him) and of the basic structure of political cause and effect,
largely—entirely, in the view of many—came from what he saw on
television. What was on television left a greater impression on him
than what was said to him, or what intelligence he received, or what
facts were known. Sometimes aides explained this by saying the
president was acutely visual—that is, not a reader, but that, in the new
American media mode, he had a kind of hyper–video sensitivity,
with a keen recall of image and sound. But his postmodern orien-
tation went further still: he saw television as the real battleground
and an end in itself. So, not policy debate or legislative maneuver-
ing, but television performance and the impression it left were what
mattered. He judged aides and supporters in large part by how they

did on television. And he invariably asked people around him for critiques of how the other people around him did on television.

He routinely shushed anyone else in the room when Jenna Ellis came on—high praise.

A key activity of the new election challenge was to schedule Jenna's media hits. The inner circle tried to close ranks around her, with Herschmann, in a series of calls, grilling her on an election-challenge plan she showed no sign of having, other than to stop participating in the calls.

Ten days after the election, Ellis sent out a message, appearing to take charge of the campaign and implying that remaining staffers would report to her, further telling the campaign's hair and makeup person that she now worked exclusively for Ellis. (An email was, cattily, forwarded among campaign staffers about Ellis arranging to have her makeup done the night before for early morning hits—she'd just sleep in it.)

* * *

On Saturday afternoon, November fourteenth, Giuliani gathered his team in the campaign office in Rosslyn. The mission was to build a national legal team—in a day. The rush was to get lawsuits out the door in the next twenty-four hours.

The room had not been cleaned since Election Day, eleven days before. Refuse filled the trash cans and overflowed onto the floor. There was a heavy sour or rotting smell—in the trash was a week-old Buffalo chicken sandwich—mixed with Giuliani's reliable farting.

The sweeping view from the big conference room was over the Potomac and Southwest Washington, taking in the Capitol and the Lincoln Memorial. Giuliani's back was to the window. He was holding court and juggling multiple phone calls. There was a whiteboard with seven states highlighted—PA, MI, GA, NC, NV, WI, AZ— with key counties and a list of potential lawyers in each place.

Andrew Giuliani, the former mayor's son, was there. Giuliani and his son had often been estranged—Rudy had broken up with Andrew's mother, Donna Hanover, in a famous news conference during the last stage of his mayoral term—but Andrew had gone to work in the Trump White House, and, in the Trump election cause, he had now become his father's aide-de-camp. Boris Epshteyn, a Trumpworld hanger-on who had briefly held an unspecific position in the West Wing and then had tried, not too successfully, to launch himself as a right-wing television commentator, was back in the fray. Joe diGenova and Victoria Toensing, husband-and-wife television lawyers, were on hand. Christianné Allen, Giuliani's twenty-one-year-old personal spokeswoman and another baffling presence, was, as usual, by his side. There was, equally baffling, Mirna Tarraf, a Lebanese twentysomething former real estate agent from Newport Beach, California, often with the former mayor, along with several young women who had been campaign workers but who had been repurposed to Giuliani's team overnight. And Ellis, who was across the hall in the campaign studio doing a television hit.

"What the fuck is this?" demanded Jason Miller after arriving in the room. He had pulled Boris Epshteyn aside to take alarmed note of what was obviously a potential superspreader event. Everybody was piled in close in the conference room, and no one was wearing a mask.

It was impossible to overstate the unanimity of feelings among the Trump inner circle for this new intruder circle: they looked ridiculous, they sounded ridiculous, they espoused ridiculous theories.

Coming into the building, Miller had taken a call from an upset young staffer whom Ellis had called to inform she was no longer reporting to the old campaign team; she was now reporting to Ellis and the mayor—that or be fired. Coming face-to-face with Ellis outside the conference room, Miller lost it. "You're threatening to fire my people? What is going on? You can't treat people like this."

"You're being hostile."

"This is fucking crazy. I mean this is all fucking batshit crazy. You're fucking crazy," said Miller, throwing up his hands and leaving the building.

The next day, the campaign was reorganized around arranging TV bookings for Giuliani, Ellis, Epshteyn, Toensing, and diGenova, all to get out there and argue *the steal*.

* * *

A key sign of the situation pushing quickly to the outer edge of no return was that the crazies kept identifying people who were even crazier.

"Sidney Powell," pronounced Giuliani, "is crazy."

Powell, whom the president had drafted into the election challenge effort, and Rudy had a showdown early on the week of the sixteenth, with even Rudy, in frustration, questioning Powell's most outlandish theories.

"I didn't come here to kiss your fucking ring," Powell said to the mayor. The two of them ended up in separate rooms sulking, with Ellis calling the president to moderate. The president made clear that he wanted Powell on the team. He was embracing everybody (or anybody) who agreed that the election had been stolen from him.

Powell, at sixty-five, had had quite a long and serious career, with ten years as an assistant U.S. attorney and then in private practice handling some big cases, including parts of the Enron defense. But along the way, there had been a drift into right-wing politics—or, perhaps more to the point, into right-wing media. Powell wrote and self-published a book about the Enron prosecution, *Licensed to Lie: Exposing Corruption in the Department of Justice*, which led to Fox News appearances. She added two and two together for other conspiracies and views of the deep state: Andrew Weissmann was the Enron prosecutor and, subsequently, Robert Mueller's deputy in the investigation of the president. See? It was all connected! Ever-larger conspiracies earned her more Fox airtime.

The president noticed Powell on Fox, and called. So did Michael Flynn. Flynn was, briefly, Trump's first national security advisor, bounced out in an FBI investigation in the first weeks of the administration. Represented by an established law firm, and pleading guilty, he would later fire the firm and hire Powell to try to reverse his plea. In Powell's defense of Flynn, he was a victim of the worst deep-state abuses, a narrative that would be embraced by the president and the Trump Justice Department. Indeed, it would result, not long after Election Day, in Powell being fully signed on to the election fraud and recount team and, shortly, in Flynn's pardon by the president.

Powell had moved beyond Flynn, into deeper new conspiracies. In the days immediately following the election, she was the author on Fox of operatic new conspiracies, going much further out than anything the president had yet reached: computer systems had been programmed to switch Trump votes to Biden votes, with the CIA in on it. Now she had been telling Giuliani and the team that the conspiracy ran even deeper: Trump's landslide victory was upended by an international plot. Former Venezuelan president Hugo Chávez (dead since 2013), George Soros, the Clinton Foundation, and the Chinese had masterminded the plot to steal the election from him. Oh, and the voting software routed the results though Germany, exposing the tabulation to nefarious elements there!

There was no doubt among Trump's White House staff that things had gone seriously over the edge. The presence of Sidney Powell was not necessary to confirm this. But she did become the tipping point into utter flapdoodleness. All in Trumpworld with any amount of professional concern and grounding now stepped pointedly aside, became only observers of the circus.

* * *

The law firm Porter Wright, which Matt Morgan and Giuliani had agreed to hire for the Pennsylvania lawsuit, bailed in the days before the hearing, one among many firms that quit the election challenges. Campaign and West Wing lawyers started to refer to being "ghosted" by the various outside counsels.

Rudy moved to step into the case. He had not argued in a courtroom in almost thirty years, and even his bar association standing was unclear, but he had convinced the president that he could no longer rely on his own campaign lawyers.

On November seventeenth, Giuliani appeared in federal court in Williamsport, Pennsylvania, before Judge Matthew Brann, joined by local counsel, radio host and lawyer Marc Scaringi. Giuliani presented a broad conspiracy of voter fraud and alleged that as many as 1.5 million votes might need to be invalidated.

The confused judge pointed out that the filing hadn't argued voter fraud.

And, indeed, over the weekend, the campaign lawyers had removed the fraud charges because arguing fraud demands a far higher level of scrutiny, and they had deemed their case to be based on a woeful lack of evidence there. "I am not going to lose my fucking law license because of these idiots," a disgusted Matt Morgan told White House colleagues.

Giuliani now asked the court to let them amend the complaint and refile those same outlandish claims. The judge turned him down. Giuliani argued massive fraud anyway, returning to his stacks of affidavits. "These ballots could have been from Mickey Mouse. We have no idea," Giuliani told the increasingly irritated court in a hearing that was streamed online—with #mickeymouse soon trending on Twitter. (This, in turn, irritated the president: Giuliani was referencing Mickey Mouse! Why would he mention Mickey Mouse?)

Well, if you are arguing fraud, shouldn't the stricter standard apply? the judge pressed.

They were not arguing fraud, because the court wouldn't let them amend the complaint to include their fraud charge. Therefore, argued Giuliani, in sophist-absurdist style, reminiscent of his many cable television appearances, they should not be held to the fraud standard in their fraud claims.

* * *

As was so often the case, the president wasn't happy with his legal team: They weren't fighting hard enough. The message wasn't clear enough. They needed impact. There wasn't enough impact. Everybody was coming up way short in their defense of him. He was alone and let down.

"People have got to know this was stolen. This was taken from us. It was organized. It wasn't even a close election. It was a landslide. We won by a landslide. A *landslide*—and it was taken. This is what people need to understand—it was a landslide."

Among remaining aides, there was a slow-motion sense of threading the needle, of trying to meld the right thing with the tenable thing with the Trump thing. In politics, the smart move is not to say no and to know how to finesse yes. Miller proposed a press conference to lay out, state by state, the strategy and the multiple (however remote) paths to victory. They would hold it at RNC headquarters, to help suggest that this was a partywide effort.

Rudy and Andrew Giuliani and Ellis, Kerik, Toensing, diGenova, Epshteyn, Miller, and the rest of the Giuliani entourage gathered in an RNC conference room beforehand—one where the air-conditioning was blasting in late November. Around the conference table, Rudy, shivering, suddenly announced that he had asked Sidney Powell to participate in the press conference.

Ellis tried to argue against this, saying that Powell's conspiracy theories, to which Powell was now tying ranking Republicans, made her look completely nuts. "We're going to own her if she speaks," protested Ellis. "She'll be on our team."

"We need to lay it all out," said Rudy. "Let's not be afraid of the truth."

"It's not true," said Ellis.

Miller reminded Giuliani that even he had recently called Powell crazy—at which point, the six-foot Powell showed up wearing a leopard-print cardigan and a leather jacket that made her look like something out of the Michael Jackson 1984 Victory Tour.

The group shortly filed out of the cold conference room and into the small room reserved for the press conference, with fifty or sixty people and the heat up high and no ventilation. Giuliani introduced what, in Ellis's characterization of the new Trump lawyers, was being called "an elite strikeforce team": him, Powell, Ellis, diGenova, Toensing, and Epshteyn, each vastly more familiar with a television studio than a courtroom.

In fact, Giuliani's presentation, departing from his often more manic turns, was mostly procedural and straightforward—he was getting good at ticking off the long, long list of minor and massive state-by-state fraud claims. He stood beside a poster board with a U.S. map and the legend "Multiple Pathways to Victory." Six states were highlighted in red: Pennsylvania, Wisconsin, Michigan, Georgia, Arizona, and Nevada. Giuliani seemed to make an effort this time to stay focused and buttoned up . . . but for the heat.

Three minutes into his presentation, sweat started to bead on his forehead. Over the next fifteen minutes it sprouted on his cheeks, then on his chin. He had to take his glasses off because they were slipping. Then, thirty-two minutes in, a rivulet of black hair dye started to run down his face. Then the rivulet grew wider, tributaries of black and deathly gray. Curiously, you could not immediately see it from the in-person seats. But you could see it on television, and in seconds, Twitter lit up in wonder and incredulity. Everybody in the audience in person, agog, was pointing at their phones and then looking up and pointing at the mayor.

"No," said Miller in the back of the room to Sean Spicer, the president's former press secretary, now covering the press conference for Newsmax, "this isn't happening."

And it happened for a long time, with Giuliani, deep in his dirge of abuses—they were becoming singsong-like—unaware that his sweat was washing away his hair dye.

And then it got much worse: Powell came on and let it all out, uttering virtually not a single word that had any basis in reality or even possibility:

What we are really dealing with here, and uncovering more by the day, is the massive influence of Communist money through Venezuela, Cuba, and likely China in the interference with our elections here in the United States. The Dominion Voting Systems, the Smartmatic technology software, and the software that goes in other computerized voting systems herein as well, not just Dominion, were created in Venezuela at the direction of Hugo Chávez, to make sure he never lost an election after one constitutional referendum came out the way he did not want it to come out . . .

Now, the software itself was created with so many variables and so many back doors that can be hooked up to the internet or a thumb drive stuck in it or whatever, but one of its most characteristic features is its ability to flip votes. It can set and run an algorithm that probably ran all over the country to take a certain percentage of votes from President Trump and flip them to President Biden, which we might never have uncovered had the votes for President Trump not been so overwhelming in so many of these states that it broke the algorithm that had been plugged into the system, and that's what caused them to have to shut down in the states they shut down in. That's when they came in the back door with all the mail-in ballots, many of which they had actually fabricated, some were on pristine paper with identically matching perfect circle dots for Mr. Biden. Others were shoved in in batches; they're always put in in a certain number of batches, and people would rerun the same batch. This corresponds to our statistical evidence that shows incredible spikes in the vote counts at particular times and that corresponds to eyewitness testimony of numerous people who have come forward and said they saw the ballots come in the back door at that time.

Powell's delivery was precise and articulate. The disturbed, paranoid, hallucinogenic, and ludicrous in the mouth of a composed spokesperson made this seem all the more like a put-on. (And, months later, trying to defend herself from a defamation lawsuit by Dominion, Powell would seem to admit that it *was* a put-on, or theater, or burlesque, and not something that a reasonable person ought to have believed.) Indeed, Powell's tale of a worldwide conspiracy to subvert the U.S. presidential election was, after the confusion and disbelief, gut splitting.

And yet it now entered the election conspiracy bloodstream. It was Dominion that did it.

Some White House aides, in trying to understand how they'd gotten here, would agree that the tale of the frog in the pot of slowly heating water might describe their situation: somehow they did not realize they were being boiled alive. But now they knew, and nearly all marked Rudy's hair dye press conference as the moment when they could no longer, in any fashion, deny that the Cartesian world had ended.

* * *

The next day, Andrew Giuliani popped for COVID. The Rudy superspreader team was thereupon banned from Virginia headquarters, however mostly empty it was now, and forced to relocate to rooms at the Mandarin Oriental Hotel, overlooking the

Jefferson Memorial. The superspreader team now moved between Giuliani's and Kerik's suites.

* * *

Trump was pissed off. "What's going on with this shit dripping off his face? And they're killing Sidney in the press for what she's saying—saying crazy shit . . ."

And yet, somehow, the lesson he took from this was that his people weren't being aggressive enough. They weren't on the offensive. He had bad lawyers. Rudy was fighting, yes . . . but with shit dripping down his face.

5

WHAT'S BLACK IS WHITE

The president's estimate that they might have a 25 or 30 percent chance of prevailing—contradicting Justin Clark's estimate that, at best, they might have little more than a 5 percent chance, itself a bow to the president's need for the most inflated view of his situation and advantage—was now magnified exponentially by Rudy.

It was much more likely, Rudy told him (and Trump willingly believed) that the president would be able to overturn the election than that Joe Biden would be able to hold on to it. Giuliani argued that, in this conflict, Trump was the more tenacious, gifted, and brazen fighter. Here was the bedrock of Trump's belief about himself, and Giuliani now unctuously reinforced it. This, in addition to Giuliani's growing pile of affidavits, was the basic premise of Trump's incredulity that anyone anywhere might think that Joe Biden was a plausible winner in a match with Donald Trump—he just simply couldn't lose to him. That wasn't believable!

The president, the people closest to him knew, was highly susceptible to what, for whatever reason, and against whatever logic, he *wanted* to believe—in other words, he frequently stood on the edge of a separate reality. The fault, therefore, lay not precisely with him but with whoever pushed him over.

The fault was Rudy's, people closest to the president concluded.

The Trump family put it on Rudy because Rudy was crazy, or drunk, or opportunistic, or all three. Don Jr. assessed the obvious to a confidant: "Rudy isn't capable of winning these cases." Jared, in his particular style of disapproval, no longer mentioned Rudy or commented upon him when the subject arose. Meadows tried a more sophist approach of separating the "real" issues from the "Rudy" issues.

In other words, Trump *wasn't* to blame because Trump was Trump, but Rudy *was* to blame because Rudy was Rudy.

* * *

Rudy had two strategic paths to victory. In fact, there were no paths to victory, but Giuliani kept hotly outlining his two-pronged attack: They would go through the state legislatures, where they would present their evidence and where Republican legislators would throw out the Biden electors and send Trump electors to Washington (the actual procedures and precedents for this being nonexistent). Or: federal courts, acting under Article II of the Constitution, which gives the power of regulating each state's elections to the state legislature (and only to the state legislature, which now became the Trump legal team's rallying cry), would throw out millions of votes where decisions had been made by election officials instead of the state legislatures.

In Giuliani's analysis, the Supreme Court was their true ace in the hole. It was simple: the Trump administration, with its three appointments, had a lock on the Court.

"In our pocket," Trump now repeatedly said.

"We'll win when we get to the Court," Rudy repeated, steadfast and, to most others, harebrained in his confidence.

Since the first days of the administration, personal loyalty had been a consistent theme in the Supreme Court nominees presented to Trump: here were judges who would be on his side. It was his litmus test: Will they support me? The Federalist Society and the White House Counsel's Office, which proposed nominees and coordinated the confirmation process, walked a fine line between support for conservative views and support directly for Trump. Trump, without interest in the Court or much (or any) background in its traditions, found it easy to believe the Court was wholly stacked in his favor, and when push came to shove, would surely have his back. "We've got the Supremes," Trump assured various of his callers.

The old Rudy—Rudy the Justice Department hand, Rudy the prosecutor, Rudy the occasionally diligent student of government— would have known that even a stacked Court was going to go out of its way not to cast its fate with this mess, this crazytown mess, that the rule of institutional self-protection would surely win out. But Giuliani was now unequivocal that this was a certain path. Giuliani might not have argued in court in thirty years, but he had come out of his television defense of the president during the Mueller investigation—even in Trump's characterization, "playing a lawyer on television"—with new confidence in the power of his own posturing and aggressiveness. The Supreme Court would play its part in the Trump drama. He described what he had come to see as an inevitable decision in their favor as "the ultimate showstopper."

But the other aspect here, itself an inherent part of continual conflict, was just about living another day—"kicking the can down the road," in the understanding of other White House advisors, distressed and disbelieving that the fraud campaign was continuing with no letup in sight. Everything was, empirically, collapsing around them; there were no hopeful signs for any way forward. No matter: in the war room in Trump's head, and in Giuliani's increasingly fevered imagination, the Supreme Court was out there. They must not let up, because that was where they would prevail.

On Saturday, November 21, two days after Giuliani's hair dye meltdown at the RNC press conference, U.S. Court District judge Matthew Brann, in Pennsylvania, denied the Trump effort to have millions of mail-in ballots thrown out because of small inconsistencies, from county to county, in the filing process. (For instance, some counties had allowed voters to correct mistakes on their ballots where others had not.) The legal arguments, Brann said, were "without merit" and based on "speculative accusations." The claim, "like Frankenstein's monster, has been haphazardly stitched together." The court had "no authority to take away the right to vote of even a single person, let alone millions of citizens," Brann wrote in a model of the scoffing and incredulity that many of the decisions in the Trump election cases would express.

But, in fact, they hadn't lost at all, according to Rudy. They had just quickened the pace to victory: "Today's decision turns out to help us in our strategy to get expeditiously to the U.S. Supreme Court," said Giuliani and Ellis in a statement after the Pennsylvania court smackdown.

* * *

The breadth of the legal effort needed to overturn the results in at least three states—Wisconsin, Georgia, and Arizona were now the favorites (after the court made it clear that the road to invalidating more than a million votes in Pennsylvania was closed)—to achieve an Electoral College majority, and to accomplish this in no more than a few weeks, would have been, even in more favorable circumstances, an improbable feat. In the week after the election, the president kept insisting that they had to do what Bush had done in Florida after the 2000 election, a matter involving a few hundred votes shifting either way. And, indeed, that effort had been a massive one in a single state with a razor-thin outcome, whereas this was three states with vastly larger vote gaps to overcome.

Who were those lawyers? Whom did Bush have? Trump demanded to know, casting about in his almost entirely impressionistic view of history and events. He kept returning to the question, leading Kushner to publicly declare that they were looking for a figure like James Baker, who had run the Bush recount effort, to run theirs—soft-pedaling to the president the ninety-year-old Baker's disparaging public remarks about the Trump election challenge and making no real effort to find such a party eminence to lead the challenge.

Trump was back in a place where, in his career, he had often found himself: All his problems could be solved with the right lawyers; all his problems were the result of having the wrong lawyers. There were, out there, brilliant, canny, cunning, hugger-mugger lawyers who could fix any problems, and then there were his own flat-footed, unimaginative, wimpy, and exhausted ones.

In this sense, he was correct. Both the White House Counsel's Office and the Justice Department had turned their backs on his electoral quest. No lawyer with normal career prospects, it seemed, would go there.

Even before this, Trump had come to the breaking point with the Counsel's Office and the Department of Justice, frequently talking before the election of his post-victory plans to replace both Pat Cipollone, the White House counsel, and Bill Barr, the attorney general.

Cipollone, a devout Catholic and pro-life lawyer, had first come to Trump's attention in 2016, when the conservative radio and television host Laura Ingraham brought him as her uninvited plus-one to a debate-prep session. A dead ringer for Milhouse Van Houten, from *The Simpsons*, Cipollone replaced—in fact, was one of the few people willing to replace—Don McGahn, the then White House counsel, whom Trump had come to despise. And shortly, he would come to despise Cipollone, too.

In one midsummer encounter, as protests raged in Atlanta, Minneapolis, Portland, and other cities, and with the president watching

Fox's coverage of the rioting on an endless loop, Trump summoned Cipollone to the Oval Office, launching on him as soon as the out-of-breath lawyer (running down from his second-floor office) got to the doorway.

"So, Pat, what have you been doing all day? Like, just tell me, what time did you get in? Filing any lawsuits against Antifa?" His diatribes against Cipollone were traded both as cautionary tales—it could get that bad for anyone, if they weren't careful—and models of the Trump insult oeuvre.

Barr, too, who had distinguished himself beyond any attorney general in recent history as the president's accommodating water carrier and whose intervention had arguably saved Trump's presidency after the Mueller investigation—reading the special counsel's damning report in the most fulsome way; indeed, reversing its thesis for public consumption—now was the target of a withering attack.

Here was another presidential litany: "Took forever for the IG [Inspector General] report [on the Russian investigation] to come out ... Durham [an investigation of the Russian investigation led by John Durham, a federal prosecutor] thing spins on forever ... not charging anyone for Black Lives riots ... Never took fraud seriously ... Doesn't he get it that this is a massive problem? ... What happened to that guy? ... I wish I had great lawyers ... I have terrible lawyers."

In a meeting called to mobilize remaining White House and campaign staffers, the attendees arrived in the Oval Office to find the president talking to Elliot Gaiser, a 2016 law school graduate. Not only was Gaiser one of the youngest people on the president's legal team, but he looked like he was still in high school—junior high even! He had a memo or letter in his hand, and the president was pressing him about it. And now, creating confusion in the room, Trump was pressing everybody else about what to do with it—with everybody else now trying to figure out what the letter was.

"It's an executive order," said Trump, "to get the DOJ to take voter action."

"So, this is from the Counsel's Office?" asked one of the uncertain staffers.

"No, no, no," said an anxious Gaiser, holding the page away from him.

"What do I have to do to put this into effect? Do I just sign it?" Trump demanded. "Do I have to put it on letterhead?"

"How long have you been working on this?" another staffer asked the young lawyer.

"No, no, I just got it from—" Gaiser said with mounting panic, indicating the president. "I never saw it." Plaintively, he asked the president or, broadly, anyone, "Don't we have to run it by Pat?"

"Molly," Trump called to his assistant. "Get Pat down here."

Cipollone arrived seconds later, out of breath.

"I'm sitting here with my *new* lawyer, Pat," said Trump, with a pointed smirk, although others in the room surmised that he didn't know Gaiser's name.

The now-terrified young lawyer passed Trump's executive order to the White House counsel. Cipollone, himself confused and, as always, in panic mode, seemed to snatch the paper away and then, with a hurried excuse, withdrew, taking it with him for further study.

In other words, the effective status of one of the most complex and resource-demanding legal challenges perhaps in U.S. history continued to be that no one was really in charge—and the president was crowd-sourcing his own legal work. The suspicion was that the executive order now being passed, like a hot potato, around the Oval Office was the handiwork of Kurt Olsen, one of the growing number of right-wing conspiracy-minded lawyers vying for the president's attention. The effort was ad hoc, free-floating, decentralized, on the fly, and an open invitation for anyone with a grievance or a hopeful personal agenda to join in—and send along their own legal theories.

In this, the shark had already been jumped by Sidney Powell.

Tucker Carlson, the Fox News host, always pleased to undermine his Fox colleague Sean Hannity (who had relentlessly championed Powell) and miffed that among the dead voters on the list supplied by the campaign, which the Carlson show had scrolled through on the air, a number had turned out to be alive, went after Powell on November 19 after the hair dye press conference earlier in the day. She was portrayed as a grifter and fantasist.

Then, on the twenty-first, Powell went on Newsmax to accuse Georgia Republican governor Brian Kemp, still at this point allied with the White House, of being a key agent in the Dominion–Hugo Chavez–George Soros conspiracy. (Curiously, the show was hosted, in a downward spiral of political fortunes and a world of reverse respectability, by the former network news political heavyweight and presidential campaign chronicler Mark Halperin, caught out in his own #MeToo disgrace and reduced to the media fringe.)

On November 22, a reluctant Trump, otherwise defending her for her "fight," agreed that they might need some distancing from Powell. Hence, she was now designated an "independent lawyer," not acting as a lawyer for the president.

* * *

External validation was, to say the least, hard to come by—and yet the president found it.

He grilled Secretary of State Mike Pompeo, National Security Advisor Robert O'Brien, and Kushner and Meadows, during the days after the election on his support in foreign capitals. After November 7, and the calls by the networks for Biden, the four men each tried to prepare him for what was characterized by Meadows as "diplomatic tightrope walking." Foreign leaders might be forced to make ritual bows to Biden's election.

This was hardly the case. Across the world, there was, with detectable relief, a public embrace of the Biden victory by all but the most retro regimes (notably, Russia and Brazil).

It was startling to aides, however much they were anticipating an eruption, that Trump's wrath fell on Bibi Netanyahu. The Israeli prime minister's reach out to Biden (some twelve hours after the U.S. networks called the election, arguably a begrudging reach out) coming even before, Trump now repeated, "the ink was dry," was an ultimate betrayal.

As in all Trump reactions, a variety of grievances welled up here. There was his belief that he had singularly done more for Israel than any American president—and that therefore he was owed. And now sold out. Trump also conflated this with his own increasing anger at his failure to much improve his standing among Jewish voters, even with what he regarded as the quid pro quo nature of his support of Israel.

At the same time, aides were bringing him any indication possible from other leaders that their congratulations for Biden were lukewarm. He was assured, the European leaders, along with Putin in Russia and Bolsonaro in Brazil, were sending messages of support. Such "messages" mostly seemed however to be in the form of politic ambassadorial conversation and polite well-wishing. But this became a further part of his foundational belief: Angela Merkel and Emmanuel Macron and Mario Draghi, each of whom he'd had difficult issues with in the past—a segue here, as always, into his complaints about them not paying their fair share of NATO—were very supportive of his election challenge. Their countries ran much more secure elections than ours. And Boris Johnson in the U.K. was looking at some of the exact same problems we were having here. Months later he would yet be convinced leaders of the Western world and U.S. allies—save for Bibi—had stood with him.

* * *

Kicking the can down the road involved extending the effective deadlines for the race. You had to move the election from being a snapshot in time—musical chairs when the music suddenly stops—to being a moving target and an ongoing campaign. If the campaign before the election was about who should win, the campaign after, redefining basic terms, was about who had won. For Trump, the conflict, like all conflicts, should just continue, with the winner being who could stay in the fight the longest.

Trump, again with his wholly impressionistic historical recall, had become taken with the idea that his was one in a long line of stolen elections—he was just willing to stand up for himself, unlike the others.

In calls with various friends, he fastened onto the close American presidential races, historical retellings that, in part, seemed to come from Giuliani's efforts to galvanize him. In considering the razor-thin 1960 Kennedy-Nixon race, Trump seemed to go back and forth between admiration for Kennedy's ability to steal the election from Nixon and contempt for Nixon's refusal to challenge the outcome. But then, in the telling, he had Nixon stealing the election in 1968 and Hubert Humphrey lacking the support to fight him. ("Nobody liked Humphrey—so weak.") As for the 2000 election, Trump saw Al Gore as a victim of bad lawyers and Bush as the beneficiary of good ones—or Gore as having cautious lawyers "trying to look good" and Bush as having aggressive lawyers "who knew where the bodies were buried."

Elections themselves, certainly close elections, were, he now took as obvious, fundamentally corrupt: *of course*, in a close election, somebody's thumb would be on the scale. You weren't supposed to fight about it—or you weren't supposed to be *seen* fighting about it; you just let the heaviest thumb win, "but fuck that."

To do this, though, to have this fight, you had to argue against the very nature of an election: that at an appointed moment, it was a fait accompli, counted, done, decided, agreed. That was part of the reason the Fox News call in Arizona had been such a betrayal. You had to keep the election in play. You had to keep the dispute going, just like they had in Florida in 2000 (although, in fact, that dispute ended after thirty-six days).

By the Saturday after the 2020 election, with all the networks calling it for Biden, the election was, practically speaking, not in play.
One function, then, of the more or less screwball Trump-Giuliani
lawsuits was at least to create the sense that a contest was still in
progress. The courts were Rudy's PR operation, convincing both
the media and the president that the fight continued and the outcome was in doubt. Hence, Election Day was no longer the goalpost. The goalpost was when the election was certified by individual
states by December 8. And then, not even then: it was when the
electors gathered in their respective state capitals, on December 14.
Or not even then: it was when the votes were counted in Congress,
heretofore a wholly ceremonial occasion, on January 6.

Meanwhile, before those new goalposts were reached, there was
the overtime campaign to be staged and waged, the Rudy (and
Jenna) Road Show.

* * *

The premise was that Giuliani and Ellis would appear before the legislatures in disputed swing states, pitching a legal and evidentiary
argument about why the legislatures (in each instance, Republican-
controlled legislatures) should not certify their electors. Pennsylvania, Arizona, Michigan, and Georgia were on the list.

In fact, none of the targeted state bodies was willing to convene
a formal hearing. The best Giuliani could summon was, to anyone
except the most dedicated, a wackadoodle and disorganized show of
informal meetings with subcommittees at remote locations in hotel
meeting rooms far from the capitals.

It was quite a traveling circus. In the tent were, in addition to
Rudy and Jenna, Bernie Kerik, Rudy's traveling assistant team, and
his girlfriend, Maria Ryan. (Ryan would shortly submit an invoice to
the Trump campaign for her services. The remaining campaign officials would take some pleasure in refusing to pay it and in conveying
to a very sour president that Rudy's girlfriend had put in for her fees.)

Each hearing was a three- or four-hour session consisting of Rudy, in courtroom fashion (or, at least, television courtroom fashion) laying out his case, the relentless, shocked, hell-and-brimstone prosecutor quite seemingly having the time of his life. Then there followed a man-on-the-street group of witnesses, recruited (in part through Rudy's election fraud hotline) to testify to myriad instances of blatant and shocking behavior, teased out by Rudy, a Broadway cast of everyman characters.

In a media world preoccupied with a pandemic, with the new president-elect and his forthcoming administration, and with a daily debunking of the Trump election claims, Rudy's sideshow was too weird and obsessive and in the weeds to get much airtime. Even Fox was barely covering the hearings.

But Newsmax and OAN were.

Here was something of a paradigm for people involved in the election-challenge effort. If you were on the margins of media, political, and legal life, far from Main Street and big-league opportunities, election fraud was an avenue for you: supporting the president as he was abandoned by anyone with better prospects.

Up until now, Newsmax and OAN, both conservative wannabe networks, had barely managed to register against Fox News. Each had limited carriage on cable systems and had to depend mostly on internet audiences and low-margin advertising. Notably, parts of Newsmax's revenue came from selling diet supplements. To the extent that it and OAN had any business standing, it was as dedicated Trump supporters. Newsmax's CEO, Christopher Ruddy, largely unknown before the Trump election, but a West Palm Beach resident and Mar-a-Lago member, had branded himself "a Trump friend," becoming a permanent spokesperson for the president.

Here was another subtext of the election-challenge campaign: Fox's own internal angst. A vehement and wrathful Rupert Murdoch was open in his contempt for the president whom he deemed stupid, venal, ludicrous, dangerous. Murdoch was furious, too, with his own anchors, sending the message, in every way short of confrontation, that they had to get right on this: there had been no fraud. Biden would be president.

This made for glee and opportunity at Newsmax and OAN. Ruddy, at Newsmax, privately downplayed his own support for Trump's election challenge. But at the same time, he clearly reveled in the drama and the outlandishness of it. It was good television.

Newsmax and OAN broadcast the hearings live—every hour of them. Giuliani and Ellis, already far out on the edge of reason, were now, with hours and hours of live television coverage, turbocharged into new galaxies of certainty and conspiracy. They were on television three or four hours every day, with Trump watching every minute. Three weeks beyond Election Day, and Trump had put aside every other presidential function except the election challenge—or, more specifically, watching what his supporters were saying on television about the election challenge and what other commentators were saying about his supporters. He couldn't get enough of his own spectacle. How was Rudy doing? How was Jenna doing? Who else was defending him? Who else could they get on the air?

White House advisors, including Kushner and Meadows, continued telling congressional leaders that the president would sooner or later concede; it was inevitable, obviously. He just needed to get there on his own.

As it happened, Giuliani and Ellis were not convincing any state legislatures. Rather, they were discovering political cowardice everywhere, cowardice even greater than the conspiracy. And the state legislators were stupid: "Just no fucking idea of their power or obligations," stormed a disgusted Kerik.

At the same time, Giuliani and Ellis, through their television performances, were certainly convincing the president (if he had any doubts) that he should surely not concede. He repeated Giuliani and Ellis's case to virtually anyone who would listen.

And, too, the hearings were working.

"Big, big ratings," said the satisfied president.

No matter how peculiar and far from prime time the show was, people were watching. In the spring of 2018, when Rudy had taken over the president's defense in the Mueller investigation, he had, in a day-after-day schedule of television appearances as strange and alarming as anything most political professionals had ever seen from a senior presidential advisor, led a clear public mood swing from general approval of the Mueller investigation to growing doubts. Giuliani's manic certainty—eyes popping, mouth going, voice rising—worked.

Again, in Rudy's hours on Newsmax and OAN, his case, no matter how loopy, was moving public opinion in the Trump base from weariness or skepticism to a growing sense of widespread hinky stuff in the election and a new shared resentment with the president. As the case became more oddball and a favorable outcome more implausible, and as political and legal professionals of all stripes grew more disdainful and more and more conventional Republicans personally horrified, support for the president within his base hardened.

On November 25, the day before Thanksgiving, a legislative hearing was scheduled in Pennsylvania. Of the outstanding states, Pennsylvania represented the lion's share of votes. The Pennsylvania numbers had been particularly bedeviling for the president. Pennsylvania, a surprise win for Trump in 2016, was going to give him his 2020 victory, but this was where, hour by hour, he saw victory slipping away. It had become fixed in the president's mind that he had been ahead by a million votes, a landslide in Pennsylvania, and that then, somehow . . . somehow those votes had disappeared. *Just disappeared.*

What Rudy had managed to put together was a "field hearing"— far from anything like a real hearing, one that state reps might actually participate in or listen to. It wasn't even in Harrisburg, Pennsylvania's capital. It was in Gettysburg. But this was going to be the culminating hearing of the road trip. Giuliani and Ellis would close out the campaign before the Thanksgiving holiday. Trump announced that he would be there in person. He had not been out since the election and was pressing for a rally with the belief that there was popular sentiment to be roused that, despite all votes being counted, could still influence the outcome.

"The people haven't yet spoken," he took to saying, as though oblivious to the election that had in fact just taken place.

Meadows and Kushner, viewing the hearing as a hopelessly smalltime affair, hardly worthy of a presidential last stand, convinced Trump he ought not attend. Instead, he dialed in, and Jenna Ellis held up her cell phone to the mic as the cameras rolled so the president could broadcast his stolen-election pitch.

* * *

It wasn't just Republican state legislatures that were not getting it; Rudy and Jenna and, indeed, the president were fighting the Republican establishment, too. During a dinner in DC with the mayor and Bernie, Jenna got an email forwarding a note from Justin Riemer, the chief counsel for the RNC. Why, Riemer wondered, writing to RNC colleagues, were they supporting this Trump election nonsense? The RNC raised a lot more money fighting Democrats than it did fighting elections.

Now Jenna had Riemer's email. She passed her phone around the table, everybody stunned at the message.

"Can you fucking believe this?" said the mayor, as though holding something like a smoking gun in his hand. "They are backdooring us . . . doing everything in their power not to help us."

This was, said Kerik, like saying, "Fuck Trump, fuck Giuliani."

The mayor, sitting in the restaurant but in full battle mode (and with a few drinks in him), damn well got Riemer himself on the phone: "Who the fuck do you think you are? How can you be going against the president? . . . You need to resign and resign tonight . . . because you are going to get fired."

And the mayor called the RNC chair, McDaniel, to make sure this happened.

Riemer remains the RNC chief counsel.

* * *

Shortly after the Thanksgiving weekend, amid all the other constant new and unlikely strategies, a different, even more farfetched-sounding one was shared by Boris Epshteyn, the more or less self-appointed go-between among the West Wing, the campaign, and the Giuliani people. The new gambit coming from the Giuliani camp posited that the vice president, due on January 6 to formally certify the Electoral College results in a ceremony of no consequence, could, in this sudden new telling, reject electors. Epshteyn related this idea without clear provenance in have-you-heard-the-theory fashion.

One Oval Office advisor brought it up with Marc Short, the VP's chief of staff, hoping its silliness was not also an indication of its seriousness.

"We're hearing this, too," said Short. "But no one has approached us yet."

Well, here was yet another bullet the vice president and his people needed to be on the lookout to avoid.

* * *

On December 1, Attorney General Bill Barr quite formally checked out of the Trump circle, announcing that the Justice Department had found no evidence of widespread election fraud.

A thematic pillar of the Trump White House was that the Justice Department worked for the president and that its independence was both Democratic malarkey and a slap in the face to Trump. Bending the DOJ was a fight he kept waging—firing FBI head James Comey in the early months of his administration, firing his first attorney general, Jeff Sessions, in 2018, stonewalling the Mueller investigation, and, finally, in Bill Barr, getting an easy soft touch. And yet total dominance over the sprawling DOJ bureaucracy eluded him, its pockets of resistance a personal affront. It was a special Trump tic: fury over lawyers who wouldn't do what he wanted.

Bypassing the attorney general—he really couldn't help himself from getting on the phone to cajole and wheedle and demand— Trump had been personally calling around to various U.S. attorneys in swing state districts, among them his appointee William McSwain in the Eastern District of Pennsylvania, trying to get them to open investigations into election fraud. It seemed both inconceivable to him that they didn't see the crime here and as inconceivable that they wouldn't do what he wanted. He blamed their resistance— defiance!—on Barr.

By late November he had expanded his rant against the attorney general to aides: "Why won't Barr investigate the fraud . . . and the *machines?* Where is Barr? . . . Why doesn't he ever do anything? . . . When are we going to see something? . . . Was Jeff Sessions even this slow?"

Given Barr's past kowtowing, the president's disdain and rage were perhaps understandable. "If I had won," the president said, perhaps, aides hoped, inching closer to acknowledging that he hadn't won— "Barr would have licked the floor if I asked him to. What a phony!" (Hardly an unwarranted insight into his attorney general.)

Trump was lashing out even more directly to the White House Counsel's Office—whose lawyers he certainly considered to be his personal lawyers—instructing them to call Barr and find out *what the fuck* he was doing. What about the machines? Impound the machines! Investigate the machines! Go after the people behind the machines! And he began to suggest that it was the attorney general—"*my* attorney general"—who was the impediment to his election challenge.

Then Barr gave his December 1 interview to the Associated Press.

"To date, we have not seen fraud on a scale that could have effected a different outcome in the election."

And Barr twisted the knife over the machines.

"There's been one assertion that would be systemic fraud and that would be the claim that machines were programmed essentially to skew the election results. And the DHS and DOJ have looked into that, and, so far, we haven't seen anything to substantiate that."

Trump was livid. There was no warning that the interview was even coming. It was, in Trump's eyes, not just insubordination, but insurrection. And in a sense Trump was right: the Barr statement, a radical reversal from his long Trump tolerance, was hardly anything less than a declaration that the president (and Rudy and the others in the clown car) were pushing fictional tales and nonsensical hysterics.

Trump demanded Barr's head. "This is bullshit. No fraud? Has he just been sitting over there doing absolutely fucking nothing for a month? We have to get rid of Barr. There's no coming back from this. Who can we put in there?" Trump asked. Meadows, Cipollone, Herschmann, Kushner—all got the rant.

For days and days this remained an obsessional fixation. He talked about it continuously, blamed everyone for somehow not preventing it, and transformed, in the telling, the otherwise dutiful Barr into one of the most disloyal members of his administration. Months later he would still be talking about this betrayal.

Trying to avoid a public firing—or, worse, resignation—the White House aides enlisted Giuliani and Ellis to provide the official pushback. But Barr's end was written, and in a race to beat Trump's determination to fire and humiliate him in his last month in office, Barr's resignation would come two weeks later.

* * *

But who was running the country?

Even in more normal times this question would not have had a straightforward answer. As a manager, Trump's own interests superseded almost everything else. Therefore, he was often pursuing a series of personal concerns, vendettas, fancies, most often figments of the moment, while the executive branch itself carried on its business. The job of aides was to snatch or negotiate time with him, or decisions from him, on pressing executive functions while he pursued his other concerns—and to do this during his 11 a.m. to 6 p.m. schedule in the office.

But now he had given up on any interest or pretense in executive matters. The election challenge, this very issue of his survival, had made everything else meaningless. All daily briefings were canceled, including national security briefings. All efforts to return his attention to pandemic issues, vaccine rollout, or critical intelligence failed. And there was, quite categorically, no possibility of engaging him in, or even discussing with him, transition matters. What's more, he had cut off all communication with the Senate leadership.

At this point, it was Meadows effectively assuming all executive functions—or at least those that could be carried on in secret and not generate a headline that might alert the president that some business continued as usual. Virtually on his own, Meadows commenced the formal transition to the Biden administration. This included intelligence briefings, which Trump had stalled, Department of Defense transition meetings, which the president had rejected, opening a daily channel to key Biden aides, and integrating the Biden team into the White House's daily COVID planning and strategy meetings.

A hobbled government was able to work under the nose of a wholly preoccupied president, but with almost everyone in the government looking into the void of what might happen in the event of a crisis. Never before, it seemed to many, had a sitting president so abdicated his proscribed and daily duties and so turned from the most critical issues of the moment.

Instead, he dwelled exclusively—shutting all else out—on the "Steal," his hard 6 p.m. Oval Office quit schedule now often running late into the night with time for almost anybody who would feed his "Steal" obsession.

* * *

As much as Trump was busy raging at and casting out anyone who doubted that this was the most massive and systematic election fraud in U.S. history, he was eager to embrace anyone who was on board with it. If you weren't with him, you were against him. But if you were with him, then all was forgiven.

Few people in the Trump pantheon had so thoroughly estranged themselves from the president as Steve Bannon, the 2016 campaign CEO and top advisor in the early months of the administration. Bannon had crossed Trump's family, leaked voluminously about West Wing struggles, and in very public and not-so-private venues, conducted a riotously entertaining monologue about Trump and his family's stupidity, avarice, incompetence, and corruption. A not small amount of the details of the four-year-negative narrative about Trump were supplied to the news media by Bannon.

But Bannon, for his own semi-ironic and nakedly opportunist reasons, had been trying to find his way back into Trumpworld. During the impeachment, now almost a year ago, Bannon, along with Jason Miller and Raheem Kassam, a Bannon acolyte and British right-winger, had launched a podcast to defend the president. In Bannon's telling, the president's fate had then actually hung precariously in the balance, with the podcast becoming a rallying place for Trump support.

Then, this spring, Bannon and Corey Lewandowski, an early 2016 campaign advisor who had remained a Trump loyalist and courtier, had joined forces when the 2020 campaign was overwhelmed by COVID and BLM protests to lobby for the ouster of not only Brad Parscale but also Jared Kushner, and for Lewandowski and Bannon to return to run the reelection effort. It is almost impossible to characterize the negligible level of chance that Trump would ever have ousted his son-in-law or, for that matter, countenanced Bannon's return in any capacity. (Better to lose than to have to give credit to Bannon for winning.)

That summer, Barr's Justice Department—with, according to some, the encouragement of the president's son-in-law—had indicted Bannon for skimming money from a not-for-profit company he had joined to raise money to actually build a border wall (not incidentally showing up Trump, whose own wall still lagged). For Kushner and various others in the West Wing, dedicated in their hatred of Bannon, this indictment was a kind of double insurance that the president, beyond even his ire toward Bannon, would not ever allow him back.

But Bannon, who had befriended Giuliani (whom he had previously and publicly described as drunken and senile), became in the hours after the election a fervent believer in the stolen vote and in the wilder versions of how it had happened. Bannon's podcast, focused on an audience of one, but with a large actual audience, too, became a platform for almost every one of the outliers who had gathered around the election challenge.

The president, who had not spoken to his former chief strategist since shortly after Bannon left the White House in August 2017, was now back on the phone with him, taking strategic advice.

There was perhaps some logic here, at least from Bannon's point of view. Bannon was one of the original authors of Trump populism. While personally ridiculing the world of conspiracies, he nevertheless prided himself on being able to propagate the kind of narrative that, by its very labyrinthine qualities, draws in an engaged and credulous audience. Elections, with their thousands of unknown hands, far-flung control, opaque counting, and with the close margins in swing states, were an obvious new gold standard of conspiracy—one that Trump, more than anyone, now believed in.

But the pure nature of Bannon's opportunism was also an important window, one that Trump insiders stood at, aghast. Bannon's self-interest had been an overriding theme since his first involvement with Trump. Trump, as an outlier largely without any insider support, was a vehicle for other outliers. Bannon, hungry and ambitious, had largely failed to go beyond the periphery of any of the worlds he had tried to enter (finance, entertainment, media, and politics). Trump, no matter his flaws—and Bannon was among the most clear-eyed, and certainly the most vocal about them—was, and Bannon repeated this as his constant rationalization, a "vehicle." He was a television star who was himself so opportunistic that he was willing to do anything to be an even bigger star. The difficulty here was that Trump was ... Trump. And the degree to which you tried to use him, for good or bad purposes or for anything other than Trump's own purposes, was the degree to which he resented you.

But the election challenge was a clean slate. All the outsiders who now joined up immediately became the new Trump insiders.

Giuliani, ever blocked by the insiders, had a route back; Ellis, never taken seriously by the insiders, had her sudden chance to be on television all the time. And Bannon, most naked in his desires, needed a pardon. All that was required was that you indulged Trump in his fantasy. Bannon could certainly rationalize that there was a limited downside: the effort would come to a natural end; democracy would not collapse; Trump would not get a second term; and yet all the game players would be left with some elevated standing in right-wing media circles. And, in addition, Bannon might well receive a pardon.

Opportunistic enablers aren't of course new in politics. But the ease with which the most desperate and shameless could come over the Trump walls was notable.

And the other fact, which Bannon perhaps more clearly appreciated than anyone else, was that for all this, no matter how loopy and farfetched and disturbed, there was a large and reliable audience. This was show business or politics, or the two now indistinguishably joined.

6

WHERE NOW?

Who was doing what? Who was speaking to whom? What was the primary area of focus? Who was prioritizing the areas of focus? What were the next steps in terms of each initiative? And who was responsible for coordinating the follow-up? What was the precise threshold of what needed to be accomplished, and what were the reasonable measures of success? What's our endgame? And where do we get a win?

These were the questions, all without answers, exchanged by the dwindling group that saw itself as the steadiest of the president's advisors: Mark Meadows, Justin Clark, campaign lawyer Alex Cannon, Jason Miller, Dan Scavino, and Eric Herschmann. To ask the questions was to understand that there was no structure to direct or support any aspect of the election challenge. To ask the questions was to draw a line between the professionals with some management sense and discipline and the whirling mass of end-runs and Trump's own defiance, dictates, and free association that had now replaced them.

The list of those who had checked out now included Kushner,

focused, as though in a parallel universe, on his Middle East nego-
tiations and, in the obvious view of all, his valedictory reputation;
Ivanka, focused on relocating her family to Florida; Hope Hicks,
unseen since mid-November; Bill Stepien, all but formally out of
the office; Derek Lyons, staff secretary (a central palace guard),
gone; Alyssa Farah, communications director, out of the White
House and quite openly interviewing for television jobs; Kayleigh
McEnany, the press secretary, home in Florida and appearing almost
nightly on the Sean Hannity show; Stephanie Grisham, the First
Lady's chief of staff and former White House comms director,
nowhere to be seen.

Morgan and Clark, in part to protect their own legal reputations
and in part because this was a fool's errand, had stepped away from
any role in the ongoing cases, except for one. Morgan had been left
in charge of the purse strings. Even in the midst of the biggest legal
fight of his life, certainly an uphill one, Trump maintained his most
consistent view: lawyers were always ripping him off. As Giuliani
encouraged a legal free-for-all and tried to recruit law firms to support his own team's lack of legal depth and talent, and as local law
firms saw a potential payday, Morgan was left, often countering
Giuliani's promises, to uphold the Trump principle of paying lawyers as little as possible, if at all.

* * *

The organizational aspect of the national effort to overturn the election was, in the kindest description, decentralized—that is, whoever
seized it in disputed counties and precincts, invariably lawyers looking for fees or television time, owned it.

Pennsylvania lawyer Marc Scaringi, an eager local conservative
talk radio host and columnist in Harrisburg, practicing family, criminal, estate, and probate law (but very much *not* election law), had
jumped the gun and declared Trump defeated after the election.

But he'd then reversed himself and joined the Pennsylvania lawsuit in its final hours, becoming the poster lawyer for local defenders, a made-for-*Saturday Night Live* figure willing to say or do anything without fear of humiliation.

In one sense, perhaps, you could argue that this was an indication of the president's strength and influence. He could say things, tweet something, and a movement would happen—or, at least, ad hoc forces would take up the mantle. But the downside here was that most of the measures were taken to please the president or to garner press for whoever was staking the new claim and were disconnected from the need to accomplish anything. It was a world of local self-promoters.

Several state attorneys general pitched a new approach. The concept went that if one state's "fraud" or bad election practices changed the outcome of the presidential race, this harmed other states, who could then sue the offending state. But this needed a goodly number of attorneys general of friendly states to get on board what was (by any estimation) a long-reach if not ridiculous legal theory. The theory, or variation of the theory, went through a series of drafts. The initial efforts getting little buy-in—indeed, several of the attorneys general thought they might be "sanctionable," that is, so ludicrous or far afield that the courts might punish the lawyers who brought the suits.

Ken Paxton, the Texas attorney general, beset by a slew of legal problems of his own (an indictment for securities fraud before taking office and accusations of bribery while in office) and therefore eager to curry favor with Trump, agreed to be the lead plaintiff. Texas would sue Pennsylvania for unfairly helping to defeat Donald Trump. The Texas suit, as soon as it was filed, was joined by seventeen other Republican AGs, almost all of them dubious about the merits, but all of them wary of a stinging tweet in their direction from the president, and conscious of the points it would win them (with at least five of them getting a personal pitch, with signature flattery and threat, from Trump himself).

"Once it was filed it was impossible not to join," noted one of the AGs, explaining to his staff why he had signed on. "We'd invite a tsunami of problems if we didn't."

Such "support," along with Giuliani's certainty that this would absolutely succeed, served to convince the president that he had a winning hand, that in fact the Texas lawsuit, quite on the outer edges of harebrained, was another ace-in-the-hole case before their ace-in-the-hole Supreme Court.

This was now the pattern: pay no attention to lost lawsuits and just file new ones. Indeed, part of the grand circular point here was that the president's confidence was maintained by local lawyers and politicians eager to curry his favor by jumping into the election fight without regard for the ultimate outcome of these battles. They all might have been far from convinced that there could be any positive outcome, but they were nevertheless ever willing to please Trump— and possibly to get on television in the process—which, in turn, fortified his certainty and confidence.

* * *

What was in Trump's mind? And who knew what was in Trump's mind?

There were people in the Trump circle who had achieved respect and standing because they had come to have fine antennae for how the president might react; they got his animal instincts. But there was no one, literally no one, who would have claimed they had any substantial insight into what Trump was thinking and feeling.

The president's reactions and his behavior were so at odds with what was recognizable or what could be accounted for—his issues with factual accuracy were as confounding to people around him as they were appalling to the liberal press—that it became logically necessary to accord him a kind of Martian status. He was simply not like anyone else. In insider political circles, almost all politicians are seen as difficult and even damaged people, necessarily tolerated in some civics class inversion because they were elected. So, Trump was compared to the most outsized of them, but he still came out stranger and more difficult and more damaged. (There was much speculation about his mother, whom he almost never mentioned, unlike his father, who was his recurring example of cutthroat accomplishment.) Or he was compared to billionaires, men who, well beyond what a politician could do, absolutely and capriciously controlled their own environments and how the world was allowed to interact with them. There was a running commentary about who might be more difficult, Trump or Sheldon Adelson, the casino billionaire and leading Trump contributor who, even in Republican circles, had achieved a fabled monster status.

The question that was asked since the beginning of the administration but that became even more urgent as Trump's single-minded and senseless election challenge progressed was: Why would anyone tolerate this? The answer was simply that, in 2016, he *had* been elected, no matter how loopy and unexpected that was, and this was the nature of politics: you bowed to the winner. (In fact, already some of that tolerance was seeping out because of the stark reality that he had not been *re*elected.) But the other answer was that, in politics, there was a whole professional class whose essential skill sets involved dealing with maximally difficult and damaged bosses. You took it and put up with it and tried to make the best of it, not in spite of everything, but because this is what you did; this was the job you had. And the more you could tolerate or accept or rationalize, the better you were at it and the higher you would rise in the universe, the brutalized universe, of power.

Still: What was he thinking? Here they were, a month in, with every single indicator having gone against them: More than fifty separate lawsuits had collapsed by early December. Anything that the election challenge needed in order to proceed had failed. The countdown to final disposition was in days—by December 8, each state would certify its election results, and on December 14, electors would meet in each state capital. They were, in terms of reason and logic and practicality, at the end of the internet. *So*: What was he really thinking? He must understand. Yes?

There was hardly any indication that he did. Trumpworld had two levels, those within the sound of his voice, a level he wholly dominated, and events and people beyond it, a level he was often not very interested in, cognizant of, or realistic about. In the first level, he had, incontrovertibly, won the election by a landslide and it had been taken from him by both blatant and unseen hands: thieves in the night and the liberal establishment. And he, by his own act of will, would get it back by demanding that it be given back! His voice defined the day and the mission.

Okay, but, possibly, he had a finer sense of the larger play, beyond what others could see. That had always been part of the surmise of a higher explanation, that he was playing three-dimensional chess. But this suggestion sat awkwardly, to say the least, with his constant binary logic: he liked something, or he didn't like something; someone liked him or didn't like him; it was good for him, or it was bad for him; he knew what he knew and had no idea or interest in what he didn't know. But perhaps the answer was beyond logic. His emotional intelligence was all about performance. He was a circus barker, the ultimate promoter personality, mass rather than class, with a genius sense of how to satisfy the audience. He was an actor playing Donald Trump the character, doing what he thought that character would do, what would most appeal to the character's audience—what would get ratings.

You could dismiss everything else about him, but you still had to respect that.

Here was a fact: his campaign had raised more than $200 million since its defeat. Us against them? Fighting spirit in the face of overwhelming odds against you? Or total reality inversion, the

Pied Piper leading the deadhead Trump children into the alternative universe?

Something was working, if beyond all sense and logic.

* * *

On December 3, Trump convened a meeting in the Oval Office to
talk about the money. What would the richest defeated campaign
in the history of political failure do with all its money? What could
it do? And where was the money? Where would it go if—perish
the thought—the defeated president was forced to leave the White
House?

It was a meeting of the campaign's money guys—at least those
who were left. Trump, in a happy surprise, seemed suddenly nearly
realistic, or at least moving off his dug-in position. It was an uphill
battle. Impossible to say what might happen. Everyone had seen
what Rudy was saying, right? *Right?* But they might not make it.
But if they didn't, they would be back "in four years and beat this
sleepy bastard."

Could he count on everybody to stick with him? To continue the
fight, now and in the future? It was heartening for some in the room
to hear this: a clear-eyed recognition of political realities. But one
of the participants noted that Trump hardly knew Sean Dollman,
the campaign's CFO, or Alex Cannon, campaign counsel, and wondered if this new seeming reasonableness was tailored for them.
But, possibly, there was a corner being turned, a sense of accomplishment about having raised all this money, and now a more realistic way of looking forward four years hence.

Still, there was that sinking sense of worlds not aligned, of Trump
in this place of his own, blind beyond the people in front of him and
deaf beyond the sound of his own voice.

"Great job. Really impressive. Boy, we need someone like you on
this. Any chance you could come in and work full time?" the president enthusiastically asked Dollman.

"But, I do," said a bewildered Dollman.

"Do what? What do you do?"

"Well . . . I'm the CFO of the campaign, sir."

"Really? How long have you been in that job?"

"Since the beginning of the campaign."

"Wow," said Trump, seeming to acknowledge the depth of his oversight. "And what did you do before that?"

"I was the CFO of the 2016 campaign."

* * *

Giuliani came down with COVID on December 6. Boris Epshteyn, the shuttle (or, some thought, double agent) between Rudy's people and the remaining West Wing and campaign leadership, who had gotten COVID days before, was blamed—probably by Rudy's people, but not inconceivably by the other side. (Two weeks before, the former mayor, who had apparently failed to catch the virus from his own son, had bragged of his indomitability.)

As much as all other factors emptying the White House, there was the fear of COVID and its persistent domino effect, as relentless in the White House as it was in many prisons and nursing homes. You could walk the West Wing halls for minutes on end without seeing another living person, other than Secret Service and the president.

Everyone sheepishly held to the president's preference that the virus be mostly unacknowledged, masks eschewed and superspreader events overlooked, but there was, nevertheless, even without a formal tracking program in the White House, a reflex to blame each infection on someone, as the president had continued, at the least opportunity, to blame his own case of it on Chris Christie.

Now, in fact, the president was worried that the press was going to leave the impression that Giuliani had gotten the virus from him. "They blame me for everybody getting it," he pronounced, looking for sympathy.

Then Jenna Ellis got it two days later (the West Wing joke being that she got it from a Giuliani fart).

Being out of the president's sight was never a good thing, not least of all because other people started to talk in your stead, often about you, and to call attention to your bad press or, in fact, to any press you were getting that might be at the president's expense. And now the press kept pointing out, and people kept pointing this press out to him, that, as Trump interpreted it, Jenna had never argued so much as a parking ticket.

By the time Ellis returned from her recovery, she was a much-reduced presence in the White House. "She was giving me the yips," said the president, meaning a combination of she was standing too close to him and she was too obviously profiting off his favor.

* * *

The Senate election in Georgia was left, much more realistically than Trump's own, hanging out there.

Georgia had become another particularly unsettled and gnawing issue in the president's mind. The fact that a historically deep-red state had gotten this close to breaking from the southern bloc and from him was another sign that pernicious and unseen forces were at work. Meadows, whose Freedom Caucus was made up largely of House members from the southern states and whose own future was tied to a certain southern hegemony, had taken over the Georgia fight, pushing Rudy, a far-from-southern conservative, out.

This was another part of the Rudy tension. While Trump needed him, other conservatives distrusted him. He might be all in for Trump, but he was yet a pro-choice, big-city, much-divorced northerner (as was Trump himself, in the not-so-far past).

Then, too, Meadows understood that it was of far more value helping to save a single Senate seat in Georgia, and therefore the Republican majority in the Senate, than spending all your capital trying to upend the results of the presidential election there, an obviously futile enterprise.

Trump wasn't making much effort to pretend his focus in Georgia was on the party's fate. The ongoing Senate races were distracting attention from him, from his vastly larger issue. Also, he was getting blamed for the fact that the GOP was still fighting those races, with the Senate majority hanging in the balance. He was sour about this, believing that he had saved the Senate, he alone, basically. Every poll had put the Senate down, but his coattails had carried them. It was further proof that the election had been stolen from him, that the Senate, which so many had written off, had been saved, nearly. Now he was expected to help save the Georgia Senate seats for the Republicans when the Republicans weren't doing shit to save Georgia for him.

Especially Georgia's governor, Brian Kemp, whom Trump had supported. (He had also, against his better judgment, supported Kemp's choice of Kelly Loeffler, at the time a tepid Trump supporter, to replace her Republican predecessor in the Senate, Johnny Isakson, who had resigned for health reasons.) Kemp was actually going so far as to say the Georgia election had been a fair one when, obviously, it had been so *unfair*!

On December 5, the presidential party took the small plane (not the big Air Force One) and flew to Valdosta, Georgia, for Trump's first rally after the election—indeed, the first time he had done an event in what might be his post-defeat status (*if* defeat happened, but it couldn't happen, because he had won, a constant qualifying and amending that had entered his permanent speech patterns), an event theoretically not at all about him. Indeed, it was one of the few events he had ever done in which, quite likely, he would get no personal benefit.

He was doing this only because incumbent Georgia senator David Perdue had been such an abject and loyal supporter. And because he'd be blamed if he didn't. But he wouldn't have done it for Loeffler—never liked her. And Kemp! No way.

Meadows was trying to manage the president's volatile mood. Whatever the president's agenda was (mostly to keep insisting he had won Georgia and to insult Kemp), Meadows was trying to shepherd his own.

Two important elements, pushed here by Meadows but certainly supported by everyone else, had been written into the president's speech: a clear endorsement of the Republican candidates, Loeffler and Perdue, to motivate rather than, as he had surely been doing with his fraud rants, demotivate Georgia Republicans to get out to the polls; and an acknowledgment, however oblique, that he might have lost, even if only in the subjunctive: *if* he had lost. Getting Trump to follow this part of the script would, in the West Wing and larger Republican circles, be perceived as great progress—that is, if everything else that might be ad-libbed in whatever direction his riffs went did not hopelessly overwhelm these two points.

You could not know where he would go.

Louie Gohmert, the Texas congressman who, even among Republicans, was a head-shaking figure of Tea Party and Trumpian thickness and folly, was on board, passing out chocolate-covered pecans—called Millionaire$—sliding more down the table as soon as anybody stopped chewing. ("Do you have an interest in this company?" one of the passengers asked. "Nope, just like 'em," said Gohmert.) So was Ronna McDaniel, the RNC chair who had cemented her position by delivering the party apparatus to Trump; and Doug Collins, who had given up his House seat to run in the Senate primary in Georgia, but failed to qualify for a runoff spot, who Trump had made his point person for the Georgia recount. Jason Miller, Kayleigh McEnany, Dan Scavino, and Brian Jack, the thirty-three-year-old White House political director (the guy the president called for

details and factoids about presidential campaigns—Trump's Goo-
gle) who was from Georgia, were also around the conference table.

It was a tricky dynamic, focusing on the Senate mission while
not in any way suggesting that the true and larger mission was not
the defense and, indeed, the reelection of Donald Trump—bowing
to the ostensible mission while at the same time having everyone
know you were really on board for the true mission.

Notably, the president kept visiting the group around the conference table. Usually not a social mixer when the presidential party
traveled, making at best a single perfunctory visit, he seemed now
to be searching for some affirmation, not so much mixing, though,
or conversing as repeating the now-familiar lines.

"I can't believe they stole this thing. Can you believe they stole
it? Georgia completely stolen. Completely. But Kemp is done, I tell
you, Kemp, he's one of the only two races I'm one hundred percent
getting involved in. He's finished. Lisa"—referring to Alaska's Lisa
Murkowski—"is the other one. I gave her the drilling, but she's always
been nasty to me. The other is Kemp. He's finished. Doug"—he said
to Collins, standing above the others sitting around the conference
table—"you would have been a better candidate than Loeffler. So
much better. So, what would you rather be, a senator or governor? I
could see you being a good governor. A great governor."

"Sir," said Collins, uncomfortably, "I just want to make sure we
get Loeffler and Perdue back in the Senate."

"But what do you think about being governor?"

"Umm . . . well, I don't—"

"You think about how that sounds, 'Governor Collins.'"

"You realize," said Miller, laughing, when the president left, "he's
going to say that during the rally? You might want to come up with
what your response is going to be, because he's saying it."

Which he did, in his two-hour speech, staking his claim on
Georgia's political future and his unhappiness over other political
concerns. Still, though he delivered his lines about Loeffler and

Perdue and referenced a world in which it was possible—not that it had happened, but with the Dems' having rigged it, that this might be the result—that he had in fact lost the election.

But there was always the discrepancy between his scripted words and his true words—the logic, or illogic, which powerfully, even rapturously gripped him and which he could not shake and to which, putting political sense aside, he needed to bear witness. Indeed, he laid out in Georgia quite a real-time sense of what he and, practically speaking, he alone had come to believe, a veritable catechism of the information he had selected and absorbed to argue his case. The manic and idiotic nature of his view is perhaps the strongest argument against his cynicism—he was in the weeds of fixation and delusion.

We won a lot of places. We won Florida. We won Ohio. Big, big. We won them big. Remember, we were going to lose Florida, they said. We were five down in Florida. We won by a lot. We were way down in Ohio, and we won by a lot. I think they say that if you win Florida and if you win Ohio in history, you've never lost an election. This has got to be a first time. But the truth is they were right, we've never lost that election. We're winning this election. And I will say, we're fighting very hard for this state. When you look at all of the corruption and all of the problems having to do with this election, all I can do is campaign and then I wait for the numbers. But when the numbers come out of ceilings and come out of leather bags, you start to say, "What's going on?" . . .

If we have courage and wisdom, I think, you know what the answer's going to be because you can't let people get away with what they got away with. Think of it, with over seventy-four million votes, over, think of that, more than . . . I got more votes than any sitting president in history. Eleven million more votes than we got in 2016. And we thought that if we could get sixty-eight million, sixty-seven million, that would be the end. All of our great, brilliant geniuses said you'd win if you get sixty-seven or sixty-eight. It's over. We got seventy-four million–plus and they're trying to convince us that we lost. We didn't lose. They found a lot of ballots, to be nice about it. And they got rid of some, too. The seventy-four, let me tell you, the seventy-four could have been even higher . . .

In fact, President Trump is the only one of five incumbents since 1912 to receive more than ninety percent of the primary vote. And again, anybody received over seventy-five percent, they won. We got ninety-four percent. President Trump set a record for the most primary votes ever received by an incumbent, ever. And nobody that's received all of the primary votes, nobody's received at a much lesser level than what we—they always won. But we didn't, according to what they say. It's rigged. It's a fixed deal. Nationally, initial numbers show that twenty-six percent of President Trump's voting share came from nonwhite voters. The highest percentage for a GOP presidential candidate since 1960. That's a long time ago. President Trump won . . . Think of this one. President Trump won eighteen of nineteen bellwether counties. You know what a bellwether county is? It's a big deal. So, I won eighteen of nineteen, a record, never happened. That between 1980 and 2016 [these bellwether counties] voted for the eventual president in every single election, and before that, it was almost every election. And we won a record eighteen of nineteen. Never lost. Nobody's ever lost with anything like that . . .

President Trump won. President Trump won as we said both in Florida and then Ohio. And by the way, won by a lot. Remember the fake polls where they said he's down by four in Florida, and I won by a lot. He's down by two in Ohio, and we won. I think we got eight or nine or something, up. But nobody's ever done that. Those two very powerful, big, important states. And the beauty is that we also won Georgia, and that was good. We won South Carolina, and we won Iowa. Remember, we're not going to win in Iowa, they said. We're not going to win. I think the farmers like Trump a lot, right? Well, we

won in Iowa by a lot. We won in Iowa by close to record numbers. I
think I have the record. And we won all over the place.

And many of these swing states, it's a very interesting statistic.
President Obama beat Biden all over the country, except in some
of the swing states, where Biden beat him badly. How does that
work? And they say it's statistically impossible. He beat Crooked
Hillary. Think of this. He beat Crooked Hillary in the swing states,
but she beat him everywhere else. Let me tell you, this election was
rigged ...

At virtually every point where Trump stopped to take a breath,
the crowd responded, heartily and furiously, with shouts of "Stop the
steal"—it, too, committed to an ecstatic view of Trump's reelection
and its righteousness and overpowering emotion.

* * *

On December 8, Jason Miller learned from a contact on Capitol Hill
that a briefing booklet had been sent to Republican congressional
offices under his name, titled "Five States and the Illegal Votes:
Why the November 3, 2020, General Election Was Not Won by
Biden." Miller discovered that the booklet had been written by Cleta
Mitchell, a longtime fixture in conservative Beltway legal circles.
Meadows had brought Mitchell into the election challenge, but she
seemed to be doing this work under the radar of her partners at Foley
and Lardner, a major international law firm.

The booklet outlined a series of specific claims, including 66,247
underage voters in Georgia and 305,701 people who had applied for
absentee ballots prior to the eligibility period; in Michigan, 500,000
mail-in votes were counted without "meaningful" Republican observation; in Pennsylvania, it was 680,000 mail-in votes that had been
counted without Republican observation; in Arizona, more than
700,000 mail-in votes were counted without Republican oversight.

The charges were drawn from the salad of numbers and allegations floating in from the Giuliani team, from many of the various lawsuits that had been rejected, and from rump local initiatives and complaints. In other words, there was no central source, no true vetting, and no clear provenance for any of these numbers.

Mitchell told Miller that she thought the campaign should be more out front in terms of informing people, and that the booklet should go out to every name on the nationwide Trump list, arming them with the facts. Equally though, it also seemed that she did not necessarily want *her* name on the "facts."

Miller said he needed to have the campaign research team review it before they blasted it out—and there it died.

* * *

On Friday evening, December 11, three days after the individual states certified their electoral votes and three days before electors were to meet in their respective state capitals to cast their votes, the Supreme Court perfunctorily dismissed the Texas-initiated lawsuit. Filed on Monday, the seventh, the suit the president had taken to calling "the big one," which he seemed to see as a kind of rising-up of red states—quite a Fort Sumter moment—was dead by the end of the week.

The idea that one state or a group of states could object to how another state conducted its elections did not even merit an argument before the court.

The president, who some had thought, perhaps wishfully might have been moving toward acceptance, reverted to high and bitter dudgeon. This was betrayal by the three justices he had personally appointed: Neil Gorsuch, Brett Kavanaugh, and Amy Coney Barrett. He reserved particular bile for Kavanaugh, whom, he now noted, he had not wanted to appoint in the first place. "There were so many others I could have appointed, and everyone wanted me to. Where would he be without me? I saved his life. He wouldn't even be in a law firm. Who would have had him? Nobody. Totally disgraced. Only I saved him." It was another persistent theme: he resented that he had been forced to appoint strangers rather than people he knew he could have depended on; he was annoyed at Giuliani for repeatedly assuring him that their allies on the Court would carry the day, and he was now annoyed at all the people who had prevented him from appointing Giuliani to the Court.

Again, it was a stark split screen.

The Supreme Court's decision was a cringing embarrassment—or, reasonably, ought to have been for any lawyer involved in it, the attorneys general of the various states, and, presumably, the 126 members of Congress—many with law degrees—who had signed on in support of it. The plaintiffs had no standing in bringing it, said the Court, as almost everyone who had weighed in on the issue had said it would say. The two conservative members who said they might have allowed it to go forward, Justices Alito and Thomas, said that, even so, they would ultimately have ruled against Trump and Texas. The media and the Democrats could not have been more vicious in their mockery of the legal stupidity here, with the conservative Court concurring.

It was simply not possible that so many people with a basic legal understanding would have held this position—except if they weren't actually holding it. They seemed to take two leaps of logic. In the first, it was obviously ridiculous—ridiculous to anyone with any empirical reasoning capabilities, ridiculous to the various state AGs who had dragged their feet in support of it, ridiculous even to a deeply conservative Court. But, in the second step, it was necessary and productive to support Trump's asinine and hopeless suit because Trump had mustered so much support among so many voters with no interest in or capacity for empirical reasoning, or, at least, who were preoccupied with other issues.

Here was another central fact of the moment: a lot of lawyers who knew that their stuff was full of shit were telling the president it anyway, because he expected them to. This was deeply disturbing for many of the remaining White House staffers still trying to hold on to basic political and bureaucratic craft—that is, what passed for basic Washington reality (i.e., you didn't want to be laughed out of the Supreme Court). This was a group most closely identified with Kushner. Indeed, what sustained them here was, in part, that Kushner, communicating this by his absences, understood the folly.

Again, everyone understood. And everyone understood that everyone else understood.

Even those who had adopted support for Trump's unreality as the existential condition of modern Republican politics understood that the Trump legal case was not viable or even intelligible and, for that matter, that nothing would keep Trump president beyond January 20.

In a sense, this was good news of an equivocal sort: everybody in a position of power and authority, no matter how signed up to Trump reality they seemed to be, grasped the true reality.

At any rate, the Texas attorney general's bid to the Court to extend the December 14 certification of electoral votes in the four crucial states pending further investigation was denied, which meant that this goalpost, like all the previous goalposts, wasn't budging.

* * *

Giuliani, from his quarantine, ever attentive to the president's moods and to the necessity of feeding Trump what he wanted to hear, sent in the conservative California constitutional lawyer John Eastman, who, to Trump's pleasure, had written an article claiming that Kamala Harris wasn't a natural born citizen and therefore couldn't be vice president. Eastman had turned opinions on a variety of hot-button conservative legal issues into many television appearances. It was Eastman's theories about vice-presidential discretion that Giuliani had been floating and that had made their way to Marc Short.

On January 6, the vice president would preside over the counting of the electoral votes in the Senate Chamber. This was, heretofore and by all, widely regarded as a ceremonial duty with no real function or discretion on the part of the vice president. Eastman, sitting in a chair directly facing the president behind his desk, now argued, to the discomfiture of Pat Cipollone, sitting in on the meeting, that in fact the vice president had wide powers. Eastman told the president that the vice president could reject any of these votes and simply replace Biden electors with Trump electors. Or, he could send the Biden electors back to their respective state legislatures for further consideration and scrutiny, where they then might be replaced. Either scenario could give Trump his Electoral College victory and the presidency.

Hence, the only issue was convincing the vice president to exercise this power.

The increasingly fitful and surly president was suddenly full of exclamations and murmurs of pleasure and oohs and ahs. Indeed, Trump had a notable lack of a poker face, his glee as evident and as uncontrollable as his scowl.

"So, all Mike has to do is object?"

"All he has to do."

"He doesn't have to—"

"All up to his discretion."

"Totally up to him to send these votes back?" His elation was filling the room.

"Totally."

The president was meeting with an academic who was offering, at best, an academic theory. But here was one of the most promising meetings the president had recently had. He was as spun up as he had been in several weeks. If things had been looking bad, now they were coming up roses. Here was all he had ever needed: a lawyer who could solve the problem.

"But do you really think this could happen?" Cipollone asked Eastman as they left the Oval Office.

"Theoretically, maybe," said Eastman, "but not likely."

"You just told the president of United States this is a doable thing," said a confounded Cipollone.

"Well, worth a shot," said Eastman, shrugging—and departing, having dismissed his own theory, which would become the predicate for the events of January 6.

7

THE ENDGAME

Yes ... there was zero doubt about how this was going to turn out: Joe Biden was going to be the president. It was not a political contest or a courtroom drama whose outcome hung in the balance. Some people tried to find parallels with Watergate and Nixon's effort to hold on to power as support drained. But then there were opportunities for doubt and reversal. Here, beyond the fantastic and apocalyptic, there were none. Not in anyone's mind except Trump's and those of the people almost everyone else considered hopelessly sycophantic or unglued who had gathered around him, some hardly capable of walking a straight line.

Oh, and apparently in the hearts and minds of untold millions of Americans.

Here was a mirror-reality mash-up that Trump effortlessly attached to the narrative, a fight against the swamp, corrupt Dems, media elites, woke corporations, all trying to undermine him and get him out of office—hence, election fraud. Why did a large majority of Republicans believe, against the reasonable evidence, that there had been widespread fraud? Because he had said there was. As succinctly as the pollster Tony Fabrizio had put it when he urged Trump to support masks—"Mr. President, your voters believe whatever you tell them to believe"—they now believed in a massive election conspiracy. And, what's more, Trump was telling people to switch from Fox News to Newsmax and OAN, giving each network a great new audience and a reward for its slavish adherence to this new Trump narrative.

For this reason—the awe and devotion of the Trump base and the equity you could purchase in it with your own acts of awe and devotion to him—a portion of Republicans in Congress (again, understanding that there was no danger that anything they did would have any practical effect at all) rushed to stand by the illusory election challenge.

At the same time—because this was the end, and the king was practically dead, and precisely because of the vexing awe and devotion so many party regulars had for him—other Republicans were taking this opportunity to try to put a stake in his heart. For a month, Mitch McConnell had been nearly monosyllabic about the election challenge, withholding congratulations from his old colleague Joe Biden, with whom he'd had a long and even fond relationship, but offering no more support to Trump than not publicly rejecting his election challenge, itself a clear message. McConnell had spent a happy 2020 Election Night watching Senate seats he had every right to expect to lose hold (and with Perdue in Georgia a whisker from 50 percent, it looked like the Senate would hold). His only annoyance with the evening was to have Trump do better than expected—although, aside from a worrisome hour or so during the evening, McConnell had little doubt that Trump was going to lose.

Asked by a variety of friends (each of whom knew the answer) which he would prefer, a Trump victory and a Senate majority or a Trump loss taking the Senate with him, McConnell confirmed, quite as though the question did not have to be asked, the latter. McConnell had already absolved himself of the loss, sending out

Kevin McLaughlin, his handpicked head of the National Republican Senatorial Committee, days before the election to blame the Trump stain for the loss—another issue of bitter enmity for the president, who believed that the election had clearly shown that he had saved or nearly saved the Senate for McConnell, quite arguably true.

McConnell might fairly seem to be a pure Machiavellian player singularly focused on his own power and on his Senate majority, a backroom tactician of the kind that doesn't much exist in a theatrical age. But the animosity between the two men, Trump and McConnell, was total—and for McConnell, an emotional reveal for a cold man. The Republican leader's view of Trump was as virulent as the most virulent liberal's view: Trump was ignorant, corrupt, incompetent, unstable. Worse, he called into question the value and seriousness of every aspect of McConnell's Machiavellian achievement—what good was power if you had to share it with people who had no respect for it? Every day for the past four years, McConnell had struggled not to bend—at least not privately to bend, as so many others had—to the headbanger in the White House. The price of private virtue was to endure the humiliations of having to, begrudgingly, publicly bend (further complicated by the awkward fact that his wife, Elaine Chao, was Trump's secretary of transportation—an earlier Trump effort to buy off McConnell). McConnell had a coat of impervious armor like a Marvel comic character; little ever got through. But it was impossible to overstate the hatred he had for Trump, a central, if unseen, drama of the Trump years. It was of an ultimate kind in politics—it was, that is, personal—and not just a hatred of Trump but of his allies and staffers, too. Politics is tribal, and those in the Trump camp understood that if a propitious opportunity presented itself, McConnell would deal with them as he would like to deal with the president.

And yet, on McConnell's part, it was in the weeks after the election still a standard, if increasingly strained, Republican leadership Trump response: placate, humor him, and assume he would lose focus and that the crisis would wane with his attention span. It was a waiting game for the courts to rule against the president, who would then move on to some other outrage to distract from that. McConnell had really not figured that even Trump would be capable of ignoring the reality that every single court that the election challenge had come before had ruled against him. He would—he must—fold, however huffily, at some point, McConnell assumed.

On December 15, after the formal certification of electors by their respective state legislatures, McConnell, in a move about which no one could doubt the meaning, reached out to Biden. "Our system of government has processes to determine who will be sworn in on Jan. 20. The Electoral College has spoken. So today, I want to congratulate President-elect Joe Biden."

Of all the thresholds Biden had so far crossed in the election challenge—and, for that matter, the thresholds Trump had failed to get over—this was perhaps the most significant. Trump's challenge, McConnell was saying, would get no help from the Senate. Even its tolerance, bare tolerance, for his acting out was over.

The election challenge, if anyone had any doubt, had failed.

That day, Trump and McConnell had a conversation, with McConnell absorbing Trump's abuse—for the last time. Indeed, they would not speak after that, or, McConnell aides assumed, *ever* again. The conversation was as much a break from the language of politics, even at its most bitter, as there might be. It was a road-rage confrontation, escalating in seconds from zero to sixty, with Trump heaping obscenities on the Republican leader and assailing his honesty, competence, patriotism, and manhood. In the days after, McConnell seemed to regard the conversation with something between horror and awe. And fear, too. He had so often danced around it, but here it was: one of the three branches of government was run by someone unmoored from his constitutional and public responsibilities; the president was deranged, no longer in control of himself, if he ever was, no longer with the capacity to accept reality, if he ever could.

The past four years had been, for McConnell, a game of running the clock out, of letting Trump destroy himself without first letting the ever-increasing devotion and awe the party regulars had for him destroy McConnell or the party. And now, finally, the clock had all but run out. McConnell was letting it be known—seldom the tip of the spear, he allowed Senate allies like John Thune and Roy Blunt largely to speak for him—that he wanted nothing less than a straight-up ratification of the Electoral College tally on January 6.

On the call with the Republican caucus after the certification of the electors cementing Biden's victory, McConnell reinforced his clear position: The Senate would not aide Trump's specious challenge or his ludicrous theatrics. It was all over, but for the final ceremony (one that McConnell would particularly enjoy).

There was no pushback from anyone on the call.

* * *

But, curiously, the very fact that the Trump gambit was not going to succeed, that the election challenge had failed to advance and that all the checks against it had become only more formidable—and now, with the second-most-important person in the Republican Party and the most powerful Republican on the Hill standing against it—only made it easier to support.

So much of Trump politics was a public bow and a private guffaw. You could, apparently, fool most of the people most of the time.

It was always a safe place to be: to wave the flag for a symbolic stance that might seem popular but for which, because it would never happen—beyond the tweets, so much in Trumpworld never actually happened—you would never be held to account.

It was for the show of it.

Again: the singular point was that everyone knew that nothing was going to alter the election results. The *New York Times* and MSNBC and the liberal echo chamber would predictably get its collective panties in a twist, generating gratifying right-wing push-back for Republicans standing up for the president. But the Electoral College count would take place on January 6, and Joe Biden would be certified as the next president. And on January 20, he would be sworn in as the president of the United States. Everyone knew this—everyone but the president. A political party, or a large faction of it, was indulging its leader's fantasy. The paramount leader was unaware that he stood naked in the crowd before everybody.

* * *

Mo Brooks, a sixty-six-year-old congressman from Alabama, was a figure of high standing in a somewhat dubious club called the Dead-Enders, a rump Republican Party faction legacy from the introduction of Tea Party members to Congress in 2011. "Dead-Enders" was once a name applied as a negative, but like that other once-negative name, "deplorables," it had become something of a term of affection. Along with Brooks, other members included Louie Gohmert, from Texas; Andy Biggs, from Arizona; Matt Gaetz, from Florida; Paul Gosar, the dentist from Arizona; and Jim Jordan, the former wrestling coach from Ohio. Their résumés were unimpressive; their general intelligence raising many eyebrows; their social skills limited. Still, in the purity of their own self-caricatures, they achieved quite an outsize portion of media notice. They would, given the opportunity, push ever further for that attention. Effectively, that's what they were doing in Congress: they were character actors playing the role of right-wing ghouls, martyrs, heroes, disruptors. But since Trump's election, they had promoted themselves from mere character actors to leading roles.

On December 16, Brooks announced his effort to overturn the election by challenging the certification of electoral votes in various key states. This had been done before, as protest or stunt, notably by several Democrats when Trump's own count was certified in 2016, and, in 2004, by former California senator Barbara Boxer, indeed over allegations of rigged voting machines. The procedural hurdle, to take the next step beyond merely standing up and saying your piece, was that a challenge from a House member had to be joined by one from a Senate member—precisely the step McConnell and his posse were trying to warn members away from.

It is a further curious note that the symbolic nature of this, its entire lack of practical or even procedural significance, seems to have been understood by the president's own legal team. Or, as another telling note, this was how disorganized and ineffectual the legal team was: Nobody reached out to Brooks. Nobody from the White House was actually in touch with him. Nobody was coordinating with anybody. Nobody from the White House was managing what in a real world would need to be one of the greatest congressional confrontations of modern times.

Except the president, sort of. In a conversation with Tommy Tuberville, Trump proposed that Tuberville speak up on his behalf. Tuberville, a former college football coach, had, with Trump's support, entered the Alabama Republican Senate primary in 2020 against Jeff Sessions, the former Alabama senator (and the first senator in 2016 to endorse Trump) who joined the administration as attorney general only to become, for various perceived offenses against Trump, a public enemy. Beating Sessions in a race most characterized by Trump's continued abuse of Sessions, Tuberville then ran in the general election against the Democrat Doug Jones, who had slipped into office in this overwhelming Republican state because his Republican opponent, Roy Moore, was found to have cruised for underage girls in various Alabama malls. At any rate, Trump, never reticent on this account, had in many ways handed Tuberville the Senate seat—one that Tuberville would not formally take until next month (and he was, therefore, not yet under McConnell's watch)—and now suggested what Tuberville could do for him in return.

Still, because he was not actually yet a senator, Tuberville, who now at the president's behest offered himself up as possible objection to certification in the Senate, seemed like an outlier taking an eccentric and even loopy position.

* * *

One of the odder figures in the Trump White House—and this was saying a lot—was the president's trade advisor, Peter Navarro. He was distinguished by his abject desire to curry favor with the president, permanently stationing himself in the outer Oval Office, and by being so disagreeable, abrasive, and contrary that he was unable to get along with anyone other than the president.

Navarro was one of the few remaining holdover figures from the Steve Bannon era in the White House and was still thought of by some as a Bannon sock puppet, Navarro's voice a baroque mix of deep-state, anti-China, return-to-manufacturing-nirvana gobbledygook.

In the sweepstakes of who lived in the world farthest removed from reality, Navarro's planet was often singled out. If he could have initiated a war with China, he would have—but failing that, he lived in a constant state of agitation and paranoia that he was being spied on by all those less hostile to China than he was.

But none of this yet explained why Navarro, the trade expert, became the White House's go-to expert on election fraud. Similarly, he had once taken it upon himself to research and identify "Anonymous," the administration figure who had written contemptuously and covertly about the White House in the *New York Times*—which he got wrong.

On December 17, Navarro issued—in what he described as his capacity as a private citizen, but what White House aides observed was researched and written on White House time—the first of his reports on the stolen election, *Volume One: The Immaculate Deception*. (This would be followed by *Volume Two: The Art of the Steal* and *Volume Three: Yes, President Trump Won*.) The reports made the case against "the authoritarian—nay fascist—behavior of a small group of social media oligarchs," the larger Democratic Party, and all other elements of the Republican Party skeptical of the claims of election fraud. Even the *Washington Examiner*, the conservative DC paper almost invariably friendly to the president, could only take mocking and derisive notice of Navarro's claims and numbers.

The "Navarro Report" promptly became the standard Trump and Giuliani bible in their version of the 2020 election.

* * *

The ongoing struggle from the Oval Office to reverse the election results was on a parallel track with the struggle of much of the rest of the West Wing against those same people empowered by the president to attack the election.

On December 18, a meeting was held in the Oval Office that was not all that dissimilar from the constant chaotic and disorganized meetings in the Oval, but in counterpropaganda fashion, it would become memorialized in the election-challenge saga.

What happened in the Oval Office that day (or on any other day) was not so much an indication of a strategy or even part of the process of formulating a plan, but instead, consisted of the random comings and goings of random people. Protocols, priorities, chain of command—all were largely absent. There was no functioning calendar, no real process for vetting people. Seldom, if ever, was there a strict agenda. At any given time, people in the West Wing with visitor passes might easily wander into the Oval Office, which itself would almost invariably be populated by an ever-revolving group of West Wing kibitzers, gossipers, backstabbers, and those eager or willing to hang on the president's every word. It was not unusual to find the youngest West Wing staffers in with the president, listening to his catalogue of complaints and resentments and media critiques.

Perhaps above all else, the operative principle of the Trump government was that the president could not be alone—the more crowded the Oval Office, the less alone he felt. This might not have allowed more people to have an influence on Donald Trump—he was not so much listening to people as having them listen to him— but it certainly allowed more people to *think* they had an influence.

Eric Herschmann had known Trump and the Trump family from his work with Trump's law firm in New York. Then, as a no-salary retainer, he had signed on to help with the first impeachment trial. In this, he was on the Kushner side, part of the self-appointed adults in the room. That is, he shared the belief that beyond the outward fire and fury, Trump was in fact quite a cipher. Hence, you wanted to be there to guide him away from the people who might otherwise encourage his fire and fury.

On the eighteenth, a collection of the irregulars showed up in the Oval after hours, including Sidney Powell, former national security advisor Michael Flynn, and former Overstock.com CEO Patrick Byrne. It was quite a group: Powell, a lawyer so mired in fantastic conspiracy theories that almost everyone in the White House, including the president, questioned her mental competence; Flynn, a QAnon favorite, himself spiraling ever deeper into conspiracy (he would argue that COVID was a liberal plot), who had pled guilty to lying about his contact with the Russians and had then, subsequently, been pardoned by the president; and Byrne, an anti–deep state conspiracist who had been romantically involved with Maria Butina, whom federal prosecutors had accused of being a Russian spy trying to seduce powerful men.

The regulars, who would leak copious details of the scene to Axios reporter Jonathan Swan, one of the leading Trumpworld leak transcribers, would portray this as a showdown:

The crazies would be beaten back by responsible White House lawyers. According to the Axios report, Powell "proposed declaring a national security emergency, granting her and her cabal top-secret security clearances and using the U.S. government to seize Dominion's voting machines."

Herschmann, according to Axios, faced her down:

"Hold on a minute, Sidney," Herschmann interrupted from the back of the Oval. "You're part of the Rudy team, right? Is your theory that the Democrats got together and changed the rules, or is it that there was foreign interference in our election?"

"It's foreign interference," Powell insisted, then added: "Rudy hasn't understood what this case is about until just now."

In disbelief, Herschmann yelled out to an aide in the outer Oval Office. "Get Pat down here immediately!" Several minutes later, White House counsel Pat Cipollone walked into the Oval. He looked at Byrne and said, "Who are you?"

Flynn went berserk. The former three-star general, whom Trump had fired as his first national security advisor after he was caught lying to the FBI (and later pardoned), stood up and turned from the Resolute Desk to face Herschmann.

"You're quitting! You're a quitter! You're not fighting!" he exploded at the senior advisor. Flynn then turned to the president and implored: "Sir, we need fighters."

Herschmann ignored Flynn at first and continued to probe Powell's pitch with questions about the underlying evidence. "All you do is promise, but never deliver," he said to her sharply.

But perhaps the most telling line in the Axios story was the following:

Trump was behind the desk, watching the show. He briefly left the meeting to wander into his private dining room.

Trump, according to the story, would shortly return to engage in the discussion when the issue became the typos filed in one of Powell's briefs, traversing in the blink of an eye from martial law to misspellings.

The point here, in the telling of the insiders, was in part to absolve Trump of direct responsibility: he's a passive party to the crazies. This account made him a kind of Chance the Gardener figure, from the Jerzy Kosinski novel and Peter Sellers film *Being There*. But it missed the larger truth: that Trump was the orchestrator of the chaos. He thrived in the middle of it. Indeed, there existed the possibility that overturning the election was not even his main goal. Rather, the joy and energy of the resulting chaos was.

Fight, fight, who was ready to fight? More fight was what was needed, was the president's message, more attitude than plan. Cipollone, as always, and here this evening, was called out by the president as the man with the least amount of fight.

"You can't count on Pat," said the president with a shrug.

As the meeting got hotter, Trump added more people to it. He got Meadows by phone, and then Giuliani (clearly in a restaurant somewhere, amid the din of conversation and clinking ice), and then, failing to find Clark, he had the White House track down Morgan. Each of the new participants was patched through to a voluble Oval Office full of people. It was hard to figure out who, in the cross-talk. The president seemed to be the instigator in chief, a kind of Jerry Springer, polling people in the room to express themselves and egging them on to take pot shots at one another. At the center of this was a genuine discussion about having the military seize voting machines, with the president entertaining this in some blank-canvas, we-can-do-anything-can't-we? sense. The president seemed entertained, continuing to poll the room and the people on the phone.

"Do we know that we can do this? I think we can. Don't you?" he pressed.

Meadows kept trying to change the subject.

Herschmann, trying to be lawyerly, kept pointing out the discrepancies between what Powell was saying and Giuliani's position.

An excited Giuliani wanted to know if he should run over from the Georgetown restaurant where he was having drinks and dinner.

"The more bizarre shit becomes, the more Trump likes it," one

West Wing aide analyzed. It was only everyone else who, panicked, seemed to believe they were on the verge of either declaring martial law or holding back the forces of the political apocalypse. Trump himself seemed happy in the moment.

It was impossible to know who was ahead in this argument, or even if, in any sense, the argument was real.

When Giuliani got there, Powell was yelling at the group that she had five affidavits, waving them in the air, which would conclusively prove her claims that the Dominion voting machines were a tool of a wide conspiracy. Giuliani grabbed the affidavits from her and quickly surmised that all five were from the same source. Code-named "Spyder," Powell was billing her source as a "military intelligence expert," but, in reality, he was an IT consultant in Dallas named Joshua Merritt who had failed to complete his entry-level training course in military intelligence, and that was fifteen years ago.

"This is gibberish, nonsense," said Giuliani, prompting someone else in the room to note how far out there you had to be to lose Rudy.

By the end of the meeting, some in the room were convinced that Trump was going to give Powell a White House position, as special counsel overseeing an election investigation, or even thinking they would wake up to find that she had replaced Cipollone.

In fact, the next day was as chaotic as the night before; there was no new direction. Both Meadows and Giuliani had rushed into the Oval; perhaps their intervention had kept Powell, as outré and preposterous a figure as had ever been in the Oval Office, from becoming the most significant legal figure in the Trump administration. Or, as likely, this was all a passing diversion for the president. A fancy in the moment.

Herschmann, intent on protecting not only the president but himself, essentially posited that the crazies might well have been able to push the president "to invoke emergency national security powers, seize voting machines, and disable the primary levers of American democracy" if they had not been opposed by White

House lawyers. But this elides the point that the nature of the Trump chaos is that, beyond his immediate desires and pronounce- ments, there was no ability—or structure, or chain of command, or procedures, or expertise, or actual person to call—to make anything happen. How exactly would the Department of Defense be sub- orned to seize someone's property, and where would that property be taken? And what would be done with it?

The crazies in and out of the Oval Office, with everyone else who was in and out of the Oval Office, were far closer to court jesters than generals in charge. As much to the point: there were no gen- erals in charge.

* * *

Shortly before Christmas, it was finally impressed upon Trump— Meadows's voice was prominent here—that the Senate races in Georgia were in deep jeopardy, and that he would be blamed for the loss. Certainly, he had seemed to do everything possible to inhibit the chances of a Georgia Senate victory.

If he needed a Senate majority to push forward on his election challenge on January 6, he could lose it after January 1.

Trump believed he had an easy fix: he denounced the stimulus agreement his own treasury secretary, Steve Mnuchin—and his own administration—had negotiated with equally resistant Republicans and Democrats through the autumn. That agreement gave individuals gifts of six hundred dollars. In an overnight inspiration undercut- ting Republicans and his treasury secretary, and delighting Dem- ocrats, Trump, focusing on the Georgia races, now wanted to raise the amount to two thousand dollars.

Cash in the pocket, in the best political tradition (cash with his name on it), could well make the difference in a tight race.

"I simply want to get our great people $2000, rather than the measly $600 that is now in the bill," Trump tweeted.

Not incidentally, the two thousand dollars was also aimed directly at McConnell, who would either have to bow to Trump and accept the new number, exactly what he had been negotiating against, or reject it and be blamed by Trump for losing the Georgia races. Mnuchin, collateral damage, was now open in the contempt for Trump he had long struggled to keep private. (Trump aides, keeping track, would move Mnuchin into the uppermost ranks of Trump haters among current and former Trump officials, a large club.)

McConnell marked this as a final indication that it had become a White House of one—no voice meant anything but Trump's. McConnell conveyed his rejection of the two-thousand-dollar scheme through one of his aides to one of Trump's—using the same language Rupert Murdoch had used on Election Night when Fox had called the Arizona race against the president: "Fuck him."

* * *

On December 23, Trump left for Mar-a-Lago with the vice president, a man he had never given all that much thought to, keenly on his mind.

Most people credited the stable relationship between president and vice president to Pence's artful loyalty. But Trump, too—while not so privately marveling at Pence's ass-licking qualities and with an oft-spoken distaste for Pence's wife, Karen, who he accurately suspected did not like him—nevertheless seemed to appreciate that a conflagration with Pence of the type he had had with so many in his administration might just be a kind of third rail for evangelicals and for the bedrock conservatives in Congress. The vice president and the president each did his part in avoiding the obvious contradiction between heartland religious conservatism and Trumpism, and between a follow-the-rules vice president and a break-everything president. In a sense, this was the paradigm relationship of the political era, neither wanting to fully test who might represent the stronger force—and in this, the two forces converged.

The vice president was a disciplined man, and this had surely helped him in observing the key attribute needed as Trump's vice president: to separate your knowable actions and opinions from what you were otherwise thinking. Most others in the Trump White House, outside the small group of family and devoted soldiers who saw Trump as their necessary North Star, could sooner or later no longer keep those two things separate, and fell from favor. But the vice president had fashioned a public face that was both inscrutable and benighted, and seemingly as unwavering as the Queen's Guard. The fly that had landed on Pence's white head during the 2020 vice-presidential debate without effecting the slightest response from him summed up both his stoicism and his imperturbability.

Even Trump seemed to find Pence too good to be true, wondering how he could be such a "stiff" and a "square." And likewise, as though a corollary, he regarded Pence as someone not tough, as someone who, he increasingly pointed out, could be "rolled."

It was perhaps the greatest thesis-and-antithesis duo in the White House since cool and ironic John F. Kennedy and coarse and self-pitying Lyndon Johnson. Pence was contained, orderly, controlled, and reticent, rigid in his religious beliefs and doctrinaire in his pro-life, pro-business, limited-government conservatism. Trump was the opposite of all those things.

In a looking-glass world, Pence was the standard-bearer of an ever-more-conservative Republican Party—and pay no attention to Donald Trump. That was how the VP conducted himself: if only you complied with all the outward manifestations of loyalty and acquiescence to the president, you could otherwise pretend that he did not exist. Republican life could go on in its dedicated fashion, with only a ritual bow to the Trump distraction. Indeed, the vice president's was the reliably functioning, professionally organized office in the West Wing. If you actually wanted something done in the Trump White House (and it wasn't a pet project of Jared and Ivanka's), a good bet was to call the vice president's people.

This seemed to hold Pence in place, this sense that he was the real thing while an illusion occupied the White House. Likewise, Trump was largely restrained, his annoyances and grievances held at bay, because Pence seemed so satisfied with his own marginal standing.

Yes, but . . . even when Trump was largely satisfied, he was still storing up real and imagined wrongs and offenses that he might put into play at any time.

Eager to downplay the COVID crisis and to push off responsibility for it, during the first spike in the spring, Trump had given the vice president leadership of the pandemic portfolio. With some obvious political sense, Pence had tried to mount a good-government show of concern. But Pence's news conferences, with the attendant experts—Dr. Fauci, a sudden hero of science and reason; and Dr. Birx, apparently unwilling to surrender her reputation wholly to the White House—then became a challenge to Trump, both for the attention they received and for the way their facts undermined Trump's frequent don't-worry messages. Indeed, many in the White House came to blame Pence for elevating Fauci and Birx, in fact, making them famous, to the president's clear detriment.

It was one of Trump's off-book advisors, the secretive Ike Perlmutter, a Palm Beach neighbor, Mar-a-Lago member, and show business billionaire (Perlmutter bought a bankrupt Marvel Comics and sold it to Disney for $4 billion) with whom the president spoke frequently, who advised him to push Pence and the other experts from the stage and get back out there himself. Trump was missing out on ratings gold.

In Trump's broad with-him-or-against-him silos, a perceptual free association that it was hard for anyone to escape, Pence had fallen into what advisors were calling COVID-land, a hostile place.

Trump's annoyance with Pence now spread into the election challenge.

Pence had been faithful in his support of the legal effort but meticulous in his language. His chief of staff, Marc Short, had crafted a fine line between pursuing all legal options, as would be the president's right, and a broadside charge against the integrity of the election process. Trump yet took seemingly hairsplitting note, and also was reminded by Giuliani and others that, after the December 14 gathering of electors in state capitals, Pence seemed to excise the world *fraud* from his comments on the election. What's more, Trump believed, Pence was hardly doing all he could do to push his friend Doug Ducey, Arizona's governor, with leverage that might help the Trump effort in the swing state to support the election challenge. ("That's Mike's friend, Ducey, he's no good to us with the steal," the president complained.)

Marc Short was regarded as one of the most competent operators in the White House. A K Street conduit with close connections to the billionaire Koch brothers' conservative philanthropies and lobbying efforts and a long career within the Republican congressional establishment, the fifty-year-old was a Trump archetype. He detested the president but saw a tight-lipped tolerance, however painful, as the way to use Trump's popularity to realize the conservative grail of remaking the federal courts and the federal bureaucracy. People often bypassed the president's chief of staff, whoever that was at different times, to go directly to Short. Short and the VP's wife, Karen, were the political brain trust that far outshone any strategic structure that the president or his aides were ever able to put in place.

While Pence had adapted to his designated role as unwavering Trump loyalist, his wife and chief of staff, tactically supporting this loyalist position, were significantly less circumspect in their views of the president. Karen Pence, it was clear, was disdainful of Trump, his family, and his aides, revolted even. Trumpworld for her was Sodom and Gomorrah meets *The Wolf of Wall Street*.

On Trump's part, he regarded Pence as malleable and his wife as a quite annoying counterweight to bending the vice president to what he wanted him to do. He considered Short a Koch brothers pawn, often seeming to forget or feigning to forget Short's name and calling him the "Koch guy."

As early as anyone in the Trump White House, quite within hours of the election, Short understood that Trump had lost and that he had no chance of advancing any of his claims of victory, and began to carefully plot the vice president's final days.

Pence's virtually unimaginable feat of maintaining a convivial relationship with the president without being directly part of his cockeyed, petulant, or, indeed, impeachable actions was now about to face its most difficult balancing act. Short was as alarmed as anyone in the West Wing by the day-by-day spectacle and increasingly aware that they might reach a countdown to January 6, at which point the tactically elusive vice president would not be able to avoid the spotlight.

The president, as it became apparent that the vice president would be his only remaining recourse, was starting to bring specific pressure, both in public, in a series of tweets and statements, and in his constant running commentary noting Pence's lack of backbone and his dependence on his wife and on Short, questioning the loyalty of one of history's most abjectly loyal vice presidents.

Short, for his part—as, by mid-December, it became increasingly clear that Trump was, if only in his own mind, turning January 6 into a make-or-break day—started to organize a process. That is, a more or less formal-seeming procedure, with various scholars, other experts, and (always) more lawyers consulted in order to justify a decision that had already been made.

The experts here curiously included Jenna Ellis, who—and here the president would see her trying to bet on two horses—in her self-appointed role as constitutional scholar, now advised the vice president that he would not have the power to contravene the electoral vote count, helping to sour her relationship with Giuliani and the president.

At the same time, both to avoid doubt on anyone's part and to make it clear, not least for reasons of personal and professional pride, that the VP was in no way part of the president's ongoing fantasy,

Short was privately telling both party leaders and West Wing aides that there was "zero debate" in the Vice President's Office about his role in presiding over the electoral vote count.

Short seemed to take not only a horrified view of the White House crazies, but a moral one: theirs was a world of cynical operators and outright lies. His job was to help the vice president navigate through the sinners and gangsters that tested them. To survive them and not to become them.

The vice president himself, whose natural countenance was to see and hear as little evil as possible, met Jason Miller one afternoon in the West Wing and asked his advice.

"Well," Miller suggested mordantly, "if I were you, I'm not sure I'd want to get between a bullet and a target." Pence would be better off getting out of the White House and pitching in for the Senate races in Georgia.

* * *

Louie Gohmert, the Tea Party Texas congressman, was known for his what-me-worry lack of concern about anyone taking him seriously. And no one did. "Louie Gohmert stuff" is nearly a term of art for doing the kinds of things no one else would do to demonstrate conservative bona fides or fealty of the most shameless and ridiculous kind—such that if there were a genuine push on a conservative issue, you would not want Gohmert involved. He discredited almost anything he touched—put an outlandish hat on the discredited. He was, and Congress has certainly always had such types, a caricature of himself—happily, it seemed. Trump, a caricature of himself, of course seemed naturally to attract other caricatures of themselves, or to turn other, formally more rounded people (for instance, Lindsey Graham) into caricatures of themselves, too.

Gohmert became one of the Trump White House's most steadfast, tell-me-how-high-to-jump, just-say-where-to-dig-the-hole, go-to guys on the Hill.

At the end of December, Gohmert filed another in the series of Trump-supporting cockamamie lawsuits, this one, by wide general agreement, even more cockamamie than the ones before (except for the ones so cockamamie as not even to be fairly included in the operative cockamamie list). *Gohmert v. Pence* sought to have the court correct the vice president's reported view that he could not reject duly certified electors and to direct him, in fact, to reject those electors if he wanted to.

Obviously, this would not succeed; certainly, it would invite wide ridicule. Gohmert himself as the agent here seemed to guarantee this—"Try to imagine a universe in which the Court would say, 'Oh, Louie Gohmert, you're right,'" said a White House aide—and it would draw attention to the vastly stronger case that the vice president could not do this. Indeed, it would, rather, force the vice president to acknowledge that he absolutely could not and would not do this.

The Vice President's Office—acting with the approval of the White House Counsel's Office, although very much not with the president's approval or even knowledge—had the Justice Department oppose this lawsuit. This put the administration on the side of believing that the vice president had no unilateral powers to act in the electoral count.

It also vastly increased the president's rancor with the vice president (and, as always, with the White House Counsel's Office). He would need to redouble his efforts to browbeat and bend the vice president to his will.

* * *

Trump returned from Mar-a-Lago on December 31, missing his beloved Palm Beach New Year's Eve party.

On January 2, the president called Georgia secretary of state Brad Raffensperger. Various states seemed to carry various levels of immediacy and insult in Trump's mind. He had won Pennsylvania by 1,000,000 votes ... only to see the Democrats produce an extra 1,000,080 votes before his eyes (this was more Trump mantra: "If I wake up in the morning and they say I'm ahead by 100,000 votes, they find 100,001 votes more"). Obviously, he had been done wrong in Arizona, in Maricopa County. But Georgia, especially, whose governor he had come specifically to blame, preyed on him.

In part because of its singular importance to Trump and in part because Georgia was included in his own southern base, Meadows had made Georgia, as he had made North Carolina on Election Night, his pet project. This was also because he distrusted Giuliani. Meadows made Cleta Mitchell the lawyer on point. "I don't want Rudy doing anything with Georgia. He'll just screw it up. Cleta is in charge. Rudy doesn't do anything there" was the Meadows instruction.

Meadows, out of a sense of duty toward the president but with his feet still in the real world, had wound himself up into such contortions and rationalizations and redefinitions and subcategorizations of the issues involved with the election challenge that his incoherence might have allowed the president to think they were making the same argument. Perhaps Meadows thought so too.

Still, it is almost impossible to imagine what Meadows, the reasonably astute politician and now-experienced Trump handler, and Mitchell, the seven-figure partner in a blue-chip law firm, thought they could get out of calling the Georgia secretary of state for help in the election challenge. How could they not have seen certain trouble in the prospect of the president of the United States lobbying a state official to interfere in an election? But indeed, they idly listened as Trump seemed to try to coax, with his heavy-pressure, wheedling voice, Raffensperger to find new votes for him.

I think it's pretty clear that we won. We won very substantially in Georgia. You even see it by rally size, frankly. We'd be getting 25–30,000 people a rally, and the competition would get less than 100 people. And it never made sense ...

We think that if you check the signatures—a real check of the signatures going back in Fulton County—you'll find at least a couple of hundred thousand of forged signatures of people who have been forged. And we are quite sure that's going to happen . . .

You don't need much of a number because the number that in theory I lost by, the margin would be 11,779. But you also have a substantial numbers of people, thousands and thousands, who went to the voting place on November 3, were told they couldn't vote, were told they couldn't vote because a ballot had been put on their name. And you know that's very, very, very, very sad . . .

So there were many infractions, and the bottom line is, many, many times the 11,779 margin that they said we lost by—we had vast, I mean the state is in turmoil over this . . .

And I know you would like to get to the bottom of it, although I saw you on television today, and you said that you found nothing wrong. I mean, you know, and I didn't lose the state, Brad. People have been saying that it was the highest vote ever . . .

So look. All I want to do is this. I just want to find 11,780 votes, which is one more than we have because we won the state.

The call went on for an hour with Trump talking, uninterrupted, for long parts of it, reciting random numbers, anecdotal evidence, leaps of logic—with, one might imagine, everybody listening at some level of alarm and incomprehension. Meadows interrupted him at several points to try to restate what he might mean. Raffensperger interrupted to flatly correct Trump's numbers—largely destroying his argument. But mostly it was all Trump, not a discussion, but a diatribe. And a loopy one. Venting, with the larger point being that he believed he had won regardless of what the vote by all other reasonable measures seemed to be. That is, it is crazy stuff. Out there. Disconnected. With everybody understanding this and taking some pity.

Part of the reason Trump aides often misunderstood their own danger was that they went along to protect the president from

himself—in Trumpworld parlance, the people with him were keeping it from being so much worse than it otherwise might be. The
other reason is that, when around it all the time, you came to regard
Trump as so much hot air—he talked for the sake of talking, without meaningful effect. He is unaware of what he is saying. He has
no faculty for processing what he is saying. He's in the ozone. In
that sense, he is an innocent.

As though led purposefully to the slaughter, Trump didn't know
he was being recorded on Raffensperger's end, and his damaging
efforts to have the Georgia secretary of state subvert his state's election—or, in the White House view, Trump's effort at charm offensive and helpless bloviation (precisely the substance of what Trump
would insist was a "perfect call")—was leaked the next day.

Cleta Mitchell, sitting in on the call, would be forced to leave her
law firm, Foley and Lardner; as would Alex Kaufman, a partner at
the Philadelphia firm Fox Rothschild, who did not say anything on
the call and was identified only as "Alex" in the transcript.

* * *

Every effort in state and federal courts and in the legislatures of the
contested states, along with efforts to get the support of key state
officials, had abjectly failed. Every significant threshold of counting
and certification had passed, giving no advantage or hope to the challenge effort. Only days remained before the ultimate, formal certification, a rite that in itself was largely meaningless to the already
certain outcome. And yet Trump was steadfast, even optimistic.

And confident about his own powers.

He was buttressed by the media in this, which, operatically, had
bought into the uncharted possibilities of his powers, wiles, mach-
inations, and demagogic evilness—the media believed he might
well have the power and will to overturn the election. He followed
his own battles closely as they unfolded on television. Even as he
lost one, the narrative offered another. This was hardly just the

right-wing media, although Fox and the satellite right-wing out-lets were on the edge of their seats in anticipation. But the rest of the media were equally on the edge of their seats in horror and astonishment—even if, in a parallel voice, there was a stricter expla-nation of the really practical impossibility that anything could disrupt what was otherwise destined to happen.

* * *

The background to the January 6 certification remained the proce-dural hurdle of needing a senator to join a House member in chal-lenging a state's electors.

The nature of such a grand stand was a complicated one.

For one thing, most notably, it would have no effect whatsoever on the election. The Democratic-controlled House would defeat any challenge—meaning none could proceed—and, likely too, the McConnell-controlled Senate would also defeat any challenge. Also, no one, save for the president, had any doubt that the vice president would not participate in the certification challenge.

What's more, any senator participating in the challenge would alienate him or herself from the Republican leadership. McConnell and company had made it clear that this was a pretty personal score. Tommy Tuberville's indication that he might join one or more of the House challenges tended to reinforce the sense that this was an outlier place to be; he wasn't even seated yet.

But then, out of nowhere, Josh Hawley stood up. Certainly, nobody in the White House had seen this coming—once again, rather than an organized initiative, it was the freelancers taking con-trol and advantage of the situation.

The forty-one-year-old Hawley, in the Senate for only two years, was marked most of all by his ambition, which was quite a thing to be marked by in the U.S. Senate. His impatience was clear; he had already and repeatedly butted heads with McConnell, and he seemed proud to let people know that the U.S. Senate was not where he wanted to spend his career. A Stanford and Yale Law School grad, he had come to the Senate from Missouri after an aggressive stint as the Missouri attorney general, where he pursued the state's Democrat-turned-Republican governor, forcing him to resign.

Hawley had quickly moved to position himself as the purest and most outspoken and most electable Senate right-winger on the populist side. This was juxtaposed with the other purest and most outspoken and (at least in his own view) most electable Senate right-winger, Ted Cruz, another Ivy Leaguer, on the conservative establishment side. Both men were widely disliked in the Senate, and both were singularly focused on the 2024 presidential race—both Ivy Leaguers privately scornful of Trump and both necessarily trying to make common cause with his base.

Cruz had been debating doing exactly what Hawley now had done—jumping out and becoming the most prominent Trump defender and claiming 2024 MAGA rights. The problem was that Cruz hated Trump (Trump, in 2016, had not only stolen the right-wing mantle from Cruz but ridiculed his wife, and, Cruz believed, planted stories in the *National Enquirer* about Cruz's sex life) and was openly telling people how nuts the whole election challenge was.

He debated too long.

Joining the House members who planned to challenge certain state electors, Hawley forced Cruz's hand. Cruz, in a panic, rushed in with ten other senators, in what now seemed like a jailbreak, to join as many as 140 House members in what would be quite a spectacular piece of theater on January 6.

So, somehow, despite the known outcome, you nevertheless had a cliff-hanger, and for no one so much as the president.

8

THE DAY BEFORE

The short background for what was to happen in the Joint Session of Congress on January 6:

The presidential race in 1876, between Republican Rutherford B. Hayes of Ohio and Democrat Samuel J. Tilden of New York, ended with disputed slates in three states and a single disputed elector in a fourth. The difference between that race and 2020 was that the four states in the Hayes-Tilden imbroglio were intensely disputed by all factions, with the electors unable to be seated. In 2020, the president was, practically speaking, the only person truly disputing the races that might yet keep Joe Biden from becoming president. But Hayes-Tilden did set up the model for a significant challenge to electors and fluid consequences from such a challenge. Indeed, the Hayes-Tilden challenge highlighted the Rube Goldberg–like weaknesses of the Electoral College system in close races and the intractable mess they might produce. Hayes-Tilden resulted in an epic political horse trade (known as the Compromise of 1877), which gave the presidency to Hayes, the more obvious loser, and ultimately resulted in the Electoral Count Act of 1887, another convoluted reinterpretation of Electoral College procedures, one that now governed the 2020 election. More than suggesting any precise path relevant to 2020, Hayes-Tilden suggested that there could be value and opportunity in chaos, and that widespread charges of fraud could deliver chaos. To the extent that Trump and Giuliani had a plan—and two months in, it was far from clear that they did—creating disorder and confusion seemed the core of it.

* * *

January 5, a slogging, gray winter day, forty degrees, rain expected in Washington, DC, and somewhere between thirty-six hours and as much as, if everyone played for highest melodrama, forty-eight hours before Joseph Robinette Biden Jr. would be formally certified as what he was already acknowledged and accepted to be by every aspect of the U.S. government (save for the sitting president) and, for that matter, most people in the world: the next president of the United States.

For Donald John Trump, however, and his advisor Rudolph Giuliani, this was the moment in which Trump forces, galvanized since the election by the belief, on the president's say-so, that widespread fraud had occurred in the race for the American presidency, would derail the process and recover their victory.

The president had returned the night before from Dalton, Georgia, making a last and begrudging appeal in the Senate runoff election in another rambling speech otherwise focused on election grievances and an effort to put more public pressure on Pence.

The vice president had also been in Georgia stumping for the Senate candidates. On the way back, from their separate planes, they had arranged to get together in the White House that evening. Giuliani wanted to have the vice president sit down with John Eastman, the constitutional scholar he was most relying on to make the case for the vice president's wide powers. Marc Short would have liked to avoid this meeting. He was adamant that there was no discretion on the vice president's part; certain that, in the vice president's mind, there was no debate or ambiguity here; and confident that they had expressed this to the president in every possible way. But trying not to say no to the president, Short agreed they'd come in for a last discussion, with the stipulation that Giuliani, who Short was convinced was wholly without sense or reason, the lead clown in the clown car, not be there.

Short and the vice president arrived with their own attorney, Greg Jacob, a Federalist Society conservative-in-good-standing lawyer who viewed the president and his lawyer's position as insupportable and fallacious, if not ludicrous.

It was the vice president himself who led the pushback.

Eastman had two equivalencies that he now tried to argue:

Thomas Jefferson, in 1801, was both the president-elect and the sitting vice president in the certification of his own electors. Jefferson, presiding over the joint session, unilaterally accepted a Georgia elector who had been excluded on the basis of a clerical error. In other words, in Eastman's example, Jefferson had demonstrated that a vice president had discretion.

A frustrated, resolute, and, to a degree that he would never show, increasingly angry Mike Pence made the two obvious points: Jefferson's decision didn't change the result of the election, and the current rules under which presidential elections were governed weren't codified until the Twelfth Amendment was passed, three years later.

The next equivalency that Eastman offered came from 1961, when Richard Nixon presided over the certification of electors in the presidential election he had lost. Hawaii, a new state, had, in a close election and recount, produced two slates of electors, one for Kennedy and one for Nixon, which, although Kennedy was finally declared the winner in Hawaii, were both presented to Congress. Here, too, the disputed electors would not have made a difference in the election. Nixon, presiding over the session, asked for and received unanimous consent to seat the Kennedy electors—quite against his own interests.

Pence, here too, dismissed this example as woefully off point, both in its effect and procedures.

It was a curiously novel moment in the Trump presidency: the Vice President standing up for himself. Trump aides, marveling at the development, analyzed that, in Pence's mind, all of Trump's acting out and offending behavior over four years was on Trump himself—a cover that worked for many Republicans. But taking this action now in the Electoral College count would be on Pence, and he would go down ignominiously in history for it. He had finally, and belatedly, drawn his line in the sand.

By the time the meeting was over, the Pence team came away believing that Eastman had done the best he could to come up with relevant examples that might justify the vice president's discretion, but that even Eastman was far from convinced and that, in fact, he seemed mostly to concede all the vice president's points.

Once again, Pence and Short believed they could not have been clearer about their views and about the actions the vice president would take, and those he would not.

The president, however, was yet somehow much less clear, or was merely refusing to accept what was clear.

* * *

Trump was up early on January 5, tired from his trip to Georgia the day before, but focused now entirely on what would happen in Congress the next day. Making his calls, he was not so much seeking information as reconfirming his belief that things would happen in such a way, by whatever means, to support his cause—to which he was still counting on the vice president to bend.

Jason Miller was up early, too. He did Maria Bartiromo's show on Fox Business from campaign HQ, talking about what might happen the next day. Miller's take with Bartiromo was actually quite a step from the Giuliani-Eastman-Trump line. In effect, Miller described the coming objections to the electoral count as a procedural and symbolic exercise: the idea was to call attention to election fraud and Article II violations and not, by inference, actually overturn the election. Miller tried to coax this into something that sounded reasonable.

Again, as Miller and everybody was aware, nothing was going to happen, and nobody was seriously trying to make it happen. The very process of making something happen had collapsed—to the degree it had ever started.

The continuing effort to pressure state legislators, who were still, in the president's mind, poised to rise up, had ended with Giuliani's girlfriend, Maria Ryan, supplying the wrong cell phone number for Michigan House Speaker Lee Chatfield, which the president then tweeted out—resulting in thousands of calls and texts to an unsuspecting twenty-eight-year-old person named O. Rose, from Petoskey, Michigan, now living in California, who had nothing to do with state politics or Donald Trump and who identified as "they/them."

"Do we have clear t[alking]p[oint]s on the VP role tomorrow? Just a few topline would be helpful," one of the aides in the campaign communications office plaintively wrote Boris Epshteyn, the go-between to Rudy's people, less than a day before the most consequential showdown in modern democracy was to take place.

Epshteyn fudged, supplying talking points vague enough as to be almost meaningless:

- The VP has a significant constitutional role at the Joint Session under the Twelfth Amendment;
- The key is the interplay between the Twelfth Amendment and the Electoral Count Act;
- In the end, the Constitution controls the process of the selection of the next president.

After more coaxing, Epshteyn finally forwarded over a collection of Giuliani's largely unsourced numbers and a copy of the report prepared by Peter Navarro.

This comprised the effort to manage and lobby Congress.

* * *

As sure as the sun would rise, Congress would certify Joe Biden's Electoral College victory. So, for Trump and Giuliani, this was either an attention-grabbing last hurrah—both men would of course do almost anything for attention—or part of a kind of elaborate charade of saving face and creating a historic political martyrdom. Or—and this was the "Emperor's New Clothes" situation that most political professionals were steadfastly trying not to acknowledge—it was mental derangement of a kind and at an intensity never before known at the highest level of the U.S. government.

Almost everyone who remained around the president understood that he, along with Rudy, did in fact *actually* believe that there was yet a decent chance of upsetting the electoral count and having Trump declared the Electoral College winner or, failing that, prolonging the election and returning the fight to the disputed states. The president's aides (and family) understood, too, that he was the only one (granted, along with Rudy, which only made the situation more alarming) in any professional political sphere to believe this. Hence, although they did not call it such, and tried to see it as more nuanced, derangement.

This derangement was certainly encouraged by the various members of Congress and the Senate who were saying they would participate in the melodrama—for their own attention-getting or symbolic reasons. It was not, though, shared by them. No one in Congress, not even among the most spirited or yobbish of the Dead-Enders, actually believed there was any imaginable chance that certification would be delayed (at least for more than a few hours) and that Joseph

Robinette Biden Jr. would not be the president of the United States in fifteen days.

To the same degree that Republicans were rushing to line up with the president, many seemed to rush to assure colleagues that they, personally, thought it was all, well, nuts.

At the same time, this derangement was evidently shared by many of the groups and individuals converging on Washington for the next day's protest. Here was yet another inexplicable divide between the political class and the people who had elected them. It was also another demonstration of Trump's almost otherworldly connection to the latter, a connection at the heart of this very derangement. Trump and his people—"my people"—*believed*.

Still, the protests, along with the arrival throughout the day of the vast and devoted throng, however reaffirming to Trump, was only a sideshow to the main event in Congress, which was receiving all his attention.

There was hardly a waking hour in the past forty-eight during which he and Giuliani had not been on the phone in pent-up nervousness and excitement over the coming battle in Congress on January 6. They were two generals poring over a map of the battlefield.

At the same time, it was noted by all in the White House that the president and his lawyer had in fact no plan for what do if the sun did *not* rise. There was no script here. No agents in place. No network ready to go. No plan if dog caught car. Neither the president nor his lawyer had any more of a grip on what might happen, given a favorable outcome, than anyone else. Because it absolutely wasn't going to happen, no one was considering the contingencies if it did.

Still, Hayes-Tilden and the election of 1876 did suggest the possibilities for endless and, for Trump, hopeful complications. For several weeks, Trump had kept asking various lawyers and advisors for a brief on Hayes-Tilden. He did not, though, ever apparently manage to sit through a complete retelling of the complicated tale.

What was *likely* to happen today, when the electors were counted before Congress, as the Constitution provided—"the President of the Senate shall, in Presence of the Senate and House of Representatives, open all the [electoral] Certificates, and the Votes shall then be counted"—was that, as the vice president read the vote count for the individual states, there would be objections to the tallies in at least four and as many as seven states. These included Arizona, Georgia, Pennsylvania, Wisconsin, and possibly Michigan, Nevada, and New Mexico. The fact that no one actually knew how many was just another aspect of the disarray.

In 2016, there had been two objections from Democratic congresspeople to the certification of Trump electors. Those had failed, however, to attract the support of at least one senator to advance the objection to debate and a vote. But now, with a handful of senators, including Hawley and Cruz, on deck to support objecting House members, an objection could proceed. The first contested state would likely be Arizona. At that point, with the House-Senate objection jointly registered, each side of Congress would adjourn to its respective chamber to debate the issue for, by law, not more than two hours. A majority vote by each branch would be necessary to disqualify the electors—and in no imaginable scenario would that happen. (Although, if the Democrats had lost another five seats in the House, and hence their majority, and with the Republicans, with Georgia in abeyance, still holding a Senate majority, this could theoretically have turned out differently.) And yet, this process itself—counting, objecting, each chamber caucusing, then voting again, then returning for another objection and a repeat process— might extend the certification for hours, even into the next day. The possibility of more time, and a sense of the game's never ending, somehow added to the confidence of the president and his lawyer.

Both men, egged on by hypotheticals ever nearer to fantasy and after exhausting all other options, had come to take it as an article of faith that the vice president could simply reject Biden electors in favor of Trump electors and thereby hand the election to Trump; or, falling short of that, the vice president could determine that a state legislature ought to give further consideration to possible discrepancies in the state vote and send back the questioned electors to their respective states for a reconsideration of their certification. Were any of this *actually* to happen, it would certainly be contested in courts that had shown no interest in supporting the president's election challenges and in state legislatures that had also shown no appetite for this fight. But much more to the point, the vice president had again and again and *again* given every indication that he was having none of it and that there was no room for doubt or further discussion.

Marc Short believed that there was no way, this side of open insult and public break, to make their position clearer.

Truly, there were no variables.

Still, Trump and Giuliani continued to game how to play the vice president.

It was a hothouse conversation—the two true believers in a deep dive into what no one else believed. Meadows, one of the last remaining West Wing officials still at work, was staying clear of whatever the president and Giuliani were plotting. Kushner was, to his own great relief, in the Middle East, wrapping up what he saw as his historic mission, his peace deals—this last one with the Qataris—and was not scheduled to return until the following day. The president had all but banished the White House counsel, Pat Cipollone (who was grateful to be banished), and was speaking instead to Herschmann. Herschmann, believing he understood how to move the president, tended to offer objections that sounded awfully like the plaudits of a yes-man. Kayleigh McEnany had been strategically

missing in action for several weeks. The remaining campaign officials (Miller, Justin Clark, Alex Cannon) tended to be merely on
the receiving end of Trump's calls and opinions. And everybody else
was, effectively, cleared out.

White House wags noted that Treasury Secretary Steve Mnuchin
had fled as far as Sudan—where he was negotiating a good-behavior
economic pact with the former terrorism-sponsor nation—to get
distance from this last election gasp.

"There is no question, none at all, that the VP can do this. That's
a fact. The Constitution gives him the authority not to certify. It goes
back to the state legislatures," said Giuliani, as though on a loop.
He kept repeating this to the president and to the others who were
part of the continual conversation on his cell phone. ("Yes . . . yes . . .
yes . . . here's the thing . . . hold on a second . . . hey, let me get back
to you . . .")

The president, in his own loop, kept similarly repeating this back
to Giuliani.

And they both similarly repeated this to everyone else with such
insistent and repetitive determination that it overrode any opportunity to disagree with them or in any way even to engage in the
conversation. There it was: the vice president could, and Trump
and Giuliani believed likely would, defy all precedent, all available
advice, as well as his stated position, and upend his own career to
nullify the election. Truly.

About this, they continued to weigh the odds that the vice president would come along: sometimes fifty-fifty, sometimes as much as
sixty-forty, even somewhat more. At the grimmest, thirty-seventy.
But always a solid shot.

That this had no basis at all in sense or reality—no one in the
U.S. government (no one *anywhere* in the government) regarding
this as having any chance at all of happening, literally a zero-chance
shot—contributed to letting the two men persist in their delusion.
Why interfere with their delusion if it was a pointless one? Their

delusion would change nothing. And why interfere if neither the president nor his primary advisor was going to listen anyway?

Hence, Trump and Giuliani were left to plan for what the president would say to fortify the vice president in this historic overthrow when Pence was scheduled to arrive for their last meeting.

This all then prompted the question as to the extent and nature of the president's delusion: How far had he left reality? And to what extent had the government itself become a charade to support his delusion—not that the delusion, mind you, would ever become reality. But the checks and balances of government would not discourage it, either. The president would just simply float, disconnected, out there.

* * *

There was the world within shouting distance of the Oval Office—privy to the president's monologues, catalogue of resentments, agitation, desires, long-held notions, stray information, and sudden inspirations, with little practical relationship to the workings of government—and then there was the world beyond that. Early in Trump's presidency, aides noted that a second-floor office, where the likes of Stephen Miller and Kellyanne Conway worked, meant a degree of exclusion but also protection: Trump would never climb the stairs (and by the end of his term, he never had).

The Trump White House, cabinet offices, and agencies may not have been staffed by top policy makers or the most astute of bureaucrats, but most were professional or career-minded enough, save for a few notable instances, to turn Trump's gut calls, free associations, furious resentments, and wide-ranging balderdash into something that resembled a presentable policy with a legal framework.

The Obi-Wan of this process was, again, most consistently Kushner. While he might absent himself from the fights that he was most clearly going to lose, he was careful to be on the scene when his own interests were at stake and, knowing the nature of Trump's attention span and impatience with detail, when he could reasonably enough change the thrust and form of his father-in-law's orders and directions. Kushner's oft-stated view of his moderating effect on the president—*if you thought this was bad, it could have been much worse*—seemed, considering how bad it was, to be an odd stretch of self-congratulation, and yet it was probably true.

Kushner and his wife were still trying to keep their people around the president, and were certainly receiving hourly reports from them. But at the same time, they also seemed clear-eyed as to how little an effect anyone could have on the president at this point, hardened as he was in his irrational beliefs, and they were keeping their distance—indeed, with Kushner now in Doha, seven time zones away.

To the degree that Trump had, for four years, been running the government with scant idea of the rules and practices of running the government, he was doing that now without virtually anybody who did have some idea and desire to protect both him and themselves from embarrassment or legal peril.

The person he did have, Rudy Giuliani, was drinking heavily and in a constant state of excitation, often almost incoherent in his agitation and mania, over maintaining the president's favor by doing his bidding and feeding his obsession.

It really was one of those what-if moments. Not: what if the president of the United States were revealed to be an evil despot, moving the nation to the type of fascistic dictatorship hotly anticipated by MSNBC. But, rather: what if, stripping all protection and artifice away, he were revealed to be incapable of separating the fantasy of what he believed possible from the practicalities of accomplishing it? Indeed, aides noted that, on the eve of a consequential legislative battle, the White House would ordinarily have been burning up the phones, but Giuliani, in effect the president's singular operative, barely had contact information for most people on the Hill.

The good news here is that the irrational president could actually not accomplish anything very much. He was just one man, without a plan, nor with much knowledge of how the government worked, whose staff had almost entirely deserted him. The bad news was that his fantasy, given his self-dramatization and moral authority, as it were, with his base, was now shared by millions of people.

* * *

For most politicians, vox populi is a pretty remote concept, one brought home only with polling, press, and elections. Trump's regular and, during some periods, nearly constant performances at stadium rallies gave him a greater direct route and connection to his base than any politician in the modern television age. It was a fan base of adulation on a par with that of a pop star—a massive pop star. ("The only man without a guitar who can fill a stadium," he liked to say about himself, in one of his 1960s-stuck references.) Unlike most politicians, who polled for the most effective issues and the cleverest nuances in wording, Trump, in his hours of dominating stadium stages, surveyed the audience in an emotional real time. He threw out gambit after gambit, line after line, calibrating the response. And when he hit the note, the magical note—Obama's birth certificate, the wall, taking a knee, fake news, and now the stolen election—he repeated it again and again, with there being little light between what he most believed and what most moved the crowd.

He took his legitimacy from these rallies and the crowd's febrile response. He knew he would win the election, and he would believe he had won the election, not least of all because the rallies, four or five a day in the week before the election, had been so beyond anything the Democrats and Joe Biden could ever in their wildest dreams have mustered. And they were happening during the pandemic!

In some vital center of his appeal—and what distinguished him was that he understood this while almost nobody else did—he existed not in the professional zone, with all the other careerists in the federal government, but in the emotional zone of his fan base.

This was a real and exceptional sort of populism. He egged the

fans on, and they egged him on. He knew nothing about government, and they knew nothing about government, so the context of
government itself became beside the point. It was one-on-one, direct.
He had charisma in the Christian sense.

At the same time, he was the star—never forget that—and the
base was his audience.

Trump often expressed puzzlement over who these people were,
their low-rent "trailer camp" bearing and their "get-ups," once jok-
ing that he should have invested in a chain of tattoo parlors and
shaking his head about "the great unwashed."

* * *

On Saturday, December 12—little more than three weeks before
rioters and revelers would disastrously appear again in Washington
on January 6—several thousand Trump fans and fanatics had
gathered in the capital. The Trump fan base here was segmented
down, post-defeat, to impassioned supporters of the election challenge, its most self-dramatizing and ecstatic core.

There were the Proud Boys in elaborate dress, ZZ Top beards
and tie-dyed kilts—Enrique Tarrio, a Proud Boy organizer, got
in line and took a public tour of the White House—who seemed
to have appointed themselves Trump protectors and vanguard as
the Hell's Angels had once done for the Rolling Stones. There
were Trump impersonators and a wide variety of other made-for-
the-cameras MAGA costumes. There were veterans—or people
in military gear trying to suggest patriotism and firepower. There
were old men and women, too—more Las Vegas than Altamont.
Virtually all without masks.

"It's like *Let's Make a Deal*," said Trump the next day to a caller,
referencing the long-running game show from the 1960s—
somehow yet his psychic era—where audience members dressed
up in foolish costumes to get the attention of the host.

The speakers at the December 12 event were themselves a retinue of Trump attention seekers: Michael Flynn, the former general
who had briefly served as Trump's national security advisor before
being rolled out of office for lying to the FBI, had, after pleading
guilty, reversed himself and abjectly reaffirmed his Trump loyalty,
finally getting his pardon just days before the rally. Sebastian Gorka,
a figure of uncertain provenance and function in the Trump White
House during its first months, was one of the early oddballs to be
pushed out when John Kelly became chief of staff and had pursued
a Trump-based media career ever since. Also speaking, Alex Jones,
the conspiracy auteur, and MyPillow entrepreneur Mike Lindell, a
former drug addict and a current fevered conspiracist.

Four people were stabbed and thirty-three arrested in the December protest, most in the several-hour melee that took place after
sundown. Three weeks before January 6, the end of the Trump
administration was already being greeted with riots and violence.

"Seems like quite a few crazies," said Trump to aides the next day.

This was, in hindsight—or might have been recognized as such
in hindsight—a run-through for the groups who would be gathering in Washington on January 6. But it was also a pretty good
insight into Trump's view. The fan base was always peculiar. Stars
needed fans, but this did not mean that a fan was not a strange
thing to be. The more devoted the fan, the odder the fan. Like any
megastar, Trump saw his fans from a far distance out. Certainly,
there was no personal connection. A star could not assume responsibility for his fans, could he? Indeed, the fans were not the star; the
star was the star. Never forget.

* * *

But it wasn't just the crazies. There was method here, too. The January 6 march on Washington, in the subtle variations among the organizing groups, was, for many, an effort not so much to keep Trump

in power as to find the best position for when he was no longer in power.

Here was the math: He was going to lose the White House; that was certainly sure. But he was going to be left with enormous reach and sway and influence. Every member of Congress now supporting his electoral challenge was thinking forward to Trump's future usefulness to them.

Likewise, for the organizers of the Washington march.

It was the singular difference between Trump and former presidents that his power and standing might not largely depend on the White House, that he could go on being Donald Trump, with the awe and devotion this involved, without being president.

And the money that flowed through him, that flowed because of him, wasn't going to run dry simply because he was not in office.

As the great unwashed were gathering, on the evening of January 5 there was another gathering, at the Trump Hotel, of ranking Republicans, all primarily there to plan and to fundraise for 2022. This included a circle of top-draw Trump celebrities, Don Jr., Michael Flynn, and Corey Lewandowski among them, and presentations by groups, like the Republican Attorneys General Association, looking for 2022 funding.

The primary organizer was Caroline Wren, the most prodigious fundraiser in the Republican Party. On the eve of a protest over the 2020 election, Wren had assembled thirty to forty major Republican donors to hear about political investment needs for 2022.

Wren was a contract fundraiser, hired by groups or candidates to raise money through her own efforts, out of which she received a commission that could run from 15 to 40 percent. Wren, close to Don Jr. and his girlfriend, Kimberly Guilfoyle—Wren raised money for Guilfoyle's Mar-a-Lago birthday party—was a key fundraiser for the Trump 2020 campaign. Now, she had raised much of the money to fund the next day's rally at which the president would speak. She had, in other words, raised money for an event that would bring people to Washington, which would in turn become an opportunity to raise more money.

She was hardly the only one. The organizers of the rally where the president would speak included Amy Kremer and her daughter Kylie Jane Kremer, Tea Party and pro-Trump Super PAC activists, organizers, and fundraisers; Ali Alexander, another right-wing organizer and Trump fundraiser; and Alex Jones, the conspiracist media personality—each of them with a direct financial interest in the day's events and in future dealings with the Trump money machine.

Their connections to the Trump campaign would further implicate the president in the next day's events—Wren helped fund a robocall encouraging protestors to march on the Capitol—but certainly, given their broader financial interests, their involvement here suggested as much about business as it did about rioting.

January 6, for many, was about the money.

Trump aides would label each one of them grifters (a key word in the Trump White House to apply to others so as to not be described that way yourself) and hangers-on. Trump himself would take sour note of the money they were making off of him. But this was yet a hunger game of Trump loyalty as measured by money raised and crowds produced. What was being foreshadowed here were the coming claims on the Trump franchise.

This was the prize: to be at the head of the class among the solicitors for the Trump cause. Here, at its professional core, distinguished from the interests of its mere attendees, was what the January 6 rally was about, a hierarchy of players looking to maintain and strengthen their ties to the ongoing Trump political enterprise.

* * *

Trump wasn't devoting much thought to the groups amassing for the next day's rally.

What the vice president was going to do in Congress—the right thing or not—was at top of mind. In the many times he had already spoken to Rudy that day, the rally—at which, the next day, Rudy would also speak—had not come up more than in passing. The farther, though at some distance, item on his mind was the Georgia run-off election and how, if it went badly—and it seemed to be going badly—he could shift the blame where it belonged. This was another refrain he played all day: if McConnell had only supported his two-thousand-dollar stimulus check idea—he rendered this in the third person: "*Trump's* two-thousand-dollar stimulus check"— they would have won in Georgia.

"Fucking Mitch . . . even a dummy can figure it out . . . he's trying to lose . . . I don't think he wants to win . . . he wants to lose these seats . . . dumbest thing I've ever seen . . . these people are so stupid . . . Dems do a much better job of sticking together . . . run circles around the Republicans . . . dumbest thing I've ever seen . . ."

But Georgia was certainly not as important as what the vice president would do; nor as important as the final plans for how to get the vice president to do what he needed to do.

Ross Worthington and Vince Haley, on Stephen Miller's speech-writing staff, were drafting the president's remarks for the next day's rally, but they were having trouble getting Trump's attention. Miller himself, following the birth of his first child, had been another largely absent presence for many weeks. Neither Worthington nor Haley sensed that the rally was on anyone's main radar. For them, it was both a sentimental effort, the president's last rally, and a whistling-past-the-graveyard exercise. The brief was just to use Rudy's stuff to make the election case.

Trump had, starting weeks before, continued to nod to the event in a series of tweets: "JANUARY SIXTH, SEE YOU IN DC!" But this was not a White House event. Even if they had wanted to, there was no one in these final days in the White House capable of organizing a major rally or even coordinating with anyone who was. And the president was always halfhearted at best when he wasn't in control of an appearance—meaning the look and feel, the staging and the lighting, and the run of show would be off, you could guarantee. (Nick Luna, his body man, had once doubled up the number of flags behind Trump on the stage, at the expense of people standing behind him, on the assumption that flags looked presidential. "I'll tell you what looks presidential," remonstrated the president. "People standing behind me cheering.")

At the same time, the rally was happening, organized by the White House or not. If anyone had been paying attention (Trump and Giuliani, anyone else in the White House, Nancy Pelosi or Mitch McConnell), it should have been clear that this had the makings of a shit show, particularly with the December 12 rally just a few weeks ago as a living example.

The *Washington Post* outlined in quite extensive detail what was going to happen on January 6, although this was played as a local story, and you had to scroll pretty far down to find it. There would be four different rallies on the sixth, the *Post* reported, each with different organizers, each set to protest the election results and to demand an overturn of the Electoral College vote. Key gathering points would be the Washington Monument, Freedom Plaza, and the Capitol.

There was Women for America First, a group associated with the Kremer mother-daughter duo. There was something, said the *Post*, called the Wild Protest, slated for the Capitol lawn. A Trump supporter named James Epley, unknown to the White House, had filed an application to march from the Mall to the Capitol. A breakaway member of Women for America First, Cindy Chafian, had asked for her own permit for an organization called the Eighty Percent Coalition—some polls had nearly that many Republicans saying they didn't trust the election results—for a venue near the Washington Monument.

Said the *Post*:

... online forums and encrypted chat messages among far-right groups indicate a number of demonstrators might be planning more than chanting and waving signs.

Threats of violence, ploys to smuggle guns into the District and calls to set up an "armed encampment" on the Mall have proliferated in online chats about the Jan. 6 day of protest. The Proud Boys, members of armed right-wing groups, conspiracy theorists and white supremacists have pledged to attend.

For Trump, and for everybody who had grown used to him, this was in some sense just more of the same—here was the impassioned, quirky, voluble, "a bit too crazy," great unwashed group that had filled his stadiums. For Trump, these people were the background to his main event. They were props for him. They were not the story. He was the story.

The main event, his main event, even if only in his imagination, was for Biden's electors not to be certified and to instead be replaced by Trump electors; or, at least, for Biden's electors to be sent back to their respective state legislatures.

The main event for nearly everybody in the U.S. government was also this ritual count, but to get that done and to have all this over with—no more so than for the people left in the White House, who were exhausted, and filled with no small amount of personal embarrassment by the election fight, and who wanted to move on.

* * *

The vice president was expected for his regular weekly lunch with the president. These were occasions pushed by the vice president and his office. It was part of Pence's disciplined plan to stay in the president's immediate circle, understanding that if you weren't within the immediate sound-of-his-voice circle you were far out of it. For the past four years, Pence had made a point of calling the president one or more times a day and to be in as many Oval Office meetings as possible—often several meetings in a day. The lunches were specifically meant to be an opportunity for Pence to tell the president exactly how hard he was working for him. He usually got ten minutes to do this before Trump snapped on the television and launched into his current list of grievances.

But today's lunch was shifted to a meeting at 2 p.m.—this was to be a calling on the carpet.

By the afternoon of January 5, with turnout reports from the run-off election in Georgia looking unpromising and with thousands of people arriving in the capital, the president, no matter how unambiguous the signals from the VP's office, more of them every day, was yet singularly focused in his belief that the vice president should and would do what he, Trump, had now righteously codified as "the right thing."

"He's got to do the right thing. He's going to do the right thing." He used the term with everyone. Before their meeting, the president tweeted: "The vice president has the power to reject fraudulently chosen electors."

Rudy, in turn, was telling everyone that they knew exactly what was going to happen. They could depend on Pence, no question at all about that. If he didn't immediately upset the election and certify Donald John Trump as the next president—still their first hope—he would at least send four slates back to their respective legislatures for further consideration. Those electors, determined to have been elected by fraudulent means, would then be replaced with Trump electors, who would return to Washington within a week to ten days, tops, where Donald Trump would be certified as the winner and sworn in on January 20.

The vice president arrived for his meeting in the Oval Office, in a rare departure absent its usual constant ebb and flow of traffic.

It was just the president and vice president alone together.

The vice president was still trying to be positive about the Georgia Senate races.

The president was wrathful about McConnell's unwillingness to back "Trump's two-thousand-dollar stimulus."

Neither man spoke about the tens of thousands of people coming into the city.

The president, with his certain sort of ADD imperiousness (impatience mixed with certainty, and not wanting to hear differently), swiftly got to the matter of Pence doing the right thing.

"You want to do the right thing," said the president.

"I very much want to do the right thing," said the vice president. "That's all I want to do."

The vice president listened to the president recount details of the stolen election—free-form, anecdotal grievances uttered and repeated. Pence didn't disagree, and he seemed to share or at least sympathize with the president's plight.

Then the vice president was subjected to the president's instructions and admonishments about what had to be done about this. Everything the vice president had previously said was ignored, with the president unquestionably assuming the vice president had the certain power to do what the president wanted done and to correct the terrible wrongs as he saw them.

As it always is with Trump, there was no real discussion. There was no response called for except to look like you were listening and to occasionally nod your head. Trump conducted both sides of the conversation.

The president, reverting to a trope he often used about the willingness to fight, talked about the vice president's heroic place in history if he stood up and did what was right, and the shame of his place if he didn't.

"Do you want to be Thomas Jefferson?" he asked, going back to Jefferson's move in the 1801 certification—the argument that Pence had explicitly rejected in his meeting with the president and Giuliani's constitutional lawyer, John Eastman, the night before.

Trump pressed further, in a line he would leak straightaway and that he would be repeating for months to come: "Do you want to be a patriot or pussy?" (The *New York Times* made this somewhat grander: "You can either go down in history as a patriot, or you can go down in history as a pussy.")

Pence, not rising to the bait, repeated that, in the overwhelming opinion of those constitutional experts he had consulted, the Constitution did not give him the authority to do what the president thought he could do. This would have been the point he had made to the president, without deviation, almost countless times, which Trump seemed to force him to make again in something like a police interrogation, hoping he might somehow, in making him repeat what he had said so many times before, catch him up on the details.

It is also likely that Trump wasn't listening. He often remarked about Pence that the vice president beat around the bush and had a hard time getting to the point.

Trump returned to talking about the "right thing," and an eager-to-mollify Pence returned to his own support for doing the "right thing."

At any rate, the upshot of what was, in theory, for Trump, the most important meeting of his presidency was, as the Vice President's Office would shortly leak to the *New York Times* in a story posted later that evening, that Pence had conveyed to the president his belief that he did not have the authority to interfere with or challenge the Electoral College vote count.

The president, for his part, immediately issued a statement directly contradicting the vice president:

> The New York Times report regarding comments Vice President Pence supposedly made to me today is fake news. He never said that. The Vice President and I are in total agreement that the Vice President has the power to act.

So . . . either the vice president or the president was lying.

Some White House aides, however much they were familiar with the president's uncomplicated willingness to dissemble, found him apparently certain that the vice president was fully on board, believing this, generously, to be a product of the vice president's comity and the president's conviction or, more pathologically the president's ability to exclude any other views and every other person from his thinking.

The vice president's side flatly rejected this view. Rather, the VP's people found the president so confident in the power of his persuasion and threats that he steadfastly believed that a campaign to pressure the vice president—via insistence, humiliation, specious arguments, warnings about a break in their relationship, and, in this last instance, straightforward gaslighting—would get him what he wanted.

* * *

Some fifteen minutes after the president's statement went out at about 9:30, an angry Marc Short called Jason Miller.

"I'm just curious about what the process is for issuing a statement about a conversation when there were only two people in the room."

"Well," said Miller, "POTUS tells me what he wants to say, and I put it out."

9

MORNING, JANUARY 6

By dawn, the crowd was building, the various organizers of the various events pulling in larger-than-expected numbers. But the protest was still just background noise, a tailgate party before the main event, the counting of the electors, which would begin at 1 p.m.—the main *non-event* more accurately.

The remaining on-call group of aides around the president that morning in the White House was down to Meadows, Herschmann, and Scavino, with Miller, Justin Clark, Alex Cannon, and Tim Murtaugh the last employees from the campaign, either working from home, or, in the case of Clark, heading to an RNC winter meeting in Florida. All of them had woken up with something close to the same thought: *How is it going to play when the vice president fails to make the move the president is counting on him to make?* And make no mistake, each fully understood Mike Pence was not going to make that move.

Just as relevant, none of the six men had precisely told the president this. Herschmann, in close touch with Kushner—traveling back at that moment from the Middle East and, likewise, by no means pressing the issue with his father-in-law—perhaps came closest to addressing the point. But far from close enough. Meadows reverted to a kind of Southern speak, so polite and genteel and sugary that no matter what he said, you might think he was on your side or at least wanted to be. Miller, Clark, Cannon, Scavino, and Murtaugh had all become expert at absorbing what the president said, ever ingesting and trying to process it in the most palatable way possible short of saying something to cause the president to turn on them.

They, along with almost everyone else in the White House, and among those who had slipped out, just wanted this to be over. It was over. Top of mind for Justin Clark, on his way to the RNC meting, was the fact that the lease on the campaign headquarters in Rosslyn was running out on January 31—everything needed to be cleared out in the next few weeks.

* * *

It was Jason Miller's daughter's fourth birthday, and he was hoping the certification of electors that day would not involve too much grandstanding. He wanted to spend the day with his family.

Miller called Boris Epshteyn for a reality check: "So . . . how exactly do we think this is going to go today?"

"Short answer: we have no idea."

"How many states are teed up?" The number of states receiving House and Senate objections would determine how long and how pitched the day's events would be.

"We're still not sure."

"And the chance of anything going anywhere? Really, ballpark me."

"Zero."

"And then what?"

"Then it's over."

* * *

It was hard to imagine what kind of confrontation or intervention might at this point have forced the president to appreciate that the vice president's course of action was set, and that everyone everywhere knew what his course was. This was rather the serious and alarming point: however known to everyone else, however absolute the vice president's course was going to be—indeed, however impossible it would have been to do otherwise and however much Pence had been clear on this point—however much it was *only* the president (and Rudy) continuing to believe that the course was fluid, there was yet nothing that could be done to make the president of the United States understand or prepare for this single, immutable outcome otherwise known by everyone.

The vice president and his chief of staff were trying. Even as the president continued to hector or shame or insult the vice president into capitulating to his effective putsch, the VP and his staff were at work on a no-wiggle-room statement that would carefully explain the vice president's position and foreclose any action on his part. They planned to release the statement just before Congress convened at 1 p.m.

So, what was going to happen when it didn't happen? When the VP did nothing more than count the votes?

There were many Democrats and pundits contemplating, even looking forward with some schadenfreude, to the president's attempting to stay on in the White House after January 20 and having to be frog-marched out by the Secret Service. Equally, there were far-right-wingers and kamikaze Trumpers looking forward to their version of a last stand. But the six remaining men closest to the situation were all purposely trying not to think about the last two weeks of the Trump presidency and what "weird shit"—in the words of one of the men, echoing George W. Bush's characterization of Trump's inaugural address of four years before—could take place.

At the moment, they were focused on how this would break—

this is, whether the president would break when the vice president crossed him.

While there were not unknowns as to the ultimate outcome, there were unknowns in the day itself that could well contribute to how the president might respond to this final, incontestable crossing of the threshold of his election loss.

For one thing, with objections by House and Senate members, it could go on for hours and hours, through the day, the night, and into tomorrow—the outcome might be known, but the suspense, independent of reality, could build mightily anyway.

And there were people in the streets. While the absolute certainty of what was going to take place was understood by every political professional on that day in Washington, except for the president (and Rudy), it was not understood by the crowd, who seemed perfectly willing to suspend all disbelief about the stolen election. This was another variable to the six men: not, at that point, that the crowd would itself be a player, but that the presence of the crowd would further convince Trump that the day would be his; not, in other words, that he would incite the crowd but that the crowd would incite him.

But this was not a sense of climax. The opposite: anticlimax. This had dragged out beyond reason. Clark, for one, was certainly relieved to be getting out of town.

* * *

And more immediately, there was the Georgia run-off election, with the counting from the day before only just finishing, and what now looked like the loss of the Senate. When Jason Miller spoke to the president at 8 a.m., he was looking for a reaction to that loss. As was their usual routine, the president, who had seen that morning's coverage, asked Miller to recap it. Who was getting blamed?

"It's all about the two thousand dollars—if Mitch had just cut those checks. Do people get this? The Dems' closing ads were all about those checks," the president rehashed. He asked Miller what he thought Pence would do, and then told Miller that Pence would do the right thing. While on the phone with Miller, the president, watching Chuck Todd on NBC, tweeted: "Sleepy Eyes Chuck Todd is so happy with the fake voter tabulation process that he can't even get the words out straight. Sad to watch!"

Getting off the phone with Miller, the president then tweeted at 8:17 a.m. his now-precise theory of how he saw the election being overturned: "States want to correct their votes, which they now know were based on irregularities and fraud, plus corrupt process never received legislative approval. All Mike Pence has to do is send them back to the states. AND WE WIN. Do it Mike, this is a time for extreme courage!"

The president continued to tweet, both about the Georgia election, the stolen presidential election, and the importance to the Republican Party in having him as president.

As the crowd began gathering at the Ellipse for the main rally— ten thousand to twenty thousand people there at this point—the president called the vice president again. A resigned, or stoic, Meadows was in the room. The president reached Pence at his residence where he was with Marc Short and their lawyer Greg Jacob and other staff members. They were trying to finish the vice president's statement that, in effect, would reject all of the president's views and desires about the vice president's power and prerogatives. But the president was now calling to restate those views anyway. It was among the most frustrating aspects of dealing with Trump. It was the very opposite of the Socratic approach, but in some sense Trump's personal version of it: merely by repeating, often word for word, what he had said sometimes countless times before he would lead you to, or bludgeon you into accepting, his position. The repetition was almost verbatim—Jefferson, patriot and pussy, right thing—but the tone, uncompromising the day before, was now even harsher, more scathing.

At 9 a.m., Mo Brooks, the congressman from Alabama, one of the Dead-Enders leading the House push to challenge the electoral count, gave an early speech at the Ellipse, just in back of the White House where the main rally was now in progress. Brooks judged it to be a happy crowd, more interested in the music than in his speech about the "Steal," and already large enough that he felt he had to yell into the microphone.

At 9:30 a.m., Miller received the text of the president's planned speech at the rally, but he didn't read it. Miller was still focused on the coming electoral count. His concern was about getting coverage of the breakout sessions, when both the Senate and the House would return to their respective chambers. Would the networks cover the House and Senate debates over the challenges to the various states? That would offer some satisfaction to the president.

When Miller and the president spoke again, shortly after nine thirty, the president continued the conversation about the great fraud and the importance of the vice president's doing the right thing and of, in general, the need to fight back against the effort to steal the election from him. What else, he wondered, could be done with the House and Senate members? They needed to be more emphatic about the steal. What were the cases they were going to be highlighting during the breakout sessions? They should be presenting the big stuff—the big frauds. In fact, the president and his legal team had little idea of what was going to happen in the arguments before Congress. Nobody was in the loop.

He was curious about the mounting crowd. How was it looking? How big was it?

It seemed to be a really big crowd, Miller told him, and getting bigger.

Miller still saw no pressing reason to read the president's speech, not just because, in front of a crowd, Trump would likely depart from it, but because, at this point, rallies were largely a set piece: he'd do his thing—probably for his last time as president.

* * *

The family arrived at the White House shortly before 10 a.m. Don Jr. and Kimberly Guilfoyle, Eric and Lara, and Ivanka, on her own—Jared was on his way back from the Middle East. It was a good-feeling gathering, even a bit of a party. The president might still be dug in but his family was moving on—and wanting to acknowledge this most remarkable four years they had experienced. No regrets. Come on . . . who would have expected any of this!

One curious point of consideration for the family that morning—prescient for how events would shortly unfold—was a follow-up to a discussion initiated some months before by aides and family. Trump representatives, working with Trump family members, had approached Parler, the social network backed by Bob Mercer and his daughter Rebekah, far-right exponents and large Trump contributors. They had been floated a proposition that Trump, after he left office, would become an active member of Parler, moving much of his social media activity there from Twitter. In return, Trump would receive 40 percent of Parler's gross revenues, and the service would ban anyone who spoke negatively about him.

Parler was balking only at this last condition.

This was now being offered by the family as a carrot to entice the president out of the White House (it was also a potential future family revenue stream): Trump could do what he loved to do most and potentially make a fortune off it. It was a given in the Trump White House that he was one of social media's most valuable assets, and that he would like nothing better than to share, monetarily, in that value.

* * *

The Giuliani group, now in its tenth week in DC, had moved out of the Mandarin Oriental Hotel and over to the Willard. Giuliani had spent the evening with John Eastman, their constitutional authority, rehashing the Pence situation. Rudy was now in hyper-drive over Pence. It had all come down to this, and it was all going to happen now—everything was on Pence. Giuliani had failed in every single instance of legal strategy and positioning in the election challenge and had now put all his eggs into the Pence basket. It might have seemed that he was trying to set Pence up to take the blame for what he himself had so abjectly failed to accomplish. To the president, Rudy was still offering good odds that the vice president would come through. To others, Giuliani was now saying that Pence just didn't have the balls to do what could be done.

Giuliani left the Willard with Eastman, Bernie Kerik, and Boris Epshteyn at a little before 10 a.m. They ran into Roger Stone in the lobby of the Willard. Stone was asked if he was going to the rally, but he said he hadn't been invited. He didn't even know who had organized it, he said.

The four men were let out of their car and had to walk across the grass to the Ellipse. They were already freezing by the time Giuliani went on, at about 10:50:

> I have Professor Eastman here with me to say a few words ... He's one of the preeminent constitutional scholars in the United States. It is perfectly appropriate given the questionable constitutionality of the Election Counting Act of 1887 that the vice president can cast it aside, and he can do what a president called Jefferson did when he was vice president. He can decide on the validity of these crooked ballots, or he can send it back to the legislators, give them five to ten days to finally finish the work. We now have letters from five legislators begging us to do that. They're asking us. Georgia, Pennsylvania, Arizona, Wisconsin, and one other coming in ...
>
> It is perfectly reasonable and fair to get ten days ... and you should know this, the Democrats and their allies have not allowed us to see one machine, or one paper ballot. Now, if they ran such a clean elec-

tion, why wouldn't they make all the machines available immediately? If they ran such a clean election, they'd have you come in and look at the paper ballots. Who hides evidence? Criminals hide evidence. Not honest people . . .

Last night one of the experts that has examined these crooked Dominion machines has absolutely what he believes is conclusive proof that in the last ten percent, fifteen percent of the vote counted, the votes were deliberately changed. By the same algorithm that was used in cheating President Trump and Vice President Pence. Same algorithm, same system, same thing was done with the same machines. You notice they were ahead until the very end, right? Then you noticed there was a little gap, one was ahead by three percent, the other was ahead by two percent, and gone, gone, they were even. He can take you through that and show you how they programmed that machine from the outside to accomplish that. And they've been doing it for years to favor the Democrats.

* * *

At 11:45 a.m. the White House entourage, including Meadows, Herschmann, and Scavino, piled into the Beast, the presidential limo and the follow-on vehicles for the two-minute ride to the rally staging area (mostly the president liked to ride alone, with the rest of the entourage following). The Trump family was already there. The greenroom tent was almost giddy—despite their ostensible purpose there being to protest the election, defend the Trump presidency, and anticipate the vice president's push to save it. Here was a celebratory sense that this might be Trump's last rally as president. Nostalgia was beginning. Elvis's last show. Don Jr. had his phone out, filming the moment.

A few days before, rally organizers had amended their estimate of the crowd size from 5,000 to 30,000. Various media reports were now putting the size of the crowd at more than 10,000. The president paused during his speech to observe that he reckoned there were 250,000 people. Best estimate put the crowd somewhere between 30,000 and 60,000—still a righteous cold-weather turnout for a defeated president.

In days to come, the president would raise his estimate to 1 million.

He came onstage to his standard anthem, "God Bless the U.S.A.," but with less swagger than usual—slower, less sure, even. He was in a black overcoat and black gloves—a strongman look.

The speech, shortly on its way to becoming the most notorious of his presidency, and the key evidence for his imminent second impeachment, was a B delivery. You could imagine that his mind would have been rightly on the vice president; whatever he said here was irrelevant compared to that.

The speech was cued up on the teleprompter. The president read most of it, a sign of disengagement.

It was boiler-plate stuff. *The media is the biggest problem we have, as far as I'm concerned, single-biggest problem, the fake news and the Big Tech . . .*

Large parts rehashing his campaign rally script:

Turn your cameras, please, and show what's really happening out here, because these people are not going to take it any longer. They're not going to take it any longer. Go ahead. Turn your cameras, please. Would you show? . . . I wish they'd flip those cameras and look behind you. That is the most amazing sight. When they make a mistake, you get to see it on television. Amazing, amazing, all the way back. Don't worry. We will not take the name off the Washington Monument. We will not. Cancel culture. They wanted to get rid of the Jefferson Memorial, either take it down or just put somebody else in there. I don't think that's going to happen. It damn well better not. Although, with this administration, if this happens, it could happen. You'll see some really bad things happen.

In a way, by this point, his unscripted speeches had become so scripted that the true eccentricities and frisson and nutty or inspiring free association were all smoothed out of it. Perhaps he was tired. Even Trump might finally become tired of hearing himself talk; it was possible. Or tired of the sixty days of tension; of keeping something in the air long, long after it should reasonably have crashed, something that now, in the next few hours, was about to come to an end.

Not long into the speech, Giuliani and his crew, with freezing toes, left and went back to the Willard. They had heard it all before.

> Our media is not free. It's not fair. It suppresses thought. It suppresses speech, and it's become the enemy of the people. It's become the enemy of the people. It's the biggest problem we have in this country. No third world countries would even attempt to do what we caught them doing, and you'll hear about that in just a few minutes.

His delivery was more singsong than bombastic and explosive. He was rushing through it. Ordinarily, he'd have thrown some red meat out and waited for the reaction—always, clearly, the moments of his keenest enjoyment—but now he was just plunging forward.

> Republicans are constantly fighting like a boxer with his hands tied behind his back. It's like a boxer, and we want to be so nice. We want to be so respectful of everybody, including bad people. We're going to have to fight much harder, and Mike Pence is going to have to come through for us. If he doesn't, that will be a sad day for our country, because you're sworn to uphold our Constitution. Now it is up to Congress to confront this egregious assault on our democracy. After this, we're going to walk down—and I'll be there with you. We're going to walk down. We're going to walk down any one you want, but I think right here. We're going to walk down to the Capitol,

and we're going to cheer on our brave senators and congressmen and women. We're probably not going to be cheering so much for some of them, because you'll never take back our country with weakness. You have to show strength, and you have to be strong.

He added that part: the walk. *After this, we're going to walk down—and I'll be there with you.* The walk wasn't in the text. The entourage heard little else—the hundreds upon hundreds of hours of Trump rallies that they all had been subjected to blurred into the usual blah-blah, but they heard that line: the walk. He did not mean this, of course. Trump didn't walk anywhere. The *we* was figurative. Still.

What was most different about this speech was that he was making a case, prosecuting an argument. Trump rally riffs ordinarily mixed the familiar with sudden bursts of new material—insults, sweeping generalizations about good guys and bad guys, patriotic this-and-that. But now he was his own lawyer. The election had been stolen, and this was how they did it.

Almost seventy-five million people voted for our campaign, the most of any incumbent president by far in the history of our country, twelve million more people than four years ago. I was told by the real pollsters—we do have real pollsters. They know that we were going to do well, and we were going to win. What I was told, if I went from sixty-three million, which we had four years ago, to sixty-six million, there was no chance of losing. Well, we didn't go to sixty-six. We went to seventy-five million, and they say we lost. We didn't lose.

Ballots everywhere. Every swing state inundated with ballots. Ten thousand here. Sixty thousand there. Four hundred thousand suddenly. Ninety-one thousand. One-hundred-seventy thousand. Everywhere, suddenly, votes for Biden materializing. You could hear now, in Trump's voice, the mad and madcap Giuliani—so much crammed into his head and his trying to get it out before it destroyed him.

> Just like the suppression polls that said we're going to lose Wisconsin by seventeen points. Well, we won Wisconsin. They don't have it that way because they lose just by a little sliver. But they had me down the day before in the Washington Post/ABC poll, down seventeen points. I called up a real pollster. I said, "What is that?" "Sir, that's called a suppression poll. I think you're going to win Wisconsin, sir." I said, "But why do they make it four or five points?" "Because then people vote. But when you're down seventeen, they say, 'Hey, I'm not going to waste my time. I love the president, but there's no way.'" Despite that, we won Wisconsin, you'll see. But that's called suppression because a lot of people, when they see that, it's very interesting. This pollster said, "Sir, if you're down three, four, or five, people vote. When you go down seventeen, they say, 'Let's save, let's go and have dinner, and let's watch the presidential defeat tonight on television, darling.'"

And, of course, it only got worse.

> ... Georgia's absentee ballot rejection rate was more than ten times lower than previous levels, because the criteria was [*sic*] so off, forty-eight counties in Georgia, with thousands and thousands of votes, rejected zero ballots. There wasn't one ballot. In other words, in a year in which more mail-in ballots were sent than ever before, and more people were voting by mail for the first time, the rejection rate was drastically lower than it had ever been before. The only way this can be explained is if tens of thousands of illegitimate votes were added to the tally; that's the only way you could explain it. By the way, you're talking about tens of thousands. If Georgia had merely rejected the same number of unlawful ballots as in other years, there should have been approximately forty-five thousand ballots rejected, far more than what we needed to win, just over eleven thousand.

The president likened the U.S. election to one where despots in authoritarian regimes supplanted the rightful vote and replaced it with fake ballots in order to stay in power. Among the fallacies here, beyond the math, the logic, and the conspiracists' view of an ever-plotting bureaucracy working together to pull off a mind-bogglingly complex plot, is that *he* was the incumbent. But somehow more powerful forces outside of the White House were conspiring to oust him.

> Tens of thousands of votes, as that coincided with a mysterious vote dump of up to a hundred thousand votes for Joe Biden, almost none for Trump . . . Over ten thousand, three hundred ballots in Georgia were cast by individuals whose names and dates of birth match Georgia residents who died in 2020 and prior to the election . . . At least eighty-eight thousand ballots in Georgia were cast by people whose registrations were illegally backdated . . . sixty-six thousand votes in Georgia were cast by individuals under the legal voting age. And at least fifteen thousand ballots were cast by individuals who moved out of the state prior to November third election . . . In the state of Arizona, over thirty-six thousand ballots were illegally cast by noncitizens . . . one hundred fifty thousand people registered in Mayacopa [*sic*] County after the registration deadline. One hundred three thousand ballots in the county were sent for electronic adjudication with no Republican observers . . . There were also more than forty-two thousand double votes in Nevada . . . More than seventeen thousand Michigan ballots were cast by individuals whose names and dates of birth matched people who were deceased . . . At six thirty-one a.m., in the early morning hours after voting had ended, Michigan suddenly reported one hundred forty-seven thousand votes. An astounding ninety-four percent went to Joe Biden, who campaigned brilliantly from his basement.

And it went on, seemingly inexhaustibly. Until, at one hour and thirteen minutes, he finished: "So let's walk down Pennsylvania Avenue . . ."

* * *

In the original schedule for the rally, the president was supposed to make brief remarks and after they were done the vice president would release his statement. But as the president spoke the vice president's people wondered if he wasn't purposely going on to hold them off—counting on the vice president not to say anything while Trump had the stage. In four years, Pence really never had—really, the stage had been Trump's for the entire time.

But at 12:30 p.m., midway through Trump's speech, the Vice President's Office released a two-and-a-half-page letter explaining that "after careful" study, the vice president had concluded that he was not able to reject votes unilaterally or, in effect, to do anything else, beyond his ceremonial role, that the president might want him to do.

"Oh, shit," noted Miller, at home, sending the statement to Giuliani, Epshteyn, and Scavino, leaving it to one of them to tell the president. Everybody else thought, *Oh, shit*, too.

* * *

Meadows and Scavino had slipped out and weren't listening to the speech. One of the Secret Service agents hurried to get Meadows aside and tell him the president said he was planning to march to the Capitol with the protestors.

"No. There's no way we are going to the Capitol," said Meadows.

Meadows confirmed this with the president as soon as he came off the stage at 1:11 p.m.

The president seemed unsure what Meadows was talking about.

"You said you were going to march with them to the Capitol."

"Well—"

"How would we do that? We can't organize that. We can't."

"I didn't mean it literally," Trump said.

* * *

By 1:30, the president was back at the White House, his family returning with him.

10

THE REMAINDER OF THE DAY, JANUARY 6

Lunch was waiting.

Don Jr. and Kimberly Guilfoyle, and Eric and Lara Trump left the White House, and Ivanka hung around.

Trump was back on the phone trying to get new information on Pence. The Joint Session had convened at 1 p.m. Arizona was the first objection. He was looking for coverage of the breakout, but only C-SPAN seemed to be on it. To the extent that aides had now come to rationalize all this as an exercise to force the voter fraud issue down the throat of the mainstream media, this, too, seemed to be failing.

Rudy, calling from the Willard, where he had watched the remainder of the president's speech and was just seeing the first mentions of disorder in the streets, gave him a breathless report on Pence, but without any new information. That said, he was also promising that as many as six states would be contested, hence a volatile situation—*we just didn't know what's going to happen* (his breathlessness was only increasing). Meadows was in close touch with Jim Jordan. But the details Jordan was offering were unsatisfying.

Indeed, the various congressional supporters seemed increasingly less excited now that their revolt would be covered only by C-SPAN.

There were initial reports about the crowds amassing at the Capitol, but the television news was mostly not yet registering a threatening sense of disorder. The president was still marveling to people about the size of the crowd, sure that the VP would understand that the base was firmly behind the president.

His focus was very much on what was happening inside the Capitol Building and on what he still believed would, or certainly could, be a radical turn in his fortunes in the coming hours.

* * *

Marc Short was standing on the House floor in the back as his boss presided. He had been taking if not congratulations at least sure signs of affirmation from both Republican House and Senate members. These were small gestures over something so large you could not make big gestures—just sighs of relief. What would have been the singular constitutional crisis in the republic's almost 250 years, averted. Even Mo Brooks, who was leading the ritual objections on the House side, indicated his thumbs up.

When the House and Senate broke to consider the Arizona objection, each in their respective chambers for the obligatory two-hour debate, Short decided to go downstairs to the Capitol grill and get a cheeseburger.

* * *

The parliamentary process just commencing represented another anomaly in this highly irregular day. The president was, in theory, waging an extraordinary legislative fight, one with hardly any precedent—the culmination of a two-month battle in which he had considered little else, on which both his immediate future and his place in history depended. But other than via his own tweets and fulminations, and his meeting the day before with the vice president, nobody in the White House was much participating or even present in this fight.

In addition to overseeing the complex and far-flung operations of the executive branch, the White House also manages a political operation whose function is to exert its influence and leverage over the legislative branch. Arguably, the Trump White House performed neither of these functions very well. But at this moment, there was no political function being performed at all.

There was nobody on the White House side whipping votes. There was nobody on the White House side who was even particularly up-to-date on who might be with them or against them other than from public reports.

True, hardly anybody was left in the White House. Still, even in the waning days of a presidency, such were the theoretical stakes that the greater Trump alumni and allies might reasonably have been brought back into action. This had not happened—rather, the opposite: even the longtime loyalists had all fled and were unreachable.

Kushner—among the key Hill contacts in the White House for the congressional leadership and the person most consistently able to efficiently mobilize White House resources, at least to the extent that anyone could—was almost entirely out of pocket on his flight back from the Middle East.

There was Rudy, of course. But the remaining insiders, most trying to keep as much distance as possible from the White House, understood that Rudy had few relationships with congressional members, and the ones he had were bad. The White House, while hanging everything on what would happen in Congress, was as remote from Capitol Hill and as disengaged with the process there as it had ever been.

To the extent, as the media darkly warned, that there was an extraordinary plot to hold on to power—an incipient coup, even— there really were only two plotters and no one to back them up. Trump had no functioning political staff, the White House

Counsel's Office had been all but shut down (to the degree the office was functioning, it was almost entirely focused on vetting pardon pleas), and the leadership of the Justice Department was in disarray.

All the same, the president and Rudy, in their bubble world, remained confident that success was there for them to grab.

* * *

At 1:49 p.m. the president retweeted a video of his Ellipse speech. At just about this time, rioters were breaching the Capitol door.

At two o'clock, the president and Giuliani—the president in the White House and Giuliani at the Willard—tried to find Tommy Tuberville, the recently seated senator from Alabama, but they instead mistakenly called Mike Lee, the Utah senator, on his cell phone. Lee, in the increasing confusion as reports started to come in of mobs breaching the Capitol fences, found Tuberville and put him on the phone. The president and Giuliani seemed to have no idea what was occurring at the Capitol, and Tuberville was either unsuccessful in telling them or thought better of trying.

At 2:11 p.m., the *New York Times* reported that rioters had entered the Capitol.

At 2:13 p.m., the vice president was pulled from the Senate Floor.

Marc Short had just gotten his cheeseburger when he became aware of the crowds and Capitol Police. Against people pushing downstairs to exit the building, he made his way upstairs, in touch with the VP's Secret Service detail, reaching Pence and his family—his wife, Karen, and daughter Charlotte and brother Greg—in the ceremonial office that the vice president, as president of the Senate, maintains just off the Senate Chamber. The Secret Service pressed for an evacuation but the vice president resisted. The Secret Service then tried to move the vice president and his family to the protected motorcade where they could wait. The vice president understood that the car could then depart at will and that would be the lasting impression: a fleeing vice president. They settled for a retreat to a "secure location"—a secret fortified shelter—within the Capitol.

At about 2:15 p.m., Boris Epshteyn, watching television in Giuliani's suite at the Willard, was one of the first people in the greater Trump circle to start, with some sense of panic, to flag what was occurring. Epshteyn spoke to Miller, who called Meadows.

"I'm sure you're tracking this," Miller said.

"Yeah, I know. Some things are moving here that I can't get into at the moment . . ." Meadows said.

Miller assumed the White House was mobilizing the National Guard. At 2:20 p.m., both the House and Senate adjourned.

At 2:24 p.m., the president, having been informed that Mike Pence had not rejected the Arizona Biden electors, tweeted:

> Mike Pence didn't have the courage to do what should have been done to protect our Country and our Constitution, giving States a chance to certify a corrected set of facts, not the fraudulent or inaccurate ones which they were asked to previously certify. USA demands the truth!

Reading the tweet in the Capitol bunker, the siege now in progress, Pence and Short, hardly for the first time, noted how far off the president could be from the page that everyone else was on. That was the generous interpretation.

In part, the president seemed just not to be grasping the facts as they were coming through—mounting crowds, breached barricades, protestors entering the Capitol. Or maybe he was simply disagreeing with them: These people were protesting the election, he was still repeating as late as 2:30. The protestors wanted Pence to do the right thing. These were good protestors, *his* protestors.

Indeed, one of the novel aspects of the breach of the Capitol was that it was filmed by so many of the protestors. This would become a subtheme to later Republican revisionism that these were just tourists, people participating in the democratic process, run amok.

* * *

"We're in! We're in!" one man with a camera shouts, as the barriers fall.

Hundreds, perhaps thousands of people, are suddenly swarming the Capitol, with a voice on the video shouting: "Let's go, let's go."

Then, "Holy shit, there are so many people, let's just go. This is ours. Fuck yeah. I can't believe this is reality. Fuck yeah, we've accomplished this shit. This is fucking history. We're all part of this fucking history."

From someone else: "WHOOP WHOOP WHOOP!" Then horns. More WHOOPs. "Listen to them all back there! Let's go. Let's go. This is beautiful shit. OH MY GOD, they are climbing up the wall. They are climbing up the wall! Let's go. Let's go. You guys are savage. We did it. We did it. Let's burn this shit down."

From someone else: "Is that a gun? Is that a gun?" Answer: "Rubber bullets."

The crowd pushing through the Capitol doors is now much smaller than the throng on the steps and seems for a moment confused and aimless. MAGA hats, camouflage jackets, and flags.

Echoing voices. "Our house! Our house!"

From the Capitol Police: "You've got to go outside. Come on. Come on. Come on, guys."

One response: "Hey, there's too many people here. You're not gonna stop this from happening. Hey, I'm just recording this. I'm just trying to record what we got going down. No freedom of the press here?"

Capitol Police: "Just hold everybody. Hold!"

Crowd: "USA! USA! USA! USA!"

Voice: "This is a scene! Holy Shit. What reality is this? We took this shit!"

"Fucking yeah, fucking yeah, fucking yeah!"

"Fuck it, we're going upstairs."

"Is there anybody on live stream right now?"

"This is 2021, you all. This is insanity. Holy shit. What is this? What is life right now? I'm shook. I'm shook. I cannot believe this shit. This is surreal, dude. I never would have imagined that we would be here. Dude, I was trying to tell you. Is this not going to be the best film you've ever made in your life? This is unreal. Wow!"

"Oh, my god. Oh, my god."

"This is surreal. But this is real life. But this seems like a movie. Treasure this moment."

Crowd: "Stop the steal, stop the steal, stop the steal."

Crowd: "We want Trump. We want Trump. We want Trump. We want Trump. We want Trump."

Protestor: "Stand down. You've got to stand down. This is not going to end well. No, it's not. The military is on its way."

"They're not going to shoot everybody."

"Listen up, we've got to be calm. We've got to be calm."

Suddenly the mob pushes forward—a sea of cameras (and MAGA hats).

"Use your crow bar."

"Back up. Back up."

"As soon as they lock down the building, we're all getting arrested."

"You'll be fine. It's only a little jail time. I do this all the time."

"The cops are leaving!"

"They are giving us the building."

"Break it down. Break it down."

"I wish somebody had a boom box. Revolutionary music."

Pounding on doors. "OPEN THE DOOR. OPEN THE DOOR."

"Break it down. Break it down."

Protestor to the Capitol Police: "I don't want to see you get hurt."

Then, suddenly, breaking glass and protestors smashing through a door.

"There's a gun! He's got a gun."

A shot is fired and a woman falls. (This is Ashli Babbit, the thirty-five-year-old air force veteran, the first person killed in the attack.)

"She's done. She's dead. Her eyes. She's dead, bro."

Protestor to one of the Capitol policemen: "You all gonna shoot everybody?"

"I saw the light go out in her eyes."

Another voice: "Infowars.com. I need the footage. It's going out to the world."

"I can't believe I saw somebody die."

* * *

Not long after 1 p.m., Mo Brooks was on the House floor trying to figure out which electoral challenges on the House side would also be joined by at least one senator, quite an unsettled state at the final hour. The number of objections dictated how many speeches would be given by House members, and Brooks was one of the people divvying out those sought-after assignments.

Sometime after 1:30, after the House and Senate had divided to hear debate in their respective chambers on the Arizona challenge, Brooks noticed Nancy Pelosi leave the Speaker's desk. Then there was a brief interruption. Paul Gosar, the Dead-Ender congressman from Arizona, was speaking. And then there was another interruption. Notable but not that unusual. Gosar returned to his speech. But then there was an announcement that protestors had entered the Capitol. Brooks found this a little more unusual, but it was hardly the first time protestors had disrupted Capitol proceedings. Brooks didn't pay a lot of attention. But not long after, there was another announcement, and members were asked to take the gas masks sealed in black Velcro bags from under their seats. And that *was* unusual, Brooks noted. There might be tear gas. On the other hand, Brooks also noted, they weren't being asked to put the gas masks *on*—or even take them out of their Velcro bags. And then, in short order, they were told they needed to vacate the House floor—one half led out one door, the other half out another door. At about this moment, Brooks heard a fist pounding on a door. There might have been shouting. But as they were led to where they would wait out the disruption, Brooks didn't see any protestors, only Capitol police. He wasn't afraid, just curious.

He would recall, in what would become part of a later Republican reinterpretation of events: "I never felt any sense of danger that whole day."

While House members were sequestered, Brooks heard some noise, but just "a little bit of loudness." He definitely never heard any gunfire. He never saw anybody panicking. He never saw any weapons. Indeed, never saw a single protestor. And no one was ever instructed to put on a gas mask. Brooks was on the baseball field in 2017 practicing for the annual Congressional Baseball Game for Charity when a gunman opened fire on him and his colleagues, wounding then House majority whip Steve Scalise. On the "scary meter," noted Brooks, that was a ten. The January 6 invasion of the Capitol, during which 140 were injured and at least five people died in connection with the riot, was, on Brooks's scary meter, a one.

Brooks says he has "no recollection" of speaking to the White House on January 6 (Meadows though was in close touch with Brooks's conservative Freedom Caucus colleague Jim Jordan). But, at least until later in the afternoon, Brooks's version was largely the view of events that the president was holding to: it wasn't that bad; the Capitol Police had it under control; everybody was safe.

* * *

Meadows, Herschmann, and Scavino began pressing the president to make some public acknowledgment of what was happening and to admonish the protestors, but his attention was elsewhere, still focused on the vice president. Fourteen minutes after his tweet attacking Pence, at 2:38 p.m., the aides managed to get a tweet out from the president composed by Scavino: "Please support our Capitol Police and Law Enforcement. They are truly on the side of our Country. Stay peaceful!"

* * *

The president spoke to retired general Keith Kellogg, who was one of his favorite military guys and was the vice president's national security advisor, to ask about the vice president.

Kellogg was in touch with Marc Short, who was with the vice president and the VP's Secret Service detail. The vice president was okay, Kellogg reported.

At least this would become the White House's stated instance of the president's expression of concern for the vice president. The vice president's team, in the secure location, registered no direct conversation with the White House until after 5 p.m.

And at no time did the president call the vice president.

* * *

Approaching 3 p.m., the pressure for the president to say something quickly mounted.

Ivanka Trump had been floating around the West Wing, chatting to a variety of people. Her children had gotten into private school in Florida, and she was pleased about this—an excited topic of conversation. She was pulled away from her discussion about schools to join the increasingly tense discussion about how to respond to the news.

The president, though, was digging in his heels. He remained singularly focused on the electoral challenge and had blinders on to everything else—at least, that was how everybody was rationalizing something close to his total failure, willful or not, to understand what was going on. At the same time, no one in the White House was seeing this as the full-on assault on the Capitol and the nail in the coffin of the Trump administration that the world would shortly understand it to be; they were, for perhaps another ninety minutes or so, still seeing this as "an optics issue," as Ivanka was putting it.

It wasn't until later in the three o'clock hour that Trump seemed to begin the transition from seeing the mob as people protesting the election—defending him, so he would defend them—to seeing them as "not our people." Therefore, he bore no responsibility for them.

Giuliani and Epshteyn were still watching television reports from the Willard. Giuliani was on the phone with the president, relating, with growing concern, what he was seeing on television, but both men were still talking about the vice president and what might happen in the electoral count.

Shortly after 3 p.m., without the president knowing it, campaign HQ cancelled all sanctioned media appearances by Trump supporters and surrogates for the immediate future.

Ivanka suggested calling out the National Guard. Meadows said they had asked for the Guard—and been rebuffed by, unclear in Meadows's telling, either the House Speaker, Nancy Pelosi, or the DC mayor, Muriel Bowser. In fact, the White House had suggested the National Guard be put on call several days before, when the president was hearing from conspiracy-minded sources, including Giuliani, that Antifa might disrupt the election challenge rallies. Bowser did reach Meadows after three o'clock to request assistance, and Meadows called Christopher Miller, the acting secretary of defense—but, in the telling, this almost immediately became a blur of responsibility: the Park Police, the Metropolitan Police, the Capitol Police, the Secret Service. The White House certainly took no leadership role.

Ivanka wasn't casting off the protestors entirely—here was the base. "American Patriots," she addressed them directly in a tweet at 3:40, which she would shortly delete, "any security breach or disrespect to our law enforcement is unacceptable. The violence must stop immediately. Please be peaceful."

The debate about putting the president out there to say something—something calming—continued for as much as an hour.

There were three views : that he must, as fast as possible, say something—it was getting serious (though no one yet was seeing this as the defining moments of his presidency); his view, that he should say nothing—it was not his fault or responsibility, and he certainly didn't want to give a speech that might imply it was; and, lastly, that anything he said, instead of helping to address the problem, might well, as it did when he was forced to make a speech condemning the racist protestors in Charlottesville, make matters much worse.

After Charlottesville, something of a dress rehearsal for the Capitol onslaught, Jared and Ivanka had urged a conciliatory, kinder-gentler approach to the president, but a furious Trump had broken his bonds with them and made common cause with the Charlottesville attackers—"very fine people on both sides."

This now was a vast multiple of Charlottesville. Or at least it was starting to sink in that this is where they were.

Meadows, who had come into the chief of staff job seeing himself as an especially communication-gifted politician, blaming much of the Trump woes on the White House's dysfunctional comms shop and vowing to get it into shape, seemed uniquely paralyzed—trying to answer both to Trump and to the real world—just at the moment when the demands to hear from the president were highest.

Aides put in front of the president two suggested tweets, written in Trump's voice, that they hoped he might accept:

Bad apples, like ANTIFA or other crazed leftists, infiltrated today's peaceful protest over the fraudulent vote count. Violence is never acceptable! MAGA supporters embrace our police and the rule of law and should leave the Capitol now!

The fake news media who encouraged this summer's violent and radical riots are now trying to blame peaceful and innocent MAGA supporters for violent actions. This isn't who we are! Our people should head home and let the criminals suffer the consequences!

He refused them or ignored them (other than Dan Scavino, Trump didn't like anyone else writing his tweets).

The challenge now became how to use Trump's own arguments to convince him that he had to do something—what passed for the Socratic method in the Trump White House. He had often said what he needed to say, so just say it again: He and the Republican Party represented law and order, so how could he not speak out about lawlessness? He should just urge his people, the good people, to go home and leave the bad people.

Still, he did not see the necessity of speaking out. It wasn't as bad as the media were saying it was. People were saying it was bad just to blame it on him. It took thirty-five minutes from his "Stay Peaceful" tweet to get him to go further—with Scavino as the author:

I am asking for everyone at the U.S. Capitol to remain peaceful. No violence! Remember, WE are the Party of Law & Order—respect the Law and our great men and women in Blue. Thank you!

But almost every stage of the panicked response, and of everybody's push to get him to understand the urgency here, prompted the same reactions from him: Denial—this wasn't on him; he couldn't control what people did; why couldn't his people protest; it was mostly

Antifa. Begrudging capitulation—he shouldn't be blamed, but, okay, he'd say something. Fighting back—why should he say anything? People were upset. The election had been stolen from him and them.

The entire election narrative was quickly being transformed: the Capitol was under siege; the "steal" was moot. But Trump remained fixed in his obsession: the election had been taken from him, and whatever happened, someone had to give it back; he could not see or think or imagine beyond this.

By 3:30 p.m., he was telling callers that, yes, he had decided to say something. He was going to speak. But he was still repeating that the election had been stolen and was seeking assurances from each caller that the protests were overblown—that it was mostly a peaceful protest, wasn't it?

A video became the plan, the safest sort of statement, with everyone in agreement: the president couldn't go live.

But back in his overcoat out on the portico, even with a script in hand, he mostly defaulted to his worst instincts:

> I know your pain. I know your hurt. We had an election stolen from us. It was a landslide election, and everyone knows it. Especially the other side. But you have to go home now. We have to have peace. We have to have law and order. We have to respect our great people in law and order. We don't want anybody hurt. It's a very tough period of time. There's never been a time like this where such a thing happened where they could take it away from all of us. From me. From you. From our country. This was a fraudulent election. But we can't play into the hands of these people. We have to have peace. So, go home. We love you. You're very special. You've seen what happens. You've seen the way others are treated. They are so bad and so evil. I know how you feel. But go home and go home in peace.

Kushner, having landed at about 4 p.m., back from the Middle East, concurred on the statement.

At 4:17 p.m., now with little question that the singular event of the Trump administration was unfolding, the president tweeted out his video with his begrudging call that the rioters go home.

* * *

Who were these people?

Every one of the people yet in the White House and those who had slipped out, along with the president's large traveling retinue, his family, the many members of Congress seeking photo ops with him, and the legions of favor seekers, had all been at rally after rally and, over and over again, had seen vivid demonstrations of the exotic, self-dramatizing, out-from-under-a-rock Trump fan base. But now, to a person, to a political professional, they were dumbfounded and awestruck—revulsion competing with incomprehension.

Even Trump himself, the clearest channel through to this fan base, seemed confused.

In part, the radically faithful had been concentrated. The merely eager party types, and the Las Vegas audience sorts, and the local business proprietors, and the family-outing Republicans, and the VFW Post members, and various church groups, the salt of the Republican earth, more or less in normal dress, all had mostly self-selected out, leaving what was generally, if abstractly, referred to in the Trump circle as the "hard core." But no one had ever come so clearly face-to-face with this pure hard core as was happening now and would happen, in video footage and in indictments, in the weeks to come.

In some sense, all the currents of the conservative movement— its way of life, its power structure, its institutional identity, its carefully assembled philosophy—had been custom-designed to avoid this moment. The weirdos and misfits; the extremists; the apocalyptic people; the paranoids; the conspiracy believers; the embattled remnants of an active racist world; the followers of Robert Welch, the John Birch Society founder; and the admirers of James B. Utt, the congressman and racist from California's Orange County (what

Fortune magazine in 1968 called American's "nut country"); and generals like Curtis LeMay, a face of the right wing in the 1950s and '60s, ready to nuke whoever back to the Stone Age—all these had been for so long sanitized out of the conservative movement. The currents of William F. Buckley Jr. (via Edmund Burke), corporate leadership, Richard Nixon realpolitik, Ronald Reagan morning-in-America politics, upwardly mobile capitalism, family values, and megachurch institutional conservatism had taken over. But now, it turned out, the real right wing had not gone away at all, but, apparently, flourished unseen, becoming ever more baroque, ecstatic, and as far from the bourgeois world as it was possible to get.

The most immediate issue was that no one, at least not in this up-close moment, was going to defend them—nobody employed in the Republican and conservative firmament. Indeed, the cadres were threatening to behead one of the leading representatives of faith-based, institutional, sanitized-to-the-point-of-blandness modern conservatism: Vice President Mike Pence!

This left the hard core with a singular point of political identification: Donald Trump. And it left Trump, at that moment, with, to every man and woman around him, the most horrifying development of his short political career: his singular connection to them.

And to make matters worse, of course, at 6:01 p.m., he tweeted:

These are the things and events that happen when a sacred landslide election victory is so unceremoniously & viciously stripped away from great patriots who have been badly & unfairly treated for so long. Go home with love & in peace. Remember this day forever!

* * *

But as he went upstairs to the Residence, he seemed, said some of the people talking to him there by phone, at a terrible loss. The monologue slowed and seemed even to cease, with a few people not even sure that this otherwise-unstoppable monologist was still on the line.

At about this time, Scavino told Trump that he had been booted off Twitter—still, a temporary suspension. For more than four years, he'd been told that this was always a possibility, and every time, he'd responded that Twitter needed him more than he needed it.

The doubtless president was, at least for a moment, someone else. "I don't know what to do here," he said to one caller not long after 7 p.m., as stark a sense of uncertainty and even crisis as the caller had ever heard the president express.

The notable thing is that he seemed to have finally recognized that the main event, the certification of the electoral votes, was now far from the main event. He may even have realized that after sixty-four days of struggle it was over.

One daily caller noted that this was the first call in weeks in which the president had not rehashed some details of his stolen election.

At 8 p.m., the Capitol was declared secure.

The vice president, McConnell, and the Democratic leaders Nancy Pelosi and Chuck Schumer were all in agreement that Congress continue that night with the electoral count, that it could not delay the certification of the new president. At about 8:30 p.m., the group spoke to Meadows in the White House—the vice president and congressional leaders relaying their decision to proceed; Meadows, while not advocating a delay, but yet standing between the president and the rest of the world, focused on the security issues and safety concerns.

Minutes later, the vice president reconvened the Senate, returning to where the session had left off, each chamber taking up the challenge to the Arizona vote.

* * *

Jason Miller, at home in Arlington, was trying to block it out—the day had already made a hash of his daughter's birthday.

He was waiting for someone else to deal with it, expecting a call, as he lay stupefied in bed with his wife, watching the video loops of the day over and over again and hoping there was a plan. But no one called. Congress was returning through the chaos. Despite everything, Biden would be declared the president tonight. How would the president respond? Still no one called. Miller considered just trying to shut his eyes and go to sleep.

At 9 p.m., he got out of bed, opened his laptop, and started to write a statement. A statement—the considered language of politics, the true mandarin's language—was the indication of ongoing business. What would silence mean?

It would leave the Trump White House on the side of chaos. They were not the government; they were the disruptors of government. Without a statement, there might truly be anarchy.

The Trump White House was the story of impolitic, incendiary, and disruptive language overriding officialese. The president considered this to be part not only of his tactical arsenal, but of his charm. Arguably, its result was now in the street. Now what was needed was to override that language, to override Trump's voice with an official government voice.

This meant doing what Trump had refused to do for the past sixty-four days: acknowledge that Joe Biden would be the inevitable president. Trump's feelings left open-ended, his denial left in place, his refusal to accept the new president—all these might well mean that the violence could go on longer and spread farther. At nine o'clock that evening, it was far from out of the question to imagine Trump's irregulars—intuiting his rage, resentment, and need—fighting through to January 20 and beyond.

But there was not going to be an abject or contrite Trump, or even a formally defeated one. It was necessary to skip over the fairness of the election and to skip over the Trump-told narrative—the election in his mind would remain stolen, forever stolen. This statement could certainly not be the official, belated concession—at least not to Trump—but it had to establish acceptance, a fait accompli, and put Trump's stamp on the new, if disagreeable, reality.

Miller was trying to get the headline, the chyron roll: the message from Trump that something had changed.

Orderly transition.

Not exactly the torch passing, and hardly a round of applause for democracy in action.

That was as far as the president could be moved. But it would work, if Trump acknowledged the importance and primacy of an "orderly transition."

Satisfied that he had navigated around what Trump would not say and had reached the reasonable minimum of what had to be said, he called Kushner and read him the draft.

"Will you call the president?" Kushner smoothly pushed Miller into the fray.

Miller called Meadows, still in the West Wing, and then the president. The president seemed eager to hear from Miller, eager to be on the phone. Most often for Trump, the phone was a one-way instrument: callers listened.

"How bad is this?" Trump asked, a stark difference from his usual opener, "How are we doing?"—which was not, mostly, a question at all, but a preface to Trump's saying how well everything was going.

"Mr. President, today is literally going to change everything."

"This looks terrible. This is really bad. Who are these people? These aren't our people, these idiots with these outfits. They look like Democrats. Hold on, our great First Lady is here," said Trump, switching to speakerphone—his overblown public language seemingly his private language, too. (He did not necessarily reserve "great" for only the First Lady but often applied it to whomever he was with.)

"Jason," said the great First Lady with a sharp note. "The media is trying to go and say this is who we are. We don't support this."

"That's what we have to make clear," said Miller, relieved that the president and First Lady were seeing the protestors as bad guys rather than good guys (and not a mix of the two). Pushing through, Miller told the president and First Lady that he had just gotten off the phone with Kushner and Meadows and that they had a proposal for later that evening if Biden reached an electoral majority. He went into reading the statement draft.

The president suggested "peaceful" transition instead of "orderly." Miller said that that called attention to the fact that it wasn't peaceful now and might not be peaceful. "Orderly," Miller did not say, suggested not just an absence of disruption, but that all the aspects of government would pass, as they should, to a new administration. "Peaceful" put it in someone else's hand; "orderly" meant cooperation, too—the Trump White House would cooperate with the incoming Biden White House. It wasn't just the protestors who needed to stop; Trump needed to extend himself, too. After all, it wasn't just the recount effort and the election challenge behind the protests, but Trump's personal intransigence.

Trump seemed to appreciate this now, to walk back, even. "The media thinks I'm not going to leave," said the president. "Do they really think that? That's crazy."

"We've never laid that out," said Miller, with some deadpan, adding, "I really can't stress enough how much we have to make it clear that we're fully on board with an orderly transition."

"We didn't tell people to do something like this. We told people to be peaceful. I even said 'peaceful' and 'patriotic' in my speech!"

"Exactly." Miller took note that there weren't the usual peaks and valleys of a conversation with Trump—the declaiming insistence on whatever point he was insisting on and the digressions to something off point.

"I'll work with Dan on getting this out," Miller told the president. Saying this, Miller suddenly wondered if they would even have the tools and channels to get it out.

Miller immediately reached a furious Scavino. "They are shutting us down. They are not letting us on. We're being deplatformed. They are completely deplatforming the president of the United States. They don't want him to say anything ever again." Facebook had pushed the president off at 8:36 p.m.

Miller and Scavino debated about getting the statement out when Biden reached 270 votes or when the full electoral count was finished. But Scavino, next to only Trump himself a kind of direct-messaging link to Trump's base, held out for letting the Republicans in Congress make their case. Miller thought they needed to immediately greet the moment when Biden achieved the threshold number.

Kushner, looped in, wanted to move even sooner. He was worried that if they waited even until the 270 point, the media's undoubtedly preferred narrative of the bitter, implacable, and unaccommodating president would already be written into everybody's stories. So, Miller started to make his calls, giving out the "orderly transition" statement, embargoed until the final vote.

Every call—to the wires, networks, and major dailies—yielded variations on the same question: When are we going to hear directly from the president? When is he going to come and talk about it? When is he going to stand in front of us and in front of the American people?

For Miller and Kushner, this was merely an invitation from the media for Trump to self-immolate further.

Catching up, Miller—not yet aware that the vice president had earlier been held as a virtual hostage in the Capitol, with the mob quite literally screaming for his head—called Marc Short to let him know that a statement would go out. A disgusted Short blew him off, curtly ending the call. Short was finished with the Trump White House.

As Miller and Scavino continued calling each other throughout the night to stay awake, as the vote dragged on, they both realized that there was no one else to call. Everybody else in the press arm of the White House or the campaign was AWOL.

This is over, Miller thought. *This is the end of the road.*

Scavino could use only his personal Twitter account to finally, at 3:49 a.m., get out the president's statement.

Of all the news outlets, Miller realized in the confusion, only Fox had never gotten back to him. Even Fox, Miller accepted—perhaps Fox most of all—was truly over Trump in a most monumental sort of way.

11

DEPLATFORMED

The story popped a couple of minutes before 11 a.m. on January 7: Facebook was blocking the president until at least the end of his term. Scavino's accounts were blocked, too.

Everybody was off television. This was now both an official White House and campaign blackout and a personally imposed one—nobody could offer a January 6 defense. The networks were wary, too: any administration voice might likely be a bilious and inciteful one.

There was silence. Nearly all communications in Trumpworld dropped to, at best, a whisper. One yet-loyal staffer, accustomed to fielding many hundreds of messages a day, received only a single email on the seventh.

The specter that the Trump administration might somehow prevent the Biden administration from taking power had now quite reversed itself. Its final two weeks had been taken from it. There was, practically speaking, no Trump administration left, certainly not one capable of any action.

Meadows came in late on the seventh. Molly Michael, the president's assistant, was in. So were the Secret Service agents. And Dan

Scavino. But there were not more than a handful of other staffers in the West Wing.

Several midlevel staffers had a back-and-forth with one another from their homes, conferring on how they might adjust their résumés to reference White House work but not specifically that it was work for Donald Trump or even for the Trump White House—yes, and about getting Trump's name off their social media bios.

The shared experience of most staffers—those still on the payroll and those who had, in the preceding weeks, quietly slipped out the back—was to watch over and over again the same video clips. All of them, accustomed to seeing this presidency through the television, were riveted to this new view of it and now seeing their own fates in it. The eternal back-and-forth over what Trump's actions might mean for the Trump White House, or for the Republican Party, or for the base, had profoundly shifted to what they might mean personally for everyone associated with him. Now everybody was going to get canceled.

The president, though, in suit and shiny solid-color tie, was still tucked in behind the Resolute desk. For a man, an 11–6 man, who liked to be out of the office, he was close to the last man left in it.

Kushner came in late on the seventh. Having largely missed the debacle—when the going got tough, Jared was nowhere to be found—he returned to his role as the adult in the room. Time for damage control, if a day late and a dollar short. It was Kushner, as he had in other crises, trying to force an awkward rewrite. Never able to specifically confront his father-in-law, Kushner depended on these vacuum moments—those rare occasions when the president was caught speechless, which never lasted very long—to rush in with something like conventional reason and wisdom.

A script was hammered out, overriding the president who otherwise wasn't changing his tune: "The election was stolen—incredible anger about people having their election stolen. Fraud like you won't

believe. Focus on that!" he repeated almost word for word to everyone he spoke to. But whereas he was usually the only voice in the
room, now, however briefly, he was reduced to a lonely voice without anyone truly listening to him.

The script was handed to him in the Oval Office, and he walked
to the East Room to deliver it. It was a body-double speech in a two-
minute, forty-one-second video clip:

> I am outraged by the violence, lawlessness, and mayhem. I immedi-
> ately deployed the National Guard and federal law enforcement to
> secure the building and expel the intruders. America is and must
> always be a nation of law and order.

This was not true, that he had immediately called in the National
Guard, but it had become certain in his mind that he had.

> The demonstrators who infiltrated the Capitol have defiled the seat
> of American democracy. To those who engaged in the acts of violence
> and destruction, you do not represent our country. And to those who
> broke the law, you will pay . . .
>
> My campaign vigorously pursued every legal avenue to contest
> the election results. My only goal was to ensure the integrity of the
> vote. In so doing, I was fighting to defend American democracy. I
> continue to strongly believe that we must reform our election laws to
> verify the identity and eligibility of all voters and to ensure faith and
> confidence in all future elections.
>
> Now Congress has certified the results. A new administration will
> be inaugurated on January twentieth. My focus now turns to ensur-
> ing a smooth, orderly and seamless transition of power.

Here it was again: "orderly."

These were perhaps the bitterest words he had ever had to speak,
and this moment was the nadir of his presidency—not because he

had been shamed by or forced to account for events, but because, at virtual gunpoint, he had been made to capitulate and, finally, concede.

Still, with his strange prescience and intuitive finger in the wind, he had nonetheless slipped into his speech a new political cry, a new flag—like birtherism, like building a wall, like China, like fake news, like taking a knee. America had a broken and corrupt election system that was robbing people, his people, of their vote and their choice of leaders. Of *him*.

* * *

At 10:44 a.m., on January 8, in his last tweet as president—his Twitter account forthwith suspended, followed shortly thereafter by a permanent ban—he announced that he would not be attending Joe Biden's inauguration, joining only three other presidents who skipped their successor's swearing in, the last being Andrew Johnson in 1869.

This was in some sense an effort to exercise his remaining power, the opposite of capitulation: "Why would I want to fucking go? They just want to attack me on TV. *Isn't it so great they got rid of Trump and brought in Biden?*" This last said in a mincing, mocking, mimicking voice.

In the media view, this was him expressing further contempt for Biden and casting doubts on his successor's legitimacy, a manifold and historic (and destructive) sour grapes.

His daughter and wife wanted him to go, but Kushner and the remaining staff felt there was little point in pushing him—there was, of course, little point in pushing a resistant Trump to do anything.

But this was all, really, just wishfulness on Trump's part, a failure of the media to read the larger room, and a willful effort by family and staff to believe in some possible normalcy. The greater truth here was that he wasn't wanted. His absence was no longer seen as a snub but as a godsend. Nobody, no Democrats, no Republicans, believed he could have gone and stood there with the new president without visibly and noisomely expressing himself—indeed, without claiming unwarranted attention for himself. His attendance would not have accorded more legitimacy to Biden, but it would, at this point, have accorded more legitimacy to himself—and no one, no Democrats certainly, but include here quite a few Republicans, wanted that.

In historic terms, his not attending his successor's inauguration should more properly be seen as his being the first sitting president not invited.

The vice president, in another offense to the president, announced he was going. That, the president decided, was more of Marc Short's doing. He blamed Marc Short for the vice president's betrayal in the electoral count. And now, egged on by Peter Navarro, he banned Short from the White House—literally barring him from the premises (not that Short, like so many others, necessarily wanted to come back in).

* * *

Those in the West Wing who hadn't yet escaped, compelled by loyalty or entropy, started to drift back in quotidian fashion on the eighth.

There was now an elephant in the room, with little or no possibility of discussing of what had happened two days before. Partly, this was simply from long practice. Trump events, Trump explosions, happened and then passed. (The world might find itself with a collective exploding head, but inside Trumpworld, moving on and doing so quickly was what you did—there was always something next.) And partly, there was the sense that, different this time, the humiliation, different from other humiliations, was simply too great to address.

Kushner called a meeting in his office to schedule the remaining days—they had a week and a half left. Again, this was seen as part of his weird pretense that, despite everything, he lived in a normal world. Hence, let's take a valedictory moment. Or, it was see-no-evil, hear-no-evil Jared, a militant compartmentalization.

The formal, if futile, point was to underline the administration's accomplishments—here was their legacy. China, the border, the American worker, prison reform, Middle East peace . . . They ought to come up with events and photo opportunities to memorialize these signature efforts and achievements. At the same time, the small group acknowledged the remote likelihood that Trump would want to do any of this.

In fact, though, he was suddenly interested—or, finding himself, perhaps for the first time in four years, in an empty Oval Office, was merely looking for company. He sent Molly Michael down to Jared's office to move the meeting to the Oval Office.

It was a strangely quiet, even eerie scene outside the Oval. Otherwise, it was constant lurkers: serial lurkers like Peter Navarro, as if always posted at the door; a lineup of aides and random visitors—it was unclear how many of them got in the building. There was always quite a town-square mood, or perhaps an eighteenth-century-court feel akin to the anteroom outside the king's chambers. In the two months after the election, it had been the many irregular lawyers hanging around outside. Now: nobody. There was a renewed and concerted effort to keep a still-manic Rudy out.

But Trump, as ever in a red tie, was crammed in behind the desk.

Without personal reflection, without (most believed) the capacity for it on nearly any level, he never much reacted in different or revealing ways. Mercurial, yes, but, oddly, extremely reliable. He swam in one direction. He yelled. He joked. He monologue-ized. He talked. Others listened. Indeed, he held court as the sun god, seeing the center of the world as his immediate circle. That was the nature of the Trump Oval Office: a man amid his admirers, flunkies, courtiers, relatives, with no restraints on his ability to bore, taunt, digress, or monopolize others' time.

So, now, this moment—being alone, having to seek company—
was out of the ordinary. He sat behind the desk with his arms crossed.
He was listening, ready to listen to aides now confused that they were
expected to do the talking.

Here was the thing, the vibe that everybody had picked up: he
was not sure what to do next.

Time, Trump time, had stopped.

The force that had propelled him since Election Day, the grievance, the impossibility of having lost (in his mind) the stolen election had, for the moment at least, died away. This was to everyone's
relief, and yet now there was a different kind of concern: What
was he feeling, and how deep did anyone *really* want to go into
Trump's psyche?

There were calls for the vice president to act to remove him under
the Twenty-Fifth Amendment—but that wasn't serious, was it?

"That doesn't have any chance," said Kushner, perhaps, tonally,
taking the idea too seriously.

The president prompted a discussion about the mounting calls for
a new impeachment—a second impeachment!

Impeachment was head scratching. Why would you remove
someone from office who was to be gone in days? The Democrats
could of course be counted on to react in their hatred both wildly
and predictably, but this was kind of *what the fuck*.

"Is this real?" Trump asked. "Really?"

Everyone seemed uncertain and generally as dubious about this
as a practical tactic as Trump.

"Well, is this good for us or bad?"

Indeed, there was some confusion here. There was, at this moment
in the Trump administration, nothing positive, nothing optimistic
at all. Except, it was hard to believe that, at just the point when
Trump could fall no further, the Democrats and the media, in one
of the weirdest reflexes in modern politics, might once again turn
themselves into bullies and Trump into a victim. No one here, or

anyone close to him, could say how he had continually been able to save himself—because maybe he hadn't. Rather, it was the strong belief, an awe-filled one, that it was the Democrats who were always saving Donald Trump.

The plan, then, was to get a poll out as soon as possible and ask the impeachment question. Everybody, putting the sixth behind them, was sure that this would be good news.

Impeachment!

Anyway, it was something to do.

And anyway, it was Friday. Thank God it was Friday, after the worst week in the history of the Trump presidency—losing the Senate, failing in an Electoral College showdown, the Capitol attack, impeachment on the agenda, *again*. In fact, it was the worst week in the history of *any* presidency.

* * *

The impeachment survey went into the field on the tenth and eleventh in key swing states.

Meanwhile, there were two days when, for the first time, there seemed to exist the actual possibility that the Republicans would break against Donald Trump. At least, this was the hoped-for story the un-Trump media was telling. Here was an old-fashioned ending: downfall.

This is how American politics is written—liberals prevail.

In the end, everybody deserted Nixon.

It was rats off the Trump ship: Betsy DeVos, the education secretary; Elaine Chao, transportation secretary (and the wife of Mitch McConnell); Chad Wolf, acting secretary of homeland security; Mick Mulvaney, the president's former chief of staff and now special envoy for Northern Ireland; Matthew Pottinger, the deputy national security advisor; Tyler Goodspeed, the acting chairman of the Council of Economic Advisors; Stephanie Grisham, chief of staff and press secretary to the First Lady; Sarah Matthews, White

House deputy press secretary; Rickie Niceta Lloyd, the White House social secretary, and the list continued, all those on it issuing chest-beating letters of resignation.

Alyssa Farah, the White House comms director and a Meadows protégée, had abandoned the White House in early December, judging the election challenge futile. (She was shortly identified as interviewing TV agents for a hoped-for on-air career.) She now returned to the air to burnish her I-got-out-early credentials. In hits on CNN, Fox, and MSNBC on the eighth, she said the president had always known he lost the election; he had lied to the American people; he should resign from office. Among all the bad news coming at Trump, among the harshest was his being attacked on television by his own people.

Jenna Ellis sent in her resignation and asked that it be dated a week before January 6.

Meanwhile, the remaining staff was trying to get the usual Trump defenders on television, but in a case of remarkable coincidence, almost the entire list was unavailable—making the *Access Hollywood* weekend, heretofore the greatest flight from Donald Trump, look something like a celebration of him in comparison. Everybody's career and future seemed at that moment to be imperiled by their connection to Donald Trump.

McConnell let it be known that he might finally turn on the president. Otherwise a hated figure in the liberal media, McConnell was now given seen-the-light kudos. Behind closed doors, or perhaps strategically half-open ones, McConnell, famously tight-lipped, was venting his true revulsion and taste for revenge. He was talking humiliation, ignominy, and criminal conviction for the soon-to-be former president.

The House would impeach; McConnell, holding enough votes in his hand to shift the Republican balance, would push to convict. Then they would further vote to strip Trump of his right to hold office ever again. After that, let the prosecutors have him. The

Republican Party would be done with him and saved. At least that's
what the liberal media was saying. It was practically over.

More immediately, McConnell was holding Trump's feet near the
fire. Even the president himself, quite loathing Mitch as much as
Mitch loathed him, got this. If he stepped out of line in the next
ten days, Mitch could well and truly blow him up. Or at least they'd
be playing chicken to the end. Jared cautioned Trump about Mitch.
Warnings about Mitch's sudden-death power over the president were
useful to Kushner, who was also seeking to keep his father-in-law
under lock and key.

Amid discussions about the Twenty-Fifth Amendment, under
which the vice president and cabinet might strip the president of
his powers, Trump met with the vice president—groveled even a
bit. Marc Short, the president said, was not really banned from the
White House. He should swing by, Trump told Pence.

Of all the other times when Trump had appeared neatly boxed in,
it now seemed that, after all his other assaults, he had finally found a
way to offend a broad American morality, and there was no getting out
of it this time. January 6 was an offense that might define a new right
of center, where the McConnell-led party could gather against him.

More than at any other point when he seemed to have committed a fatal offense—attacking Gold Star parents, bragging about
assaulting women, coddling Russia, extorting Ukraine's president,
threatening a democratic election, all just the tip of his constant
daily offenses—this one was going to nail him. He really had no
more lives left.

But when the impeachment poll came back, it confirmed his inexplicable but overwhelming support in the party. Virtually no Republican wanted him impeached; nobody even held him responsible. The
party—whoever the party was, out there somewhere—had hardly even
had a hiccup in its awe and devotion. There was almost a palpable shift
back. Republicans in Washington had been indulging a sense of a new
political elasticity, a new free-floating change in the political ether, a

Prague Spring—when in fact, delivered with a rude slap and abrupt comeuppance, there'd been no change at all. It was still a Trump world.

It was not for the first time that a Trump poll was almost magically at odds with events, or at least with the way the media portrayed events. The moral forces of rectitude and conventionality that had seemed to surround and condemn the president since January 6 were, at the very least, held in check by the countervailing righteousness of the president's broad piece of the electorate, who indeed believed the election had been stolen from him.

Mitch was not going to move against the president. The poll showed, once again, how laughably out of touch McConnell was with his own party and the nation—or, at least, half the nation.

The president, previously subdued, went back to his litany of election abuses—quite as though it were a fresh, new idea.

* * *

Kushner had started trying to put a meeting on the calendar since early in December: the post-presidency organization and agenda meeting. That had been difficult because there was not yet going to be a post-presidency, and it was impermissible to suggest as much. The meeting had been scheduled again just before Christmas and put off once more.

After January 6, Jared put it on again. Now it was disciplinary— there *would* be a post-presidency, and it was almost here. It was also what Jared called, in his repeated efforts to impose a sense of businesslike procedures—or, as some accused him, business-advice-book procedures—"landing the plane."

Something else was also suspected: Jared needed a plan in place around the president—soon-to-be-former president—lest the post-presidency fall on him. Filling his father-in-law's days, setting up his office, being the point man for . . . well, for what was unclear.

In some sense, a deplatformed former president with literally nothing to do and no way to express himself was more alarming for those close to him than a fully disruptive former president. What was Trump if he was not able to be Trump, and who would take on that burden?

The Kushner family was going to move to Florida; it was clear that exile from New York was going to be required. But Jared and Ivanka were going out of their way not to be too close to Palm Beach and the president (the soon-to-be *former* president).

Trump needed to be able to call *someone*.

The thrice-moved meeting was held on the morning of the twelfth—eight days from the end of his term. This was one day before the vote on his second impeachment in the House. That afternoon would be Trump's penultimate trip as president before flying into the sunset—a trip to the Texas border, a photo op memorializing one of the most contentious and yet defining issues of his presidency.

But first, and finally, the meeting about Donald Trump's future.

It was held in the small dining room down from the Oval, something of an overflow room for unframed photos of the president and White House gatherings ready to be reviewed or signed and sent out; and a library of hagiographic books written about the president—his former press secretary Sean Spicer's admiring memoir; Dave Bossie and Corey Lewandowski's two books about the various conspiracies to destroy the president; Fox and right-wing radio personality Mark Levin's Trump manifesto book; and a book by John Yoo, Republican lawyer and author of the Bush administration's pro-torture memo. They had all called on the president and left a book (sometimes many) behind.

The president sat at the end of the table, facing the television screen, watching OAN.

It was Bill Stepien, Jason Miller, and Brian Jack (up for a job with the House Republican leader Kevin McCarthy—but worried that it might be dashed because of January 6) at the table, the remaining brain trust, such as it was—with Jared popping into the room but otherwise careful not to be running the meeting or owning the problem. In fact, Stepien and Jack had not been around in weeks, and Jack was a late addition, recruited mainly to fill out the table.

Miller was there, held in place by both stalwart loyalty and his domestic situation—unlikely to be hired elsewhere with the continuing barrage of his former lover's militant and indefatigable tweets.

It was a sheepish meeting, with Stepien and Jack not quite sure the president had noticed their absence and not quite sure they should acknowledge the basic changes, to say the least, in the political dynamic since they last spoke.

"It might be an awkward time to chat about this now," Stepien began, with the president clearly not acknowledging the awkwardness.

Indeed, the president kept looking away to watch specific clips on OAN.

"You're sticking around, right?" He turned toward the three men.

This, too, gave a kind of odd sense that all things were continuing as before. But, yes, everyone agreed, they were sticking around, while at the same time having no clear purpose to stick around for, even if they had actually wanted to stick around.

It was a complicated dance because it seemed clear, or everyone clearly understood, that while the agenda was to plan for the post-presidency, you could not talk about Trump's not being president. The segue was instead into some further station of importance, influence, and power. Nothing diminished here.

Stepien had come prepared with PowerPoint printouts, but he seemed also careful not to lead the conversation, not to want the president to expect him to lead anything, to speak only when spoken to.

That is, the president was being humored.

And yet, too, all these men knew that much of what went on around Donald Trump at any given time was in part to humor him. Of course, such efforts to go along passively with or cater to him often took on a life of their own—so, these men proceeded carefully and hesitantly, treading lightly lest their willingness to humor him led where none of them necessarily wanted to go.

Nobody could yet imagine a post-Trump Trumpworld, either as a joke or as a new dimension in American political life.

The president, for his part, had no doubt that he would be left with control of the Republican Party. A little-known campaign feature was a series of conference calls—his "TeleRallies"—nearly sixty of them that had been set up in various congressional districts during the campaign season. These calls, promoted through the Trump list, attracted anywhere from five thousand to as many as forty thousand people, with the president dialing in to speak for five or ten minutes (or, of course, sometimes longer). This was, in his mind, the unbeatable advantage—only he could attract these kinds of numbers, and these numbers were what tipped the races. He blamed the failure to recapture the House on the failure of the NRCC, the Republican House campaign arm, and of House leader Kevin McCarthy to give him more races to swing.

"We won every one of them." He now reprised his somewhat inflated recollection for the three men.

Stepien outlined some of what they had done in the past with endorsements and how they might continue to do that now, laying out the process they had used to decide on who would get his support. Here was one of the things that the president most liked to do: hold people's fate in his hands, to reward friends and punish enemies, because whoever was endorsed paid this back not just in strict political loyalty but also with abject flattery.

Stepien's PowerPoint bulleted the House and Senate members who appeared to favor impeachment. This, in the post-presidency (or the don't-mention-that-it-is-post-presidency) was mission critical, to punish the faithless.

Trump came particularly back to Governor Brian Kemp, in Georgia, because much of how he saw his own future was in destroying Kemp's future. (In the ensuing days, he would add more such off-with-their-heads figures; it was not enough that he should live, but that they should die.)

It wasn't that different from any political discussion in Trump's White House: identifying allies and their level of devotion and enemies and their level of perfidy (pausing to tune up the television for a moment's distraction). Surreal in how normal it was.

As if January 6 hadn't changed anything.

"We can do it again," he pronounced. And then he rephrased it as a question that he had already answered: "Do you think we can do it again?" And he added: "There's nobody else."

Yes, everything continued. Everything could continue.

He was back in the driver's seat. He was questioning his campaign manager, pushing him, looking for confirmation.

Although, and this was not necessarily a departure from the past, there was still no actual battle plan, or budget, or structure—nor, in the end, was there a person to call.

* * *

Miller, still technically working for the campaign, left the White House to drive home to Arlington, while the president and his diminished party left for the round trip to Texas and remarks and a photo op at the border wall.

On the way, he took a call from Kushner.

"Can you reach out," Kushner asked, "and see if we can get some coverage for this event from the networks?"

"I'm in the car," Miller told Kushner. "Isn't there someone in the White House comms shop who can make these calls? This is an official trip, not a campaign trip."

"In fact, there isn't," said a plaintive Kushner. "Nobody. There's really nobody left."

Miller pulled to the side of the road and texted each of the networks. Only MSNBC bit, and they wouldn't consider live coverage

without an advance copy of the president's remarks and a pledge that
he would stick to them. Nobody was about to trust an off-script Trump.

* * *

On the fifteenth, there was a brief press kerfuffle when Mike Lindell, the MyPillow CEO, showed up for a meeting with the president, and reporters caught sight of notes he'd written on a yellow
legal pad that might suggest he was advising the president on a declaration of martial law.

The bedding pitchman and former cocaine and gambling addict
as a coup plotter was the kind of preposterousness that Trumpers
judged unfair for the press to take so seriously. There would of course
be no MyPillow coup. But the truer point was that Trump would
entertain almost anyone farther out and more abject in his or her
belief in the extreme than he was. It was a contrast that may have
reinforced his own sense of sanity, leaving him as a voice of mod-
eration.

It was, too, another perk of the White House. Where in other
White Houses who the president saw was closely vetted, Trump
often used the Oval Office for its fanciful possibilities—he could
invite in anyone he wanted, could divert, distract, or occupy himself with any suggestion or unconventional thought under the sun,
including, however briefly, martial law.

It was something he would miss: that any course of action he
could think of or any proposal made to him was, because he was president, at least nearly possible, even if not truly possible.

* * *

Pardons were a power that from the beginning of his term had particularly excited him because they represented unlimited power.
He could simply pardon anyone he wanted to pardon. On his own
say-so. But now they had become quite a bother—too many pardon
possibilities, too many details, too many people—and the finality

annoyed him: he needed to pardon people now because there would be no chance to pardon them later.

The traditional system of pardon recommendations coming through the White House Counsel's Office—a system through which the Obama administration issued far more pardons than the Trump administration free-for-all ever would, almost 2,000 grants of clemency to Trump's 238—suffered as all systems suffered in the Trump White House and because Trump had long dismissed the Counsel's Office as not doing enough for him.

The pardon process therefore became a function of getting his attention, never easy for something not already on his mind or not primarily related to him; or of working through Kushner, who appeared to have the unilateral ability to exercise the pardon power; or of working through the handful of people still around Trump who might, just might, have the opportunity to slip somebody in.

Trumpworld was now specifically focused on this. Everybody had a client—Matt Schlapp, the CPAC impresario, would make $750,000 for advocating a pardon for Georgia-based Trump fundraiser Parker "Pete" Petit, convicted of securities fraud. (He didn't get it; it was a wasted $750,000.)

Indeed, since the election, and with the knowledge that these were now the countdown days, pardons had become something of a Trump cottage industry. The Counsel's Office and other aides gave up trying to police the paid advocates from those trying to do what they thought was a good deed.

Matt Gaetz, the Dead-Ender congressman from Florida, who had been so slavish in his support for Trump and so out-front, if not complicit, in his January 6 participation, now sought broad immunity for not just his actions then but—given, he argued, the deep state's overreach—something close to all crimes ever. And not just for himself, but for a catchall of Dead-Enders whom the deep state might choose to pursue. As it happened, Gaetz, who failed to get his anticipatory pardon, was, at that moment—not yet publicly known, but of which he was well aware—under investigation for sex and drug charges, including allegations of sex with a minor. Indeed, Meadows, Cipollone, and Herschmann were trying to steer Gaetz away from the president. (After the Gaetz investigation was revealed, Trump, to the eye rolls of aides, would deny that Gaetz had ever sought a pardon.)

Bored by the process and the details, Trump nevertheless, in the last week, would trawl for candidates, with sudden spurts of determination not to leave this power unused. "Who do you think should be pardoned? Give me one person—who's your top pick?" became a frequent conversational interruption.

One *Oh, shit* moment involved his sudden interest in Ghislaine Maxwell, the former girlfriend of Jeffrey Epstein now facing years in prison over allegations of her role in the Epstein sex-abuse scandal. Trump had tried hard to downplay his own long relationship with Epstein "Has she said anything about me?" He openly wondered. "Is she going to talk? Will she roll on anybody?"

But pardon talk almost immediately segued to the question of if he should pardon himself: "They say I can. Unlimited pardon power."

Kushner, however, dissuaded him here: giving himself a federal pardon, which was the only pardon power the president had, might just create more reason and more motivation for various states to go after him. Still, with such a lot of people out there who wanted to hurt him, he should pardon the whole family, shouldn't he—even Barron? Kushner elided. (Other family members would note that Kushner did, though, grab a pardon for his own father.)

It impressed Trump that Rudy said he didn't want a pardon. If he got a pardon, it would look like he needed a pardon, according to Rudy. But, Trump made it clear, he *had* offered Rudy one, as though to absolve himself if, in fact, they came after Rudy.

Members of the old cadre slipped in Steve Bannon. Hard-core loyalists, the hardest core of them, had become a specific Trump pardon category: Roger Stone, Paul Manafort, Michael Flynn. But Bannon was something different. As much as he was as responsible as anyone for Trump's becoming president, and as much as he had tried to reingratiate himself after his federal indictment for skimming from a not-for-profit fundraising scheme, his frequent and public disloyalties yet rankled. Yes, Bannon could be a prick. But . . . he was still in the family.

In the final hours, Trump pardoned Steve Bannon, perhaps his only real act of forgiveness and magnanimity.

* * *

The still-president and still–First Lady were ferried at 8 a.m. by helicopter on January 20 from the White House to Andrews Air Force Base—the helicopter pulling up beside Air Force One (the big Air Force One, not the little one). The music was "Don't Stop Believin'" ("A singer in a smoky room / The smell of wine and cheap perfume / For a smile they can share the night / It goes on and on, and on, and on . . ."). The music switched to "Hail to the Chief" as soon as the president and the First Lady came down the chopper stairs, walking maskless past the masked guard and Secret Service agents. Indeed, all the attendants were in masks—the guests and family were not.

Four cannons fired a final salute.

The gathering was in the hold area. The president mounted a riser.

It was far from a Trump-size crowd—perhaps the smallest of his presidency—a Biden-size crowd, a wag remarked. Still, they were making an effort. His family. Mark Meadows and his wife. You could feel the effort. No vice president and Mrs. Pence, who were scheduled to attend the new president's inauguration.

> I want to thank you for your effort, your hard work. People have no idea how hard this family worked. They worked. And they worked for you. They could have had a much easier life, but they just did a

fantastic job, I just want to thank all of you, everyone. I want to thank Mark Meadows, who's here someplace right there. I want to thank Mark. But it's been something very special. We've accomplished a lot. Our First Lady has been a woman of great grace and beauty and dignity. And so popular with the people. So popular with the people. In fact, honey, would you like to say a few words?

[Melania speaking] Being your First Lady was my greatest honor. Thank you for your love and your support. You will be in my thoughts and prayers. God bless you all, God bless your families, and God bless this beautiful nation.

What else has to be said, right? But what we've done ... That's true, honey. Great job. What we've done has been amazing by any standard.

And then the rote recitation of accomplishments—three Supreme Court justices, creation of the Space Force (a new military command he seemed particularly proud of), a great economy, the vaccine—and a heap of blame on the "China virus" and a recapitulation of electoral math and then a casual or enigmatic sign-off.

So just a good-bye. We love you. We will be back in some form. . . .
So have a good life. We will see you soon.

* * *

Here was, it could not be missed, a send-off into the waters of oblivion—it was a sparse plane ride. There was no Hope Hicks. There was no Stephen Miller. No Jared and Ivanka. No CEO buddies. No members of Congress. No cabinet folks. The traveling adulation chorus of Air Force One had disappeared, or run for the hills.

"Can we do this again in four years?" He seemed to ask everyone on the flight. And everyone seemed to give the same answer: "Oh yes, oh yes."

He was presented with a world map with a pin in every place he had visited on Air Force One; he murmured his appreciation. Then he was given a replica of the presidential podium. "What do I do with this?" he asked with a hint of sourness. "Like a nightstand ..." But then he rallied: "Oh we can put it in the library."

* * *

The only other model for a president leaving the White House and Washington in disgrace was Richard Nixon—a reviled but tragic figure. Washington insiders, or anyone with an establishment leaning or yearning, seemed inclined to see Trump's disgrace in Nixon-like terms, the humiliated and broken man.

And yet, obviously, there was something wrong with that dramatic arc. The Trump being cast out of office was the same Trump who had come into office. There had been in the long narrative no transformational moment. People waited for his shame to catch up with him, to bring him to his knees. But this wasn't Shakespeare. He didn't learn, he didn't grow, he didn't change. He was a simple machine: he got punched, and he punched back. As long as he still stood, he was still punching.

Never admit, never apologize, never back down. Attack.

* * *

Thousands of fans lined the road from West Palm Beach to Mar-a-Lago. There were TRUMP PENCE 2020 signs with a line through Pence's name. YOU WON signs. FUCK BIDEN signs. STAND WITH TRUMP WHO HAS GRIT AND DETERMINATION. WE LOVE YOU.

12

REDUX

It was an almost incomprehensibly wrongheaded sense of story line, a fool's version, that, right away, the Democrats, not even taking the time to breathe the air without him, would bring him back again—rescuing him from the waters of oblivion.

Two weeks out of office, and he was yet dominating the news—without staff, without facilities, without even a desk—they were putting together a makeshift arrangement above the ballroom at Mar-a-Lago—and with the support of only a few ambivalent souls, he was still the superseding presence in the nation.

You could not, in fact, take away his platform.

He would be tried and *not* convicted. That was already known. The polling had scared most of the wavering Republican back into line. Yes, the case would be made: here were all the reasons to detest and heap opprobrium on Donald Trump. But, likewise, that same case would demonstrate to those who wanted to see it this way how unfairly he had been maligned and pursued and with what strength and countenance he had stood up to the witch hunters who were after him.

And by the way, the election was *so* stolen.

Nobody, apparently, could escape from this cycle. Therefore, you might assume that—even with every Democrat now praising Joe Biden's low profile, careful discipline, and policy focus—nobody wanted to escape from this permanent state of maximal righteousness and daily drama. Everybody existed, still, in relationship to Donald Trump. Hence, without him you might not exist.

Or, many could simply not exist in a world that was not trying to destroy Donald Trump, even though every effort to destroy him merely confirmed the most torturously excruciating and confounding fact of modern life, which was this: he might be indestructible.

Still, you had to keep making the effort, didn't you?

* * *

History now had to try find its footing between high crimes and misdemeanors and low farce.

If process is the true theater of government—its glue, its logic, its language—then Trump, by his disregard for it, and lack of understanding of it, and yet insistence on his own domination over it, broke the proscenium over and over again. And there was no better example of this than his second impeachment trial, wherein his defense was absent point, method, or strategy, other than that he was at the center of it.

* * *

In his first trial, the president had been accused of a complicated now-you-see-it, now-you-don't collusion with foreign actors and entities. In the second, the House of Representatives radically simplified its charges: now he was accused, more vividly, of inciting a riot. But essentially it was the same premise: of all the president's bad behavior, all of it in some sense impeachable for Democrats, here was a snapshot of behavior so outrageous that it must surely convince some Republicans to vote against him, or hopelessly shame them if they didn't. It did not.

While it did not succeed in bringing around Republicans in the House, the Democrats now proceeded to the Senate trial, with a new team of lawyers primed to make their passionate case against the president with the carefully curated and highly produced video evidence of his call to arms, and then, obvious to all for whom it was obvious, his clear connection to the conflagration at the Capitol, beginning just minutes later.

It was both a strong case, if you wanted it to be strong, and quite a weak one, if you didn't. Certainly, there was a direct relationship between a cadre of people storming the Capitol and Donald Trump's long pattern of encouragement of fringe groups and their cultural and antiestablishment grievances. But at the same time, this encouragement, this incitement, was also, in its specific form, just more Trump blah-blah—he opened his mouth and rambled for most of the hours he spoke at any given event, including the precipitating speech at the Ellipse on January 6, just filling space, ever returning to his continuing mental and verbal loop, now and then adding a new crowd-pleasing inspiration. Certainly, it was a dramatic leap to credit him with intent. It suggested an ability to join cause and effect, and the logic of a plan, that anyone who knew him or had worked with him certainly understood he did not possess. And yet, at the same time, it was surely true that the locusts would not have descended on the Capitol without him.

So, here he and the Democrats were again, with them trying to assign cause and effect to him and with most of his Republican defenders pretty comfortable in their knowledge that, in any kind of literal, screwing-in-a-lightbulb sense, he could hardly be held responsible for conceiving and executing a plan—as would be seen once again in the way he coordinated his own defense.

* * *

The few people left in the Trump White House in the final days had accomplished one last task: they had kept Rudy out, blocking a hard push from the one man who might actually have gotten Trump convicted had he managed to come in and take over the impeachment defense. Still, Rudy spread it around that he was, of course, the president's guy (telling confidants he "needed" to represent the president here, "I just have to"), spooking other potential defenders—or, at least, providing them with an understandable excuse not to join the case themselves. Who, among the right-minded and reasonably competent, would willingly work with Rudy?

This left the now-former president, in early February, blinking into the light, without any lawyers. The legislative branch of the U.S. government, with all its power, was exercising its constitutional prerogative to put the executive branch, with its coequal powers, on trial—but complicating matters, and certainly depriving him of the coequal might of the executive branch, Trump was no longer the executive. This was the favored procedural argument of Republicans looking not to convict him but not necessarily to defend him, either. But it also prompted practical questions and considerations: how does a private citizen, one without any particular expertise in government or constitutional matters or legislative process—that he happened to have been the president did not mean he had gained this expertise—and one who, for many reasons, most of his own making, had limited access to legal help, defend himself?

Now it was true that he could probably do nothing—not defend himself at all—and be acquitted. Very few Republican senators wanted to test his threat that he held their careers in his hand. He had gotten it into his head that he had the power of fratricide, nearly an absolute power to kill off any fellow Republican—and he was eager to use it. And while this might be half a fantasy, it was far from clear who would want to test which half was bluster and which was real. This reluctance held Senate Republicans in line and would keep them from convicting him, at least assuming he did not commit some further, unimaginable Trump offense. And even then . . .

At the same time, he *wanted* to defend himself. Or, at least, he wanted not to yield the limelight. He had a case to make: the election *was* stolen. Hadn't you heard? *The election was stolen!* He wanted to tell the world himself. He seemed to have an obsessive need to repeat—and then repeat again—all the rumored, purported, and theoretical election offenses. And he seemed to believe this was electrifying to people, which for many it was, although, for others, it was a reason to worry about him.

Kushner felt that this was the one defense that actually could get Trump convicted—that Mitch McConnell so hated the former president and was so incensed at what he considered the raving lunacy of the election fraud nonsense (more proof McConnell didn't need that Trump himself was a raving lunatic) that, together with the seven senators voting to convict, he could break the dam and pull in the ten more needed to convict. Mitch just might be willing to risk all-out, internecine Republican war to do this.

Lawyers were needed not just in Trump's defense but also to keep him in line. That is, as always, he stood alone at an ever-unpredictable center of events—ever the wild card. As much as possible—and often, it was hardly possible—you had to surround him with process or, anyway, with people who might, out of caution and with the confusion of many voices, slow him down. This was the only hope for blunting the onslaught. At any rate, he could not be allowed to argue election fraud in the Senate.

But the process around him was so necessarily irregular that no process people wanted in. Or he, the antithesis of process, had exhausted all of them. To a man, all the lawyers in his first impeachment trial begged off—no Jay Sekulow, no Pat Cipollone, no Alan Dershowitz, no Ken Starr, no Pam Bondi, no Patrick Philbin, no Jane Raskin, no Robert Ray, no Eric Herschmann (other than to manage from afar—and unseen). Nobody wanted to be associated with Donald Trump. Sekulow's absence particularly angered the former president. "I've given him so much fucking money, and now he's too busy? That's bullshit!" Conflicts, prior commitments, COVID—virtually every lawyer associated with the Trump White House or with Trump himself was unavailable, save Rudy. And

Rudy, if miraculously his representation had failed to kill Trump before, would surely now be the nail in the former president's coffin. So, not if he were the last lawyer on earth.

They would, Kushner was assuring Senate Republicans, put together a team of some of the country's top constitutional scholars. But not a single one materialized.

Meadows remembered that Steve Castor, the House minority counsel during the first impeachment, had a brother who was a former prosecutor. In fact, not a brother, it turned out; a cousin—in Philly. The cousin, Bruce Castor, a former prosecutor, had no particular attributes that would have recommended him as a candidate for defending a president (former president) in an impeachment trial—perhaps most notably, he was the prosecutor who decided *not* to prosecute Bill Cosby—but he was willing (although, not willing if Rudy was going to be involved). Little more than a month before Bruce Castor was contacted to defend the president, he had joined a local Philadelphia firm that specialized in personal injury cases— also not propitious, but at least it was some sort of law firm.

Meanwhile, Roger Stone, often almost as much of a millstone around the neck and threat to the president as Giuliani—aides tried assiduously to keep him from talking to the president—knew somebody. David Schoen was a solo practitioner in Montgomery, Alabama, operating without a secretary or assistant. But Stone swore by him. So, out of the blue, Trump called up Schoen. They chatted for forty-five minutes, and Trump hired him: "You're going to be my guy. You'll be in charge."

But Lindsey Graham had an idea, too.

For four years, Graham had tried to negotiate, flatter, or appease Trump to his own advantage, with highly mixed results. They had become regular golfing companions, and perhaps their bond was real. "We're golf buddies," Trump explained in a singular moment of reflection. "Something different when you play golf with someone, different than having a phone call or meeting; you spend hours with a person. When you golf with someone you get to know them at a much different level." Which possibly explained what had often seemed to be Graham's tortured or absurd efforts to rationalize the behavior of the president—golf.

Graham, on the golf course, suggested a set of South Carolina lawyers, led by a local Republican fixture, Butch Bowers. Then Graham jumped the gun and dropped the news in a Republican Senate conference call—with Trump having had only one conversation with Bowers the night before.

With Bowers inadvertently hired—not to mention Schoen somewhere in the mix—Bruce Castor was shortly notified that he was off the case before he was actually put on the case. Meanwhile, the president, who in a few more phone calls had now convinced himself that Schoen was definitely his main man, told Schoen that he would be in charge of Bowers: "You'll be the quarterback."

But Graham was telling everybody that Bowers was the president's top guy.

The collective response to Bowers was: "Who? Why this guy? What is Lindsey up to?" (Schoen was so under-profile that his name was not even coming up.) But the price was right: Bowers, in his introductory call with the president, said he'd do it for $250,000.

But a few days later, Bowers called Jason Miller, who, through the attrition of most everyone else, had become a central Trump impeachment manager.

"I've got a little bit of an issue here," said Bowers to Miller, "and I'm hoping you could help me out. It's just that I told the president it would be two hundred fifty thousand dollars, and he seemed good with that, but I didn't tell him what the cost would be for the whole team."

"And? That would be?" asked Miller, with a sinking sensation.

"Probably more in the three million area. If you could run that by him."

"You want me to tell Donald J. Trump that the cost of the deal just went up by two and three-quarter million dollars? I think you are going to have to make that call."

"And so ended," Miller reported to a friend, "the brief and terrifying glory of Butch Bowers."

With less than two weeks to go until the start of his impeachment, Donald Trump now had only David Schoen, a lawyer without staff or support or, it appeared, much self-confidence.

"You can do it," said the president.

"I don't even have a secretary," said Schoen, who, uniquely in the Trump orbit, styled himself as modest to a fault. Indeed, there was a weird and, to many, disturbing ingenuousness about Schoen. The one odd thing that seemed to be known about him was that Jeffrey Epstein had consulted him. Where the entire professional world might do anything not to be associated with Epstein—and here, particularly, when Trump himself had so strenuously tried to conceal his own Epstein connections—Schoen seemed to be proud of his encounter.

"You'll be fine," Trump assured him.

Schoen decided this would all be a wonderful civics lesson for his college-age son and daughter. He put them to work doing constitutional research. Oh, and Schoen was an observant Jew and would not be able to work on the Sabbath in a trial that was set to run through the weekend.

Panic now was official.

Herschmann, since the last impeachment, had hovered for influence in the Trump White House. While refusing the second impeachment job himself, he was telling everybody the sky was falling in. He and Meadows went back to Castor in Philadelphia. At least the unknown Castor had a firm behind him—albeit, a small, local criminal and personal injury firm—whereas the unknown David Schoen had nobody but himself (and his children).

The Democrats, for their part, had nine lawyers, most former prosecutors, from the House of Representatives, with the backing of their respective staffs, the resources of the House majority, the extra backing of the 1,200-man law firm Cleary Gottlieb, and a team of filmmakers to produce their videos.

* * *

By the agreement between Senate Democrats and Republicans, the opening day of the Senate trial, on February 9, would be devoted to the jurisdictional issue—that is, whether the Senate had the standing or right to try a private citizen. Democrats had decided that, despite the peculiarity of trying to remove someone from office who was no longer in office, of course they did. Republicans had decided that this was a much better hill to die on than to try to defend Trump's behavior and actions on January 6.

The Trump lawyers were familiar only with normal courtroom practices, as opposed to the procedures for an impeachment, where the jury effectively sets the rules. Trump's team assumed that jurisdiction would be the limited first-day agenda, enforced by . . . well, they had not gone so far as to think that through. In fact, there was no enforcer here except a majority vote. They had been briefed by McConnell's chief counsel, Andrew Ferguson, about what to expect. Ferguson, the Trumpers understood, very clearly hated the president and would have gladly pushed the Trump team in front of an oncoming bus. Still, though, the McConnell people were as anxious to get this wrapped up as anybody. Ferguson's message could not have been clearer. The Democrats were going to heavily rely on video to make their case, and their opening presentation was going to be an emotional barn burner. Plan accordingly.

Indeed, the Dems largely dispensed with the jurisdictional matter—that was beside the point. The Senate would either hold Donald Trump responsible for being Donald Trump or not. Therefore, the job at hand was to show Donald Trump in full: chaos, mayhem, death, and destruction at the president's hands.

Digital tools have made video storage and editing an easy process, turning documentary filmmaking—that is, the repurposing and quoting of archival and news footage—into the journalism form of our time. Or, as it were, the propaganda form. It may not be possible to customize any message by the selection and cutting of video footage, but close. What's more, as an emotional lever, it is far more powerful than any other evidence. Indeed, it pretends to be reality itself: better than real.

It was therefore not just the certain facts—Donald Trump exhorting a crowd and then parts of that crowd marching on, breaching the barricades, and invading the Capitol, killing several people and threatening many more—but the bloody pictures of it all.

It was Donald Trump in black coat, all grim visage, strutting affect, and extreme language, seemingly wholly unconcerned with what actions he might inspire and provoke. And then it was the day of the locust: people directly connected to the president but unrecognizable in any normal civil context, a self-styled militia or vanguard, unleashed against the U.S. government.

That was the presentation. That was the message. Those were the pictures.

The garrulous and voluble president, liking nothing so much as to memorialize or immortalize himself on television, had left an indelible video record—and not just on January 6, but through countless inciting exhortations in the months leading up to the sixth. The Democrats in their cinematic opening laid all this out with narrative rhythm, clarity, and force.

The president, said a stunned Bruce Castor, coming back into the LBJ conference room after watching the Democrats' presentation before the Senate, the large portrait of LBJ looking down on the Trump defense team, was "smoked."

"Oh, man. I just saw the way everybody was looking at those videos. Oh, man."

There were the three speaking lawyers in the room: Castor; his partner, Mike van der Veen, a personal injury lawyer—it was van der

Veen's law firm that Castor had joined in December—and Schoen. Then the support team: Julieanne Bateman, an associate at the van der Veen firm who no one would remember ever saying a word; and Adam, the law school intern, never without a piece of bubble gum, constantly getting yelled at by van der Veen. There was one outside First Amendment lawyer, David Hein, recruited by Castor and van der Veen to advise on the fine line between free speech and incitement; and Bill Brennan, another Philadelphia lawyer who had some experience with First Amendment issues. There were, also in the room, three Trump loyalists from the House: Jim Jordan from Ohio, Mike Johnson from Louisiana, and Andy Biggs from Arizona. On the Trump operations side, there were Jason Miller; Alex Cannon; Sonny Nelson, who handled TV bookings; Ben Williamson, who had been Meadows's chief deputy; and Ali Pardo, a former Trump campaign comms staffer. Ory Rinat and Sam Brown were the video team. And then there was Schoen's son, Simon.

And everybody was shell-shocked.

"They surprised us! This was unfair," said Castor about the Dems' video. "They caught us flat-footed. We didn't know!"

"What do you mean 'we didn't know'?" said Miller, coming to the end of his first week shepherding the makeshift legal team. "We knew. What did you think?"

"We didn't know they would be this good."

"You were told. McConnell's people said this was how it would play out."

"But it was so emotional," said a bereft Castor. "We got smacked with those videos. We can't pretend they weren't played. And we can't go out now with our legalistic argument."

This was Schoen's piece, the jurisdictional case, and he became plaintive and sullen.

"We have to take the temperature down," argued Castor, proposing that he, instead of Schoen, open, making what he billed as introductory remarks and an outline of their larger case.

"But that's my time," said Schoen. "You're going to cut into my time."

"No—just a short opening, just to take down the temperature," assured Castor. Everybody agreed.

Fifteen minutes into Castor's opening, Trump was putting through calls to anyone in the LBJ Room whose number he had—and to lawyers in the first impeachment who no longer represented him—pronouncing this the worst speech ever given in the U.S. Senate or, for that matter, in the history of mankind.

What's more, Castor looked like a man who'd had a *Biggest Loser*-size weight loss but who was still wearing his fat-man suit. Castor kept trying to explain, the camera added ten pounds to a person—and, apparently, three sizes to Castor's Dick Tracy suit.

And he spoke now for forty-eight minutes.

It was a free association that recalled nothing so much as Donald Trump himself, but one without forward movement, energy, or applause lines. He seemed to look up to the Capitol Dome hoping the words would drop down—and in scattered, halting fashion, they did. Compliments to the Democrats, details of government remembered from childhood civics classes, sudden juxtaposed and pointless personal anecdotes.

The last time a body such as the United States Senate sat at the pinnacle of government with the responsibility that it has today, it was happening in Athens and it was happening in Rome. Republicanism, the form of government, republicanism, throughout history, has always and without exception, fallen because of fights from within. Because of partisanship from within. Because of bickering from within and in each one of those examples that I mentioned, and there are certainly others probably that are smaller countries that lasted for less time that I don't know about off the top of my head, but each one of them, once there was the vacuum created that the greatest deliberative bodies, the Senate of Greece sitting in Athens, the Senate of Rome, the moment that they devolved into such partisanship, it's not as though they ceased to exist. They ceased to exist as representative democracy. Both replaced by totalitarianism . . .

To quote Everett Dirksen, "The gallant men and women of the Senate will not allow that to happen. And this Republic will endure." Because the top responsibility of a United States Senator and the top characteristic that you all have in common—and boy, this is a diverse group, but there isn't a single one of you who (a), doesn't consider yourself a patriot of the United States. And two, there, isn't a single one of you who doesn't consider the other ninety-nine to be patriots of the United States. And that is why this attack on the Constitution will not prevail. The document that is before you is flawed. The rule of the Senate concerning impeachment documents, Articles of Impeachment, Rule Twenty-three, says that, "Such documents cannot be divided." You might've seen that we wrote that in the answer. It might've been a little legalistic or legalese for the newspapers to opine on very much, but there is some significance.

It was incomprehensible—and, worse, he seemed to be enjoying himself. Most offensively to the former president, watching from Palm Beach, Castor had fulsomely complimented the other side for its powerful presentation.

"What does he think he's doing?" Trump demanded of one of the other lawyers. "He's not lowering the temperature. He's just making an ass out of himself. Get him off the goddamn TV. This is a disaster. What an idiot. We're getting mocked. This is a disgrace," he continued. "And what is that fucking mob suit he's wearing? He looks like Al Capone!"

Castor came off the floor and began to tell the group what great feedback he had gotten from many senators as he finished. He had really, he felt—and so many senators confirmed this—done what he had to do.

"Why did he say I'm giving a scholarly view of the jurisdictional question? That's not what I'm doing," said a morose Schoen as he went out, indignant that his time had been cut short.

* * *

The grim team headed back to their meeting room at the Trump International.

Trump continued to call in. He got Justin Clark on the phone and told Clark to tell Castor he was no longer allowed to speak, with Clark and an incensed Castor suddenly facing off.

But the president's aides suddenly feared that van der Veen might pack up and go back to Philadelphia with Castor, leaving them only with the hapless Schoen.

The basic politics remained: if they made the minimal effort, the Republicans would hold, and the Senate would acquit. No one could quite game out what would happen, though, if it became clear that they could not rise even to a minimally proficient effort. (Although there was, too, the thought that reasonable people might conclude that this was just more proof that you obviously couldn't hold Trump responsible for executing on anything, much less an attack on the U.S. Capitol.)

By the next morning, Trump still wasn't able to get off the issue of Castor's suits. "Al Capone. He's Al Capone. Those are Al Capone's suits. Do something about those suits."

In college, Miller had worked at Wm. Fox & Co., a haberdashery in Washington on G Street. Before Castor was even down for breakfast, Miller had the owner bring over everything they had in navy and gray in a size forty-eight.

"You're making me change how I dress?" said a wounded Castor.

"This is Washington, DC," said Miller, "you can't wear gangster pinstripes," and he got van der Veen, the senior partner, to write a four-thousand-dollar check to the clothing store.

They returned, glumly, to the Senate Chamber.

Wednesday and Thursday were entirely the Democrats' days, with ever-more-vivid video of the January 6 attack, while Trump's circle tried to figure out what they were going to do. It was now an open question about who would deliver the presentation, Trump's basic defense, on Friday. As invulnerable as Donald Trump should have been, there was a sinking sensation that the legal team could actually find a way here to snatch defeat from the jaws of victory.

Trump suddenly decided he wanted Schoen to take over everything—but Schoen was now resisting, saying, in the middle of the most important trial of his life, he really didn't know the case.

"You should let Castor do it—he has a whole firm. It's just me and my son."

"I've seen you on TV," Trump tried to bolster him. "You're a good lawyer. Just do it. Why are you so afraid of Castor?"

"Because I'm a wimp, sir," said David Schoen to the president.

"What? What did you say?"

"I'm a wimp sir. I'm a pushover. That's me. I can't stand up for myself. That's just who I am."

"A wimp? You're supposed to be defending me in an impeachment trial? My lawyer's a wimp? A wimp? Did you just call yourself a wimp? A wimp? I want you to do it. You do it. Man up."

With no place not to be overheard, the Trump aides found themselves in the anteroom to the Senate women's locker room, huddled together, away from both Democrats and Trump's own lawyers, trying to map out a desperate last-minute plan. Writing and organizing key parts of the presentations, for whoever would deliver them, fell to Ory Rinat, who had gone to law school before bailing on a legal career and becoming a videographer.

They needed somehow to keep Castor out of the president's view. So, the plan, going into Thursday, was for van der Veen, who Trump now decided might be the only competent one in the bunch ("One of the all time greats," he promoted him to), to do the opening; then for Schoen to take on the due process argument; then van der Veen to cover the First Amendment case; and then, briefly, for Castor to close, so as not to make it look like he had deserted the team.

Except the president wouldn't have him. "No way, no way. I never want to see him at the podium again."

But meanwhile, it became clear that Schoen had little prepared and was now balking at the videographer's script. "I haven't had any time to do anything. I don't have any paralegals. It's just me. I was promised a brief writer, a serious constitutional scholar. I was promised." The implication being that, in lieu of a scholar, he had gotten a videographer.

"Yes, but—it's tomorrow. You're up," said Miller.

"I'm just not going to do this," Schoen suddenly told Miller on Thursday night.

"What do you mean?"

"I'm not going to do it."

"You can't just not do it."

"Yes, I can. You can't tell me what to do, you can't tell me what to do. I can do whatever I want. You're not in charge of me," said Schoen, heading quickly into what seemed like a breakdown and saying he thought Miller and Alex Cannon, with Justin Clark now joining them, were thugs.

"No, I'm telling you. You can't quit. Because you'll look like a jackass."

"Don't tell me that. Don't tell me that. I can look like whatever I want to look like," said Schoen, now storming off.

But Alex Cannon intercepted him. "David, we can't let you leave."

"What does that mean?" demanded Schoen.

"I'm not sure, but I wouldn't try to leave now."

Cannon and Justin Clark then followed Schoen to his room to keep him from fleeing.

But at 10:42 on Thursday night, Schoen bailed anyway, sending an email saying he'd sit at the table, but he wasn't going to do anything more.

The plan, then, with no alternative, was to bring back the benched Castor to deliver Schoen's part, using the videographer's script. Castor was walked through the speech for most of the night, but, as though he'd ingested Donald Trump, he seemed unable to keep himself from off-point digressions and spontaneous ad-libs.

Shortly after dawn, the president called to say that Schoen had just called him and said that they—Miller, Clark, Cannon, and Herschmann, the thugs—had refused to let him give his speech. "Work with him. Come on, work with him," Trump insisted.

"I didn't even call the president," said a still-petulant Schoen to the Trump team. "He called me to say he wanted me to do it. He's pushing me to go do it. I don't even want to do it."

In the second impeachment of Donald Trump—the fourth impeachment in the history of the republic—David Schoen, never having finished writing his own remarks, delivered the videographer's argument.

Castor, who had been read in, was then read out—but shortly read in again, because while Schoen would do his opening part, he had to be out by sundown, for the Sabbath. Castor would therefore— even as, at the moment, Trump's most scorned lawyer, a position occupied over the years by hundreds—get to deliver the closing remarks.

In his new gray Samuelsohn suit, Castor almost immediately rambled off script. On live television, he could be seen being handed a note and ignoring it—it was a pointed prod from Miller, telling him to stay on script. Ten minutes later, still rambling, looking this way and that, he could be seen receiving another note and looking at it:

Get back on script and read the speech as written or I am going to come out there and pull you. Jason.

Castor hesitated for a second and then put his nose down in the prepared speech and read it out to the end.

* * *

The real point, beyond the Democrats' continuing and wildly misguided perception that they could bring shame upon Trump, was, after impeaching and convicting, to banish him from public office. McConnell, no one questioned, would love to have joined them, with at least the sixteen other Republicans needed to convict, all whose lives would be made much easier without Donald Trump in American political life, not far behind.

But if you are going to kill the king . . .

Therein lay the problem: even conviction and banishment might not yet have made him dead enough.

Without the capacity to register shame, and ever fueled by grievance, or at least the drama of grievance, and a shamelessness that always allowed him to rewrite the grievance as an insult upon all the faithful, he was a maximally reliable phoenix. He had been impeached twice, disgraced in the eyes of at least half the country multiple times more, and defeated for reelection—without any of this seeming to much penetrate or alter his sense of self.

The fact that all the modern standards of opprobrium, obloquy, disgrace, public mortification, and general measures of accountability did not bow him was at the core of liberal rage and frustration. His ability to stand up to the moral wrath of the liberal community seemed also to be at the core of the continuing awe and devotion of so many others.

And given the incompetence that surrounded him, the stumblebums who attended him, and his own stubborn refusal to listen to more considered and cautious counsel or to tolerate anyone whose talents might actually be clear and need to be credited, the heroic point could hardly be missed: It was only him. He was a team of one.

He walked into the storm alone and came out alone.

The fact that he survived, without real support, without real assistance, without expertise, without backup, without anybody truly minding the store, and without truly knowing his ass from a hole in the ground, was extraordinary. Magical.

EPILOGUE

THE ROAD TO MAR-A-LAGO

I t's called the Living Room, but it's in fact the Mar-a-Lago lobby, a vaulted-ceiling rococo grand entrance, part hunting lodge, part Renaissance palazzo. But it is really the throne room. Court life swirls around: blond mothers and blond daughters, infinitely buxom, and men in unnaturally colored jackets and pants. Donald J. Trump presides or is on display. He sits, in regulation dark suit and shiny baby-blue or fire-red tie, on a low chair in the center of the room, his legs almost daintily curled to the side, seeing a lineup of supplicants or chatting on the phone, all public conversations.

This has included a steady stream of Republican senators and congressmen seeking his endorsement—indeed, almost every Republican officeholder or seeker, save the few opposed to him, who can make the trip seems set to come to Mar-a-Lago to slavishly attend to him. During a spring afternoon, he takes twenty minutes with Jerry Moran, the senator from Kansas—"We have the longest unbroken chain of Republican incumbents," says Moran. "You don't say," says a less-than-interested Trump. Moran presses on to lavishly thank the former president for his support. Rick Scott, the Florida senator, got a dinner invitation—joined by the actor Jon Voight, a Trump devotee. Wilbur Ross, the former secretary of commerce, in a bright-green jacket not quite the color of money, stands at his shoulder for a moment. Sarah Huckabee Sanders, his former press secretary, running for governor of Arkansas, is holding a fundraiser at Mar-a-Lago that evening. Dan Scavino, his former golf course manager, social media tender, and closest White House aide, is in the house. Sean Hannity, the Fox anchor, calls, and Trump shares the call with those around him—and, effectively, with anyone at Mar-a-Lago who wants to listen in.

Some Mar-a-Lago members try to keep a respectful, albeit rapt, distance. But one after the other of the more or less forward stop to express fulsome admiration, if not nearly teary awe, with the most forward asking for a selfie, which, begrudgingly, he grants. Each greeting and genuflection becomes an opportunity for him to comment to the other people in the tighter circle of genuflection on how much he is loved and how much they, the people, have been hurt by the election that has been stolen from him. This is not, however, said in bitterness, but with some sense of the expansiveness and majesty, even transcendence, of a regime and court that have merely shifted to a better location.

Trump lives here now—here in the middle of a country club. He and Melania are its singular residents. Or, well . . . maybe Melania lives here. For four years in the White House, it was never quite clear how much time she was spending at the White House or in a house in Maryland where she had settled her parents. Aides were careful not to closely inquire or openly wonder. Here too, in Mar-a-Lago, it was unclear.

Trump had bought Mar-a-Lago, the 1920s parvenu creation of Marjorie Merriweather Post, the socialite and cereal heiress, in 1985, during the first peak of Trump mania, meaning it to be his Palm Beach estate. But with his vast debts closing in on him in the early 1990s, he converted the place to a private club for paying members.

Old-fashioned club life dominates: wine tastings, Croquet Singles, Asian Night, Italian Night with an accordion player, Prime Rib Night, an Easter egg hunt, Mother's Day brunch. Hand-lettered poster boards spell out the schedule.

The only membership qualification now, beyond the actual cost ($250,000, up from $150,000 before the presidency, plus a hefty yearly fee), is to be an abject Trump admirer. This may not be so much a political statement as an aesthetic one—the thrall of a supercelebrity.

In a sense, Trump is Rick in Rick's Café Américain in *Casablanca*. Of course, a Rick without quite so much conscience or heart—though the Palm Beach set seems to believe in his heart (if not his conscience). Or, maybe it is more akin to Jack Dempsey's bar in Times Square. Trump's the fighter, sitting on his bar stool perch. Or, going bigger, he's Sinatra, and Mar-a-Lago is the Sands Hotel in Vegas.

Out one door of the great room is the "Liberty Bar" with a formal portrait of Trump as a young man posed in tennis whites, a brilliant sun breaking through the clouds over his head, which does not seem to be treated as a kitschy joke—there might even be some reverence attached to it. Out the other door is the grand dinner patio—you can see the water in the distance. There are fifty or sixty tables. Trump has his dinner here most evenings. He appears just as the patio has filled, at which point everyone stands and applauds. Often, when Melania is here, they eat alone at a roped-off table in the center—looked at, somewhat, like zoo animals. No, no, that's not right. They are like a newly married couple: every night is a wedding at which they spend their dinner greeting friends and well-wishers.

Mar-a-Lago is in the flight path of Palm Beach International

Airport. All traffic was rerouted during the presidential years, but now it's noisily back.

This, then, is the setting, the redoubt, of one of the most powerful political movements in the Western world—waiting only for its leader to decide on his next move.

* * *

He absolutely believes he has been forced out of office by an election coup that involves almost all aspects of modern society and its coordinated power centers organized against him. At the same time, he absolutely believes he is the single most powerful political entity in the United States, holding the power to anoint or de-anoint any Senate or House member in a Trump state. He is motivated by revenge—eager to punish and strike down anyone guilty of major or minor disses to him—and obeisance. With a little critical interpretation, it is not so much broad power that he seeks as much as specific submission and adulation.

Likewise, it is also clear to those around him—those concerned for him (and themselves)—that he faces serious legal issues. He might be indicted—for financial issues, for his call to Georgia secretary of state Brad Raffensperger, in the ongoing investigations of January 6. People around him surely will. This is further proof of the collective campaign against him—just part of the larger "steal." The witch hunt. And, not incidentally, the fundamental reason for his political strength. Indeed, it's his central issue: Terrible and corrupt people are against him. The swamp. The deep state, the fake news media. That's why his movement must continue. That's why he might have to run again in 2024. To fight back against the people who would destroy him. To attack him is to attack his people. He fights for them. Not incidentally, the more he is pursued the stronger he remains.

Notably, he faces his legal challenges without any real lawyers in place, going so far as to ask random visitors if they know any good ones.

Rudy Giuliani has again been cast out, cut off by Trump family members. Trump is annoyed that he tried to get paid for his election challenge work—and for his girlfriend putting in a bill! Giuliani, now beset by crushing investigations and potentially millions of dollars in legal costs, has publicly implored the Trump family and aides (and with further pleas from his girlfriend, and not so subtle public threats) to have the Trump campaign, with its great wealth, indemnify him—and has gotten only the cold shoulder.

The former president is of course lionized by the Trump establishment—the conquering hero of CPAC (though on one of his first postpresidential trips, his plane, for the first time in four years, had to wait in line for take-off). He remains largely alienated from the political establishment—but he more and more successfully casts this as them being alienated from him, forcing them to crawl back.

House Republican leader Kevin McCarthy came down to Mar-a-Lago to kiss the ring, and Trump seemed briefly to consider letting signs of something-less-than-absolute-loyalty slide, let bygones be bygones. But that is something that he really can't do, and sourness about McCarthy continues to move through his body like an uncomfortable meal. McCarthy, in turn, has gone from trying to maintain a cooler deference to the former president to a full-out panic not to be on the wrong side of him.

Senate Republican leader Mitch McConnell now occupies the highest-most place of contempt in the Trump universe. To the extent that Trump is motivated by revenge fantasies and score settling, as he overwhelmingly is, McConnell provides a constant target.

The liberal press writes wishfully about Trump being silenced and forgotten—squeezing their eyes closed and putting their fingers in their ears. What is he without his social media platforms, after all?

Right? Who can hear him? Many Republican professionals believe, on the other hand, that he may now be more central to their lives and careers in defeat than he was in office, with his singular focus on their loyalty, preferably abject, to him.

The Trump proposition is that he is the Republican Party. It simply has no future without him. If he runs again in 2024, he wins the Republican nomination in a "landslide," says Mitt Romney (reduced by Trump to a lonely martyrdom in the Republican Party). He not only controls the overwhelming share of Republican dollars—and has sent cease-and-desist letters to other Republican entities trying to poach on his brand hegemony—but he believes he has the power of life and death over every Republican officeholder. No Republican office seems too small—the Wyoming GOP chairman has received his blessing. To be near Trump is to benefit from him. Rand Paul, the Kentucky senator, came to Mar-a-Lago for a fundraiser and pulled in five hundred thousand dollars for the evening. Caitlyn Jenner, running as a Republican candidate for governor in California, has sought to hire from the Trump staff—including Brad Parscale, the president's former personal assistant Madeleine Westerhout, and Trump fundraiser Caroline Wren—with a hope for Trump's endorsement. Every Republican primary race for 2022 will have, Trump promises, a Trump candidate, with the goal of ruling out all other candidates. Forty-thousand-people Trump rallies yet remain the possible Republican future.

There was, briefly, a rumor that Trump himself would run in 2022 for a House seat and then, in the expectations that Republicans would retake the majority, have himself elected Speaker, and then commence the impeachment of Joe Biden. For Trump aides, though, this was risible. Speaker of the House is a "real job," and Trump, in no way, is going to actually work.

Rather than being scarred by his defeat, he has weaponized it. His defeat, against practically everybody's advice, is his issue: the steal. Indeed, election rules have become a central animating issue of the Republican Party. The unlikely and even ridiculous becomes in Trump's hands righteous and powerful. Trump's handpicked PAC to fight for "election integrity" is made up of many of the opportunists, freelancers, and inexplicable characters who populate this book: Jenna Ellis, Ken Paxton, Peter Navarro, Bernie Kerik, Sebastian Gorka, and Mirna Tarraf (Giuliani's entourage member, the twentysomething Lebanese real estate agent!).

There is no brain trust around him, if there ever was one. There are no real advisors, if there ever were any—not, anyway, in the sense of people he might turn to who might know better than he. There are no white papers being prepared. There are no studies in progress.

Mike Lindell, the MyPillow CEO, and Kurt Olsen, a lawyer contributing to many of the deep-state election steal theories, both among the most extreme conspiracy advocates, were hanging around Mar-a-Lago.

A group of unknown would-be financiers have launched an effort, which Trump has apparently signed on to, for the former president to front the Trump Media Group, a special purpose acquisition company, or SPAC, that will buy media outlets and social media platforms—"grifters with PowerPoint skills," in the words of one Trump friend.

His son-in-law, the most significant figure in his administration and political life, and his daughter live in Florida now, but a calculated ninety minutes away. Each of his family members, all of them with a vastly elevated stature in American political and public life, but aware, too, of its precarious balance—between power and influence and disgrace and legal exposure—are trying to be strategic and careful. Early reports were that his daughter-in-law Lara might be considering a political future, a race for the Senate in 2022, but she seems to have quietly put her head back down.

There is Nick Luna, his body man from the White House, a thirtyish former actor—indeed, the nephew of Fred Thompson, a politician who became an actor, too, and a presidential aspirant—whose wife works for Kushner. And there is Jason Miller, who lives in Washington but functions as a part-time comms director and political advisor.

Trump doesn't mention Hope Hicks anymore. Hicks had been the single steadiest figure in his daily political life, the one person most responsible for the incremental decisions that somehow got the administration to a (however stressed) natural end. But she walked away from his final fight. Now, in her stead, there is a Hope look-alike, Margo Martin, his new personal assistant, as young as Hope used to be, and as attentive.

And there is Brad Parscale, who, to wide Trump circle amazement, is back again in an undefined role—or, depending on whose Kremlinology, back again only to be on his way out again.

But Trump has never needed an organization, or infrastructure, or even a plan to make things happen. It happens because of his own stream of consciousness—his own expressiveness makes things happen. He talks. He sits in the middle of Mar-a-Lago and talks. Talks endlessly. And people listen.

* * *

The fact that he was talking to me might only reasonably be explained by his absolute belief that his voice alone has reality-altering powers.

His claim to be "a very stable genius" was a response to my book *Fire and Fury*, a tale that contributed to something of a worldwide questioning of his competence and mental standing. He threatened to sue me for it, along with other ravings and personal attacks he leveled in my direction.

"I don't blame you. I blame my people," he says now, happily dismissing any sourness—by which he means, I infer, that his "people" had talked too much to me or had not given me enough time to talk with him.

Taking his seat in the middle of the Living Room in Mar-a-Lago, he looked good, relaxed and like he'd lost weight. I complimented him without mentioning the weight.

Jason Miller was sitting on the couch taking notes, as was, next to him, Margo, the new Hope. In a brief conversation with Miller beforehand about my focus here, Miller had suggested, in the interest of keeping the conversation going, that I not bring up January 6 or another subject that I said I was curious about, and about which I had heard Trump had a conspiratorial view: Jeffrey Epstein. "I wouldn't go there, necessarily," said Miller. Otherwise, anywhere was fine.

In fact, otherwise was not really the point, because Trump was going where he wanted anyway.

* * *

If the election was rigged, I wondered, then what did he think was the real number—what had he won it by without any interference?

Into the loop—with hardly a breath:

"First of all, the primary interference was that the fact that they didn't go to legislatures having to do with all of these changes they made prior to the election; and by law, under the Constitution, you have to. And the courts didn't have any guts, and that includes the Supreme Court, which is a terrible thing, the Supreme Court, what they did. And if they ever get packed where they're going to end up with ten more judges, or five more judges, or whatever is going to happen, they deserve it, because they didn't have the courage to do what you had to do. And I say that openly, and I say that with great disappointment. And, you know, we weren't ruled against. We were ruled always on process or standing. You didn't have standing. Nobody ruled on—they didn't rule on the facts. The facts were great for us. But before you even get to the facts, whether it's the illegals, whether it's the ballots, whether it's all of the things that happened, you know, they used COVID in order to rig the election. The ballot dumps. Maybe more importantly than the ballot dumps was when you looked at the machines being turned off. You know, at three o'clock, three-oh-two in the morning. But before you even get to any of that stuff, most of this stuff, and I'm talking about swing states, because that's what really matters—I think we're systematic, but the rest doesn't matter. In the swing states where you had more votes than you had voters, if you look at Pennsylvania, you look at Philadelphia, you had more votes than you had voters. And if you look at Detroit, you had far more votes than you had voters. So, you start with that, and that's something that is very interesting. When people hear the scenario, they all say—[people] that aren't as well versed but they're smart—they all say it wasn't even close. If you look at—I mean, there are different studies that have been done now. I mean, you know, it's a big deal. It's a big deal. People aren't—it was run like a third world nation. They wouldn't let our watchers, our poll watchers in, in Pennsylvania, in Philadelphia, in Detroit—and I mean kept them out viciously and violently. So many different things happened. But very importantly, they didn't allow—and I think this is the biggest thing—I mean, the other, all the facts are great, but there was no legislature approval. They didn't get the approval from the local politicians and judges in it, and that's against the Constitution. This should have never been allowed to happen. And in all the cases, the important thing, Mike, they were game changers. It wasn't like it affected—it wasn't like I lost by ten thousand votes and this would have been ten votes. This was many times the votes necessary to win these swing states. And, honestly, it's a disgrace."

And on:

"So, first of all, COVID changed the whole ball game, but I still got seventy-five million votes. Remember, I got sixty-three. I was supposed to get sixty-six, and I couldn't lose. I got seventy-five—I got almost seventy-five million votes and probably a lot more than that. But I got almost seventy-five million votes. We were aiming at sixty-six million votes. And we had a tremendous turnout, far bigger than the other side thought possible. That's why they closed the votes. That's why they had hours of something—something went on. Because when they came back, all of sudden: What happened? Where did all of these votes come from? It was a crooked, rigged election. When I made the speech two weeks ago"—his CPAC speech—"which, by the way, had thirty-one million people online. You saw that, right? I mean, the numbers were phenomenal. And it was just about the number one show on television for the week, and it was at five o'clock on a Sunday on cable and it was beating, you know, network television. But we had thirty-one million online. A big part of that is the voter fraud. People, they're not accepting it. They're not accepting it. It's very interesting. When you had the people—when you had the largest crowd I've ever spoken in front of was down in Washington on the sixth. That was—so you can say it was a million people. Some people say more; some people say less. But that was a crowd that went to the Washington Monument. That was a massive crowd. And a lot of those people were there—I think most of those people were there because of the voter fraud. It was a fraudulent election."

It is not just a sense of grievance, or arguing a political flip side, but of steeping into a fully built alternate world. This is perhaps its appeal. He isn't really arguing issues; you don't have to parse the facts. You can walk through the door of an entirely realized, albeit parallel universe.

"Who do you think was in control of this, the real bad guys?" I asked.

"Well, it wasn't Biden because—but they just wanted him in the basement. They didn't expect he was going to win; neither did almost anybody. And when he ended up winning—don't forget, when he left New Hampshire, it was over for him, right? But in South Carolina, he got a good endorsement. Endorsements do mean something, as I think I've proven maybe better than anybody in American history. You know we just left—senators are here every day seeking my endorsement. And if I don't give it to them—Toomey left because I won't endorse him. I said, 'I'm going to fight against you,' because of his whole attitude on tariffs and stupidity. I said, 'I'm not endorsing you. I'm going to endorse somebody else. I brought him in, you know, with me.' He was not expected to win at all. 'Liddle' Bob Corker, gone. He was at one of the lowest. Look—look at this."

He picks up a booklet he's been handed—a photocopied handout. It's unsourced, with charts based on random vote counts.

"This is at three o'clock in the morning [on Election Night]," he continues excitedly. "Look at the line. Look at the spikes. That's when they dumped ballots. They dumped hundreds of thousands of ballots. This one is in Wisconsin. Look at the ones behind it. Michigan. Look at that. That doesn't happen. They had no excuse for it. They didn't know. They said, 'Oh, it's statistical, whatever.' Look at the times. They dumped hundreds of thousands of ballots."

"So, who rigged it?"

"A group of people within the Democrat Party working along with Big Tech and the media."

"Some names?"

"I can't give you names now. Names are going to be revealed. How about where the lockboxes show up days later? In other words, they're supposed to be picked up. They shouldn't even be there. That was done by Zuckerberg. But it was picked up, and it comes days later, and most of the votes in the boxes were for Biden, you know, in areas that were good areas."

"This is a big thing that happened," I pressed. "Somebody must have been coordinating this, no?"

"It's a coordinated effort, and it's also cancel culture. This whole cancel culture is a very dangerous thing. What's happening now. It used to be that I or somebody had a view opposite of one of their views. We'd fight, and I'd win or lose; in other words, it would be an argument. But now they won't put it in. There's no more argument. If we find—I mean we have so much evidence of voter fraud, they don't want to put it in. But it's coming out, bigger than anyone would imagine.

"The names will be coming out. I just can't say it now. But it's a group of people representing powerful entities. It's a disgrace."

"Can you give me a heads-up on this? On when this will come out?"

"It's not Joe Biden. He was so unexpected. The reasons they had to shut down is that I got so many more votes than they thought. I got more votes by far than any sitting president. It's not even close. You look at the some of the telltale signs, like eighteen out of nineteen statehouses—unheard-of. If you win Florida and Ohio, you just don't lose. If you win Florida and Ohio and Iowa—in the history of our country nobody has lost. It's almost impossible. I won all three by a lot, by a landslide . . ."

"Election Night—"

"I got a call on Election Night from a guy I have no great regard for, Karl Rove, and he was kissing my ass, because that's what he does; if you win, he kisses your ass. So, Karl Rove called at approximately ten thirty to congratulate me on the great victory. He thought we won the election, along with everybody else—all over by ten thirty and then . . ."

He suddenly spied a Mar-a-Lago member couple lingering nearby:

"Hello, folks . . . How are you? . . . Everything was good? . . . Have a good time?"

He's part tummler and host. In a sense, the Mar-a-Lago attention and deference is, to him, a proxy for the Republican Party and its Trump base—no matter that these are all multimillionaire-class retirees.

"These people—there has never been anything like it. They feel cheated—and they are angry . . ." This precipitates a recitation of all the Republicans now beating a path to his door: "If I don't endorse, they are going to lose."

And another couple: "Hello, folks . . . Oh, I love that mask"—reading TRUMP—"show him that mask. He's the most powerful reporter. Well, you look good in it. Have a good time"—without a pause—"Hi, Wilbur, my Wilbur Ross, how are you? Have a good time?"

I push forward: "Was there pressure for you to concede?"

"You know I've never conceded . . ."

"It's unique that you didn't. Nixon—"

"He conceded right away. And he also left before impeachment. You know his biggest regret was that he didn't fight impeachment. Did you know that? He had bad tapes. The tapes were not good. But his biggest regret was that he didn't fight impeachment. His daughters came to me—they were at a party—and said, 'My father's biggest regret, and we love that you fight it all the time.' You know I call it 'the impeachment hoax,' number one and number two.

"They said, 'Concede.' I said, 'If I lost the election, I can handle it very easily—maybe not easily—but it's fine.' When you win . . . A man comes up to me the other night, a real expert on election—doesn't work for me; you know you've got people all over the country working on this; it's not acceptable—man came up to me and he said, 'Sir, I do this professionally. I live for it. You not only won this election, you won this election in a landslide—by ten million votes. But more importantly than the ten million votes—you won all of the swing states . . .'"

"I'm thinking of calling this book *Landslide*," I offered, only slightly concerned that he might read the irony.

"Cool title. The other title I gave you, *Fire and Fury*—and by the way, look how Kim Jong-un is behaving now. Look at how hostile Iran—and I'll tell you, they were all behaving great. I did a great job with North Korea. And China was looking at Taiwan when I was there—now, all of a sudden, they got planes flying over Taiwan. But they weren't looking at Taiwan under any circumstances; now they are looking at Taiwan. It's called respect or lack of respect—for him. You know what I mean? ..."

"Who was pressuring you to concede on Election Night?"

"Primarily RINOs, of which you have many, but fewer than you used to have. I guess I could think about names—but it was brushed away so quickly by me that it had no impact. When there's theft, when someone steals something, you can't just say ... and this was stolen. Now Hillary Clinton with the Russia hoax—they like to use the term 'illegitimate president,' so I can assume I can use the same term."

"Who were the important voices you were talking to at this point? Rudy—"

"No. I had many. Probably twenty. I had a lot of support. You know, we had many good people in the administration. You read about the bad ones, and I'm the one who will talk about the bad ones. We had some real stiffs, but we also had great people. I tell the story ... I was in Washington seventeen times in my entire life. I never slept over. So, I was here approximately seventeen times in my entire life—all of a sudden, I'm driving down Pennsylvania Avenue with two hundred and fifty motorcycles—military guard and every, everything else—and I'm looking at my wife, and I say, 'You're First Lady, congratulations, and I'm the president. Do you believe this?' But I didn't know people in Washington—now I know everybody. But I didn't know anybody. The fact is, I developed a certain something. Interesting the gentleman that you dealt with so much, Bannon"—a voluble source in my books—"he shouldn't have done what he did, but nobody was more for me than Bannon in the last year and a half. Sort of interesting—well, I like Bannon. Steve was Steve ..."

With nary a segue:

"I was very disappointed in Mike Pence. We had a very good relationship. Thomas Jefferson, many years before, is a great one, despite the fact that they want to cancel him and get rid of the Jefferson Memorial. He was a great one—was in the same position with one state, Georgia. They were unable to properly calculate the vote, and they said, 'We cannot calculate the vote; there is a discrepancy in the great state of Georgia.' And then he said, 'We will take the vote.' He took the vote. I wasn't even asking to take the vote—Thomas Jefferson took the vote—and off the record"—although he had often put it on the record—"I said to Mike Pence, 'Mike, you're no Thomas Jefferson.'"

"Why do you think he didn't do it?"

"He wasn't Thomas Jefferson, what can I tell you? There was a group of legal scholars that said he should immediately. Is he a statue? He is to protect the Constitution, support and protect. So, if he knows the votes are rigged, if he knows legislatures didn't approve—without going into dead people or illegal immigrants, ballot dumping, without going into that—he knows, by that time numerous legislatures—if you look at Pennsylvania, they had riots."

"Take me further—"

"What?"

"Take me further—"

"Mike Pence had a choice. He could have said, 'It is my duty and obligation and honor to protect the Constitution of the United States, and therefore I am obligated to send these votes back to the legislatures because they did not approve all of these vast changes made to the election.'

"John Eastman—very smart guy—John Eastman said that what Mike Pence did was a dishonor to our country. A very brilliant constitutional lawyer—and he was out there—but there were many others . . .

"Oh, look at my Sarah"—Sarah Huckabee Sanders—"Boy you look so fantastic. You know Michael Wolff—"

Sanders, the press secretary at the time of the publication of *Fire and Fury* and the point person in the tumultuous week of the White

House trying to respond to the book and to brand me as enemy number one, did something of a slo-mo double take, seeing me there with the president.

The subject of Pence now led to Trump's unhappiness with Pence's job as the administration's COVID overseer; which led straight-away to Trump's own fantastic job of getting the vaccine developed in short order; and now to Andrew Cuomo, whom he had once thought would replace Biden as his Democratic opponent, and whether he would be able to hold on to his office.

"Andrew is a thug—but I'm amazed. I thought he had total control of all those upstaters. I thought he had the state totally under control." This seemed to spur him on to a free association on other political antagonists.

"Mitch [McConnell] is the most unpopular politician in the country. Mitch was losing his election—went up twenty points, and then he won. Mitch was down by three or four. I'm very popular in Kentucky. I won a lot of states by a lot. Amy McGrath [McConnell's Democratic opponent] had ninety-one million in the bank. I did a commercial for him—he goes up by twenty points. So, I'm not a fan of Mitch—actually never was—but I got a lot of judges approved. But Mitch is the most overrated politician in Washington . . .

"I might as well tell you—Kavanaugh. Practically every senator called me, including Crazy Mitch, and said, 'Cut him loose, sir, cut him loose. He's killing us, Kavanaugh.' I said, 'We can't do that because it will destroy him—he won't be able to even go back to the second-highest court, right? They used the expression 'cut him loose,' and I said, 'I can't do that,' and it was very derogatory, that expression, 'cut him loose.' And I had plenty of time to pick somebody else . . . right? But they said, 'Cut him loose,' and I went through that thing and fought like hell for Kavanaugh—and I saved his life, and I saved his career. At great expense to myself. . . . okay? I had, let's say, fifty percent of the Republican senators or more saying cut him loose—fifty percent or more—and it made sense because they were saying, 'He's killing us.' And I fought for that guy and kept him. I don't want anything—one thing has nothing to do with another—but I am very disappointed in him, in his rulings. I can't even believe what's happening. I'm very disappointed in Kavanaugh. I just told you something I haven't told a lot of people. In retrospect, he just hasn't had the courage you need to be a great justice. I'm basing this on more than just the election. And the others . . . Roberts? What's going on with Roberts? I have no idea, and nobody else does. But the Supreme Court has shown no courage and no strength, and they have been horrible for the United States of America . . ."

"Christie," I prompted.

"I've known him for a long time. He's leaving New Jersey with one of the worst popular approval ratings in history. I helped him a lot with his problems, and he's a very disloyal guy. I helped him a lot with his problems, and he turned out to be a very disloyal guy—and he had big problems. He's not going anywhere. It's too bad, because I really helped Chris Christie a lot . . ."

"Kevin McCarthy?"

"Ahhh—I'm disappointed in Kevin McCarthy. Kevin is a little too early to talk about—but so far I'm disappointed . . ."

"Who are your best lawyers?" I prompted, curious if he'd put Giuliani in there.

"I have so many lawyers. Roy for me was a great lawyer," he said, reverting to Roy Cohn and disappearing the thousand lawyers he'd had since.

"I won't ask you if you're going to run again, but if you do, how do you keep the election from being stolen again?"

But this just plunged him back into the moment and a Supreme Court—his Supreme Court—that did not protect him, such that he seemed to be suggesting that the Supreme Court would never help him, so all elections would be stolen from him. "I wanted to go in as president, and I was told by twenty out of twenty lawyers, I had no standing. Think of it, you've just had a rigged election, caught them in a rigged election, and have no standing to go before the Court. But Texas, and the reason that all happened [the Supreme Court throwing out the Texas lawsuit against Pennsylvania] is standing, and they had perfect legal standing, if almost twenty states don't have standing, and they lost those cases on standing and process. They didn't lose them on the facts; they never got to hear the facts—because the judges didn't have the guts to make the right decisions. Wouldn't it be ironic if they packed the court?"

"Do you have any regrets?" I asked, sensing the interview coming to an end.

"Of what?"

"About things you've done or not done?"

"I gave up this life"—that is, apparently, the Palm Beach life—"for a life dealing with fine people but also absolute scum and treachery and fake witch hunts. People said, 'The greatest life; look what you've given up.' But I've also done a thousand things that nobody has done. Nobody's done what I've done."

Then we headed into dinner, Melania now at his side, with the Mar-a-Lago diners, all chiffon and blazers, rising and offering a round of deep and heartfelt applause. He was home. But would he stay there?

ACKNOWLEDGMENTS

This is the third volume in little more than three years in my endeavor to tell the story of the Trump White House from inside its walls and to tell it in an account as contemporaneous with events as practically possible. This has required a publishing effort of great dedication and nimbleness, with many publishers around the world working in real time rather than traditional book publishing time. Henry Holt in the United States has led this undertaking. *Landslide* was begun in late January and delivered to the printer in early June. This was accomplished with the good humor, great discipline, inventive solutions, and unflagging support of the Holt team, Don Weisberg, Amy Einhorn, Sarah Crichton, Pat Eisemann, Maggie Richards, Marian Brown, Eric Rayman, and Natalia Ruiz. Charlie King and Tim Whiting at Little, Brown in the U.K., Moritz Schuller and Nora Gottschalk at Rowholt in Germany, and Job Lisman at Prometheus in the Netherlands have been among the stellar international partners.

Andrew Wylie, Jeffrey Pasternak, and James Pullen at the Wylie Agency have supported every aspect of this project. They are the pillars of my professional life.

Most obviously this book would not have happened without the many members of the Trump White House who have trusted me with their recollections and views. I am in their debt.

This book was a race not only to a printer date but to get there before the birth of my son in early June. My family's patience with both my constant deadlines and with yet another go-round with Donald Trump has been heroic.

ABOUT THE AUTHOR

Michael Wolff is the author of *Fire and Fury*, the top-selling book about the Trump White House, and of its sequel, *Siege*. His six other books include his biography of Rupert Murdoch, *The Man Who Owns the News*, and his memoir of the early internet years, *Burn Rate*. He has been a regular columnist for *New York* magazine, *Vanity Fair*, *British GQ*, the *Hollywood Reporter*, and the *Guardian*. He is the winner of two National Magazine Awards. He lives in New York with his family.